BAYONETS AND SCIMITARS

Bayonets and Scimitars
ARMS, ARMIES AND MERCENARIES
1700–1789

William Urban

Foreword by Dennis Showalter

Frontline Books, London

FRONTLINE BOOKS, LONDON

Bayonets and Scimitars: Arms, Armies and Mercenaries, 1700–1789

This edition published in 2013 by Frontline Books, an imprint of
Pen & Sword Books Limited, 47 Church Street, Barnsley, S. Yorkshire, S70 2AS
www.frontline-books.com

ISBN: 978-1-84832-711-5

CIP data records for this title are available from the British Library
and the Library of Congress

Maps created by Alex Swanston, Pen and Sword mapping department

For more information on our books, please visit
www.frontline-books.com,
email info@frontline-books.com
or write to us at the above address.

Typeset by JCS Publishing Services Ltd, www.jcs-publishing.co.uk
Printed and Bound by CPI Group (UK), Croydon, CR0 4YY

Contents

Illustrations

Maps

Plates

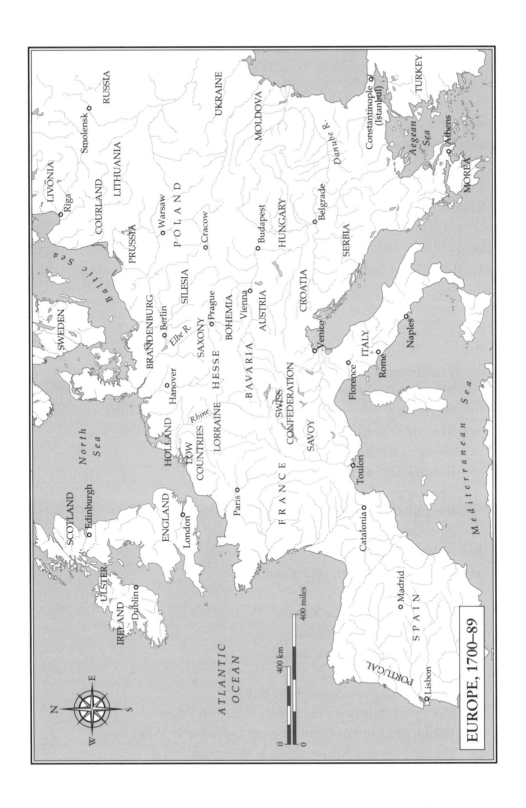

EUROPE, 1700–89

RUSSIA

Smolensk

LIVONIA

Riga

COURLAND

LITHUANIA

PRUSSIA

Warsaw

P O L A N D

Cracow

UKRAINE

MOLDOVA

Danube R.

HUNGARY

Budapest

Belgrade

SERBIA

CROATIA

Constantinople
(Istanbul)

TURKEY

Aegean
Sea

Athens

MOREA

SWEDEN

Baltic Sea

BRANDENBURG

Berlin

Elbe R.

SILESIA

SAXONY

Prague

BOHEMIA

Vienna

AUSTRIA

Venice

ITALY

Naples

Rome

Florence

North
Sea

Hanover

HOLLAND

LOW
COUNTRIES

HESSE

Rhine

LORRAINE

BAVARIA

SWISS
CONFEDERATION

SAVOY

Toulon

SCOTLAND

Edinburgh

ENGLAND

London

Paris

F R A N C E

ULSTER

IRELAND

Dublin

ATLANTIC
OCEAN

Catalonia

Madrid

S P A I N

PORTUGAL

Lisbon

Mediterranean Sea

N
E
S
W

400 miles

400 km

0

0

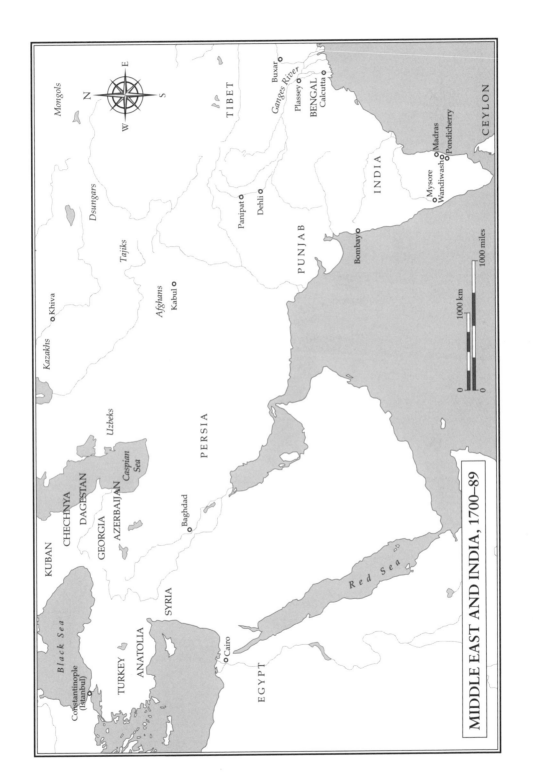

MIDDLE EAST AND INDIA, 1700–89

Mongols

Dsungars

Tajiks

Khiva

Kazakhs

Uzbeks

Afghans

Kabul

PERSIA

Baghdad

KUBAN

CHECHNYA

DAGESTAN

GEORGIA

AZERBAIJAN

Caspian Sea

Black Sea

Constantinople (Istanbul)

TURKEY

ANATOLIA

SYRIA

Cairo

EGYPT

Red Sea

TIBET

Ganges River

Buxar

Plassey

BENGAL

Calcutta

Panipat

Dehli

PUNJAB

Bombay

INDIA

Mysore

Wandiwash

Madras

Pondicherry

CEYLON

0   1000 km

0   1000 miles

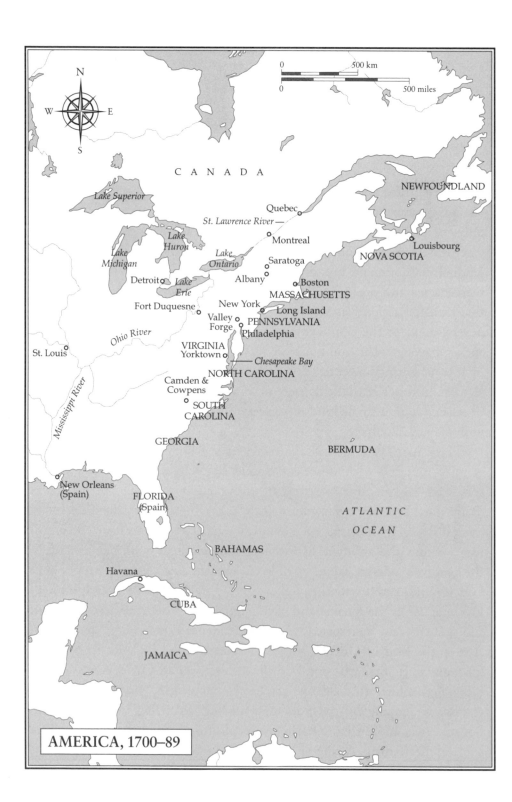

N

W   E

S

0   500 km

0   500 miles

C A N A D A

NEWFOUNDLAND

Lake Superior

Quebec

St. Lawrence River —

Montreal

Louisbourg

NOVA SCOTIA

Lake Huron

Lake Michigan

Lake Ontario

Saratoga

Detroit

Lake Erie

Albany

Boston

MASSACHUSETTS

Fort Duquesne

New York

Long Island

Ohio River

Valley Forge

PENNSYLVANIA

Philadelphia

St. Louis

VIRGINIA

Yorktown

— *Chesapeake Bay*

NORTH CAROLINA

Camden & Cowpens

SOUTH CAROLINA

Mississippi River

GEORGIA

BERMUDA

New Orleans (Spain)

FLORIDA (Spain)

ATLANTIC OCEAN

BAHAMAS

Havana

CUBA

JAMAICA

AMERICA, 1700–89

Foreword

This is the third volume in a trilogy that is an extended reflection on the changing nature of early modern war. Its ideas and concepts reflect not only the previous volumes, but Urban's long and distinguished career as a scholar of warfare on Europe's northeastern margins. His focus is the gradual development, broadly defined and at all levels of warmaking, of mercenaries into professionals in eighteenth-century Europe. The basis of that transformation was a 'military-technical revolution': the simultaneous development at the century's beginning of the flintlock musket and the socket bayonet. The combination was a weapons system that increased infantry's fighting power to a point where, for the first time since the Roman legions, Europe's battlefields were dominated and defined by a single arm of service, with a single kind of soldier able to employ both fire and shock with maximum effect.

The result was a tactical symmetry that fostered battlefield gridlock. Armies imitated each other so closely that eighteenth-century war at the sharp end became a matter of endurance rather than performance. Traditional warrior traits found little place in combat whose intensity made increasing demands on a soldier's capacity to stand firm: to control fear without the anodyne of activity. Campaigns as well, particularly in the relatively barren expanses of East Prussia and central Europe, were exercises in survival, with the pleasures of rapine and pillage severely limited. Optimal use of the musket and bayonet, moreover, depended on extensive, comprehensively synergised training. Cadenced marching, keeping in step to the beat of a drum, was a complex learned skill not to be taken for granted. Eighteenth-century drill was designed in part to condition the individual soldier to collective activity by inculcating automatic physical responses: loading by the numbers, moving according to orders. Drill, however, was more than a means of inculcating reflex behaviour. It was a survival mechanism. A clumsy or self-willed man in a musket-and-bayonet formation could initiate disorder, and that made him a potentially fatal liability. A recruit unable or unwilling to accept that concept was likely to be the subject of unwelcome attention from his fellow soldiers as well as the non-commissioned officers.

Neither conditioned reflex nor self-interested co-operation were enough to hold men in ranks under fire. A soldier's relationship to the system – any system – he serves differs essentially from all others because it involves a central commitment to dying, as opposed to accepting death as a possible byproduct of other activities like fighting fires or enforcing laws. Much of the time for most soldiers the death clause is inactive. An individual can spend thirty honourable years in any uniform and face only collateral risks such as training accidents. Even in war the commitment is not absolute. Armies incorporate a collective sense of what it is legitimate to expect under given circumstances. As casualty lists mount, soldiers are increasingly likely to begin scrutinising the moral fine print in their agreements, written and unwritten, with the state and society they fight for. Specifically, the infantry on which an eighteenth-century army depended for its effectiveness, depended in its turn on fighting spirit as well as on formal discipline. Compulsion in its varied forms might keep men from running. It could not make them fight. More precisely, it could not keep them fighting in battles that as the century progressed came to resemble nothing so much as feeding two candles into a blowtorch and seeing which melted first.

The seventeenth-century soldier had identified himself in terms of individuality. Becoming a soldier involved being able to carry a sword, to wear outrageous clothing, to swagger among the women in ways denied the peasant or artisan. The eighteenth century witnessed the development of armies as communities. To an extent that development was overlooked as long as historians focused on the socio-economic process. This small-'m' Marxism stressed military service as based on economic marginalisation, specifically unemployment and underemployment, whether structural or intermittent. 'Hunger as the best recruiting sergeant' became a scholarly meme. Recent research takes an alternative perspective: the search for behaviour's cultural origins and manifestations. Boredom, a desire for new experiences and fresh horizons, is emerging as a fundamental source of recruits. Change offered prospects for a different servitude, even for the relatively limited numbers conscripted in various forms. Europe's armies in short were, by and large, composed of men willing to fight for something other than the immediate defence of their own homes.

That did not necessarily mean desire for a completely random life. As intrastate conflict became a permanent feature of international politics – the period from 1689 to 1815 is regularly described as the 'second Hundred Years War' – states found it more economical and more functional to maintain permanent armies as opposed to raising them ad hoc. Soldiers were correspondingly able to find a literal home in the army, serving for years in stable environments, with guaranteed employment, under material and social conditions that more or less paralleled those they could reasonably expect as civilians. British army courts martial, for example, carefully regarded procedure and evidence, with military punishments in general no harsher than those the civil codes provided for similar offences. Prussia's uniforms were among the best in Europe. Its soldiers' medical care was superior to anything normally available to craftsmen and peasants. Its superannuated veterans had good chance of government employment or public maintenance in a garrison company.

Lurid descriptions of the eighteenth-century military experience as uniquely brutalising must be contextualised. Life for the common man in the eighteenth century, whether in England, Italy or Prussia, was not exactly a nursery for the finer feelings. Schools, work places and courtrooms were focal points of physical chastisement. Hogarth's *Gin Lane* and *Four Stages of Cruelty* were not abstract constructions of the artist's imagination. For soldiers the introduction of uniforms and the systematic enforcement of camp and garrison discipline facilitated an everyday stability balancing a life that at least, while not solitary, was nevertheless all too likely to be nasty, poor and short. In contrast, moreover, to the later age of mass armies, eighteenth-century soldiers were sufficiently difficult to come by, and sufficiently expensive in money and effort to develop, that they were no more casually expendable in garrison than in combat. Serious military punishments, official and improvised, bore disproportionately on a small proportion: the 5 per cent that in any closed male community create 90 per cent of the problems.

Systematic state concern for soldiers' welfare – however meagre that concern might seem today – thus generated a military commitment–dependence cycle central to Urban's presentation of the eighteenth century's transformation of mercenaries to professionals. That cycle was also a key element in a wider process that can be aphorised as the development of serfs into subjects. Western Europe's defining economic characteristic definitely by the fourteenth century was the replacement of manorialism and tenurial bonds by various forms of personal contracts: some kind of defined payment for some form of defined service. The result, in a still-hierarchic society, was networking: lattices and labyrinths of constructed relationships generating structures of patronage and loyalty that reinforced local power systems. The most familiar is the 'livery and maintenance' that in fifteenth-century England sustained the Wars of the Roses. This 'bastard feudalism' was by no means anomalous. Applied beyond its familiar English contexts, it made the development of the fiscal-military state much more a matter, in Urban's words, of 'persuasion and flattery, compromise and bribery, and mutual benefits' as opposed to a simple top-down accretion of state power through force and bureaucracy. That generalisation holds as well for central Europe, where serfdom developed late, and more in the context of providing labour for an agricultural export market than as a comprehensive socio-cultural system. Down into the eighteenth century Prussia's Junkers and Poland's gentry wore no monarch's collar lightly – if they donned it at all.

Expanding government power thus was a gradual process, based largely on extending the kinds of commitment–dependence cycles that produced professional soldiers in place of mercenaries. Mercenaries continued to exist during the 1700s, but in professionalised contexts: the Swiss, German and Irish regiments of eighteenth-century France; the subsidiary armies, for hire on long-term contracts, that underwrote the economic and social orders of states like Hesse-Kassel, Württemberg and Braunschweig. But it was only in the eighteenth century that these cycles synergised to a degree that the state could be defined by the concept of 'subject'. A subject is usually understood as a person under authority, who owes allegiance to that authority. Modern academic usage presents it pejoratively, as a state of marginalisation, in which the agency of groups and individuals is limited by lack of power and status. But subjects were not subaltern. Eighteenth-century Europe was developing a social-contract culture, pragmatic as opposed to the abstractions discussed by philosophers and political theorists. Predicated on interests rather than rights, its nexus was simple: service and loyalty in return for protection and order. This introduced a dimension sometimes described as patriotism, sometimes as nationalism, but best understood as identity – or perhaps identification – of people with states. Linda Colley describes the British version as built around Protestantism, navalism and rivalry with France. The Prussian counterpart depended on cultures of pietism and patriarchy in the context of a developing 'state of laws', a Rechtsstaat challenging and constraining, if not eliminating, arbitrary exercises of power.

This is not to say that the 'subject state' provided its soldiers with the whole-souled emotional equipment described by F. Scott Fitzgerald in *Tender is the Night*. But they were not automata. A British frigate or a Prussian battalion was a formidable instrument of war in good part because its men were positively motivated. Nor were French, Austrians and Russians held in their respective ranks only by the lash, the stick and the pistol. In presenting the eighteenth-century transformation of mercenaries into professionals, Urban describes the development of a Western way of war, not in the essentialist sense best defined by Victor Davis Hanson, but as a product of specific cultural adaptation, along lines fundamentally different even from Europe's closest neighbour and long-standing rival, the Ottoman Empire. And his analysis of the American Revolution takes the account forward, pointing towards another process with its roots in eighteenth-century Europe – the transformation of subjects into citizens.

Preface

In *The Face of Battle* John Keegan made a case for military history half-way between bloodless but often thrilling patriotic narratives and the pornography of violence. Battles *per se* are exciting, he wrote, but they explain little. However, combined with social history and the impact of technology, military history provides us with a good understanding of how humans behave individually and in groups, the process of change, and the ways peoples perceive themselves. Although Roger Chickering and Stig Förster, in *War in an Age of Revolution, 1775–1815*, warn us that the curricular segregation at universities hampers a serious study of military history, war was a part of our past that cannot be ignored by anyone who aspires to understand how we became what we are.

There were decisive changes in Western warfare just before 1700, a critical era I explored in *Matchlocks to Flintlocks* (2011). Perhaps most significant was the emphasis on discipline, then in command and control, but the most obvious was weaponry. A soldier wielding a musket with a bayonet was more deadly than either the old-fashioned musketeer or the man holding a pike – he could charge the one, forcing him to calculate whether he had time to reload or should flee for his life; he could stand off from the other, shooting him down at leisure. Nobody makes the argument better that such technology was important than Kenneth Chase in *Firearms: A Global History*, but he notes that using technology properly was even more significant. Victory went to the best army, not to the best armed one.

Since the soldier who could fire fastest during close combat had the best chance of slaying his enemies, there was constant experimentation in weaponry and its use, and with formations designed to increase the volume of fire. Deep formations did not get musketeers into firing position quickly enough, but a thin line was easily broken by a charge. Bayonet combat was relatively rare – the impact of a volley by the last side to fire, or the fear of a volley, usually caused the least steady unit to collapse. Even the steady approach of troops with shouldered arms, uniformed men marching to the rhythm of drums, often resulted in the defenders fleeing. More mobile artillery and more dependable munitions made a deadly combination when employed effectively, but it took steady men to serve them when infantry came at them with bayonets lowered, or when wild cavalry thundered towards them, dispersing their infantry screen in panicked flight.

The stress of pitched battle – confusion, noise, exhaustion, hunger and fear – caused an over-production of adrenalin that created a tremendous thirst and an extraordinary sensitivity to perceptions of likely victory or defeat. Panic was easily induced, but also acts of extraordinary valour – training and discipline could limit the first and enhance the second, but nothing could eliminate the raw fear.

Considering the horrendous casualties of pitched battle – 30 per cent of combatants or more – it is understandable that commanders resorted to harsh tactics to maintain discipline. Consequently, it may be that the non-commissioned officer, who enforced discipline, was the decisive Western innovation, not weaponry. However, like all innovations, such officers were not new. The Roman army had its centurions – and Western Europeans were reading classical historians.

The battlegrounds of this era were often familiar to the reader of classical history: along the Rhine, in the Balkans, in Italy. But other regions were unfamiliar – those to the east, in the Baltic and on the steppe. The use of the familiar to understand the new is an ancient and well-recommended practice that will be followed in this volume.

John Lynn II demonstrated in *Women, Armies, and Warfare in Early Modern Europe* that the important armies had also changed significantly in other ways between 1650 and 1700. Rulers eager to increase the number of combatants in their forces were eliminating the many camp followers who had gathered food and fodder, protected soldiers' property and shared the hard work – from carrying supplies to digging trenches and defending walls. Once rulers took upon themselves the tasks of supplying armies, they could employ soldiers in drill rather than seeking food and plunder; as a result, armies were not only more effective, but the once-terrorised peasantry came to see them as their protector. Though Lynn was not eager to engage in a debate over whether this constituted 'modernisation', he noted that the new army and state apparatus resembled today's more than they had before. A prominent example was the elimination of most private entrepreneurs from command, replacing them with officers who may have still owned their regiments, but did so at the sufferance of their lord. Brauer and van Tuyll note in *Castles, Battles and Bombs: How Economic Explains Military History*, that these 'state commission' armies were larger, more effective and logically organised – the rulers did not want to draft their own workers, because it cost them a taxpayer each time they acquired a soldier to be paid, but they wanted an effective army.[1]

This meant that the armies of this era incorporated many mercenaries, but they no longer resembled the armies of the sixteenth and seventeenth centuries described in such detail by Fritz Redlich in *The German Military Enterpriser*. There was always a demand for foreign officers in these new armies, because few nations were at war long enough or often enough to develop their own experienced commanders. There were also many men who enlisted for the pay, but they were not as cynical, ill-mannered and independent as the traditional mercenary – increasingly effective discipline curbed this significantly, as the tendency to identify with national armies limited the willingness to serve in truly foreign ones, and the growing numbers of draftees diminished the importance of money as the reason for becoming a soldier. As the 1700s progressed, we can begin looking at them as contract soldiers.

Increasing prosperity reinforced this trend towards professionalisation. Bad times were good times for recruiters, good times were not; the reverse was true for tax collectors. As wars became less frequent and caused less damage to civilians, governments poured huge sums into fortifications, hoping that they were adequate substitutes for maintaining a large standing army. Stone and bricks, it was believed, would at least buy time until troops could be raised, and they were a more permanent investment than training regiments.

Robert Citino, in *The German Way of War*, remarks on our habit of referring to the conflicts of this era as 'limited war'. The conflicts may have been limited compared to the sacking of villages and cities in the Thirty Years War, but for the soldiers it was anything but. Still, it was not 'total war'. This term, as far as Daniel Bell is concerned, means the mobilisation of the entire state's resources, as happened in the French Revolution, when soldiers and civilians alike were motivated by nationalism and ideology. Until then there were subjects and rulers, and few dreamed of liberty, equality and fraternity.

In the 1700s the lines between patriot, adventurer, contract soldier and mercenary were often unclear. Motives were mixed, and motivations changed. The draftee whose services were sold by his ruler perhaps never intended to serve in distant climes, but he might willingly have gone with his new pals wherever robbery and worse were tolerated in practice. Revenge against traditional enemies of church and nation was also important. In this the professional soldier was perhaps no worse than his civilian counterparts, but the restraints on his behaviour were primarily those which assured combat effectiveness. 'Gentlemen', naturally, emphasised the subtle but real difference between those who at least understood the principles of chivalry from those who made war only for money; therefore, they insisted, command should be exercised only by those who were, in modern terms, 'officers and gentlemen'. Not much, if anything, could be expected of the common soldier.

These points were discussed by Marshal de Saxe in *Memoirs on the Art of War*, begun in 1728. He noted that soldiers were either raised as volunteers or drafted or coerced into service, but the distinction was unimportant, since recruiting them 'by artifice' was the most common. He preferred drafting young men who otherwise would waste their youth idly or in adventures, releasing them back into society after five years. The current system, he said, enlisted only the trash of society. How much better, he said, to employ paid armies of citizens.

Drafting citizens also avoided a problem that was becoming ever more acute – the intense rivalry among recruiters working an ever-smaller pool of suitable young men; prosperity resulting from long respites from war had also eliminated the most important motivations for enlistment – poverty and wartime devastation. Also working against the wiles of the recruiter was a greater awareness of the brutal discipline, the incredible losses from disease and pitched battle, the irregularity of pay and the prospect of ending up as a cripple or beggar. Then there was the problem of desertion, especially by bounty jumpers who collected their enlistment bonus, then disappeared. Thomas Barker described three different approaches to preventing this – voluntary, cunning and forceful – none of which was particularly effective.

There were punishments, of course, but few commanders were willing to apply the death penalty except to men who fled in the face of the enemy. Mercenaries and volunteers took so long to train that it was foolish to shoot them – beatings and whippings were more plausible threats.

One issue today is deeper than whether to have armies of citizens or professional soldiers. It rests on questions about whether states should even have armies, or what role armies should play. As Dennis Showalter noted in 1996, military history today is divided between Whigs and Calvinists. A strange comment, perhaps, in an increasingly secular age that has little interest in past interpretations of human motivations, but it was to the point. Modern Whigs believe that *progress* has made war obsolete; modern Calvinists see the outcome of wars as *judgements* about the irrelevance of traditional military machines to societies evolving towards the modern world.

While comparisons of modern states to eighteenth-century ones must be made with caution, we can each think of some that are like Prussia, an army with its own country; others are like Habsburg Austria, so multi-cultural and with so many geographical challenges that economic development comes very slowly; others are like Tsarist Russia, ruled from the top, with all the advantages and disadvantages of such a system; then some resemble the Ottoman Empire, struggling with religious enthusiasts, restive minorities and outmoded traditions while being challenged by modernity.

The states of that era were evolving at different speeds. Hopes were measured against traditions and experience, but there was generally optimism about a better future. I believe that we can best understand this through a combination of familiar and new ideas, then by reflecting on them and on our widely accepted prejudices about it. Most of all, I hope that this book will be enjoyable reading.

William Urban
Lee L. Morgan Professor of History
and International Studies
Monmouth College (Illinois)

Chronology

Timeline	Europe	India	North America
1683	Ottoman Siege of Vienna broken	Shah Aurangzeb expands south	William Penn founds Pennsylvania
1686	Austrians, Germans and Poles capture Budapest		
1688	'Glorious Revolution' in England: Louis XIV seeks new conquests	The decline of the Mughal Empire begins when Hindus revolt	King William's War (British against French and Indians)
1699	Ottomans cede Hungary to Austria in Treaty of Karlowitz		
1700–15	War of the Spanish Succession		Queen Anne's War (British invasion of Canada fails)
1701–21	Great Northern War: Sweden attacked by Peter of Russia and Augustus II, Charles XII occupies Livonia and Poland		
1707	Act of Union (Scotland and England united)	Shah Aurangzeb dies; Mughal Empire almost disintegrates	
1709	Peter defeats Charles XII at Poltava	Sikh Confederacy	Tuscarora War
1713	Peace of Utrecht ends British participation in the War of the Spanish Succession	Sikhs defeated by Mughal shah	British win Hudson's Bay and Newfoundland
1715	Jacobite rising in Scotland	East India Company becomes independent	Yamasee War in the Carolinas

Timeline	Europe	India	North America
1717	Austrians take Belgrade	Maratha Confederation becomes powerful	
1725	Turkish war with Persia		
1733–5	War of the Polish Succession		
1736–9	Turks defeat Austrians and Russians	Persians capture Delhi	War of Jenkin's Ear
1740–8	The War of the Austrian Succession; indecisive war between Turks and Persians	Anglo-French War	King George's War ends in a draw
1748–54	Second Jacobite rebellion in Scotland	Persian Empire collapses; political chaos follows	Braddock routed
1756–63	Diplomatic Revolution: Austria, France and Russia join to attack Prussia; Seven Years War	Black Hole of Calcutta; Persians defeat the Maratha Confederation	French and Indian War
1757	Pitt becomes prime minister, makes alliance with Prussia; Prussia wins battles against Austria and France	Battle of Plassey; Britain becomes the major foreign power in India	French capture Fort William Henry in New York
1759	The *Annus Mirabilis* – Britain wins victories on every front – Europe, America, India		British capture of Quebec; total French defeat in Canada
1762	Russia and Sweden leave the war; Frederick II of Prussia survives	Third Battle of Panipat (1761) leaves India in political chaos	
1763	End of war leaves every power with great debts	Treaty of Pondicherry costs France dearly	Pontiac's Conspiracy; new taxes on colonies
1768–74	Russian War with Turkey		American expansion over the mountains
1772	First partition of Poland (Russia, Prussia and Austria take lands)	Hastings's reforms restore order	Redcoats sent to Boston

Timeline	Europe	India	North America
1775–81	Britain hires Hessians to fight in America	East India Company problems lead to the Boston Tea Party	American War for Independence
1778	France enters the American War	Intense conflict between France and Britain	Battle of Saratoga ends British hopes for easy victory
1780	Gordon riots in London		
1781	Spain besieges Gibraltar; Russia and Austria plot to divide up the Ottoman Empire	Second Mysore War ends French influence	Cornwallis surrenders at Yorktown
1783–4	France makes peace with Britain, but is left bankrupt; financial reforms fail	East India Company comes under royal control	American Independence
1787–92	Russia takes Crimea from Ottomans; Austrians take Belgrade; the French Revolution begins	Cornwallis's reforms	Northwest Ordnance for western settlement; Constitution signed
1789	Storming of the Bastille		Washington president
1792	Execution of Louis XVI; second partition of Poland	Colonial era truly begins	
1795	Third partition of Poland		

CHAPTER ONE

War in the Eighteenth Century

War in the Seventeenth Century

Everyone in central Europe remembered the Thirty Years War (1618–48) as one long nightmare of violence and destruction. The bloody battles in the Holy Roman Empire were followed by massacres, robbing, murdering, raping – Protestants sacking Catholic towns and villages, Catholics rampaging through Protestant communities, and both ignoring confessional identities when food and fodder were short. Marauding armies from Austria, Spain, France, Denmark and Sweden were trailed by life-hardened wives, washwomen, cooks and prostitutes, some performing all roles simultaneously; no army could survive without them. Each army was mobile, sustaining itself by looting every community in its way. One could not think of any of these armies except as a plague on everyone's house.[1] This plague then spread into the Low Countries (modern Belgium and Holland), to Poland and, in the form of civil war, to France and England.

The war in Germany was declared over in 1648 by the Peace of Westphalia, but recovery came slowly. France became the major power of Europe, while Poland, Austria and Spain declined. Minor powers manipulated the political situation for their own benefit – Sweden, Brandenburg-Prussia, Saxony and Holland being the foremost of a numerous host. Given this history, it comes almost as a surprise to see that by the end of the century the semi-disciplined armies of that era had evolved into something closer to their modern forms. This was the result of new technologies being applied to the art of killing and improved methods of training soldiers; also generals had accumulated experience in commanding large armies.

The sizes of the new military establishments were much greater than they had been, and, because soldiers could no longer subsist on plunder, they were now supported by a logistical supply line and stores kept in safe fortresses. As a result, the disorderly life of the mercenary army evolved into that of disciplined camps and garrisons. In this process the role of women in warfare declined significantly. Lynn noted in *Women, Armies and Warfare in Early Modern Europe* that this was not altogether a loss – theirs had been a life of poverty, suffering and danger. Camp life had long resembled a travelling city, but it was a very disorderly one. The women had no home, no choice, and their children would grow up knowing no profession but war. Boys would become soldiers; girls would become wives or whores (unmarried, though attached to one man) or, perhaps more often, prostitutes. Some perhaps joined the numerous body of sutlers, who supplied troops with everything the state did not, most importantly alcohol, tobacco, gambling and sex. Sutlers had come to resemble small businessmen more than pawn shop owners and fences, though they undoubtedly made much of their profits from buying soldiers' plunder; still, they were part of a process that relieved officers of bothersome responsibilities. Although there were fewer officers assigned the task of maintaining order in the baggage train, the 'whore officer' still had to face down formidable women who laughed at his efforts to intervene in their quarrels. Soldiers ordered to drive loose women from camp often married their common-law wives, which meant exceeding the strict limit of four to six women per regiment – the number considered sufficient for washing clothes and nursing the ill and injured. This was not the only reason for orders requiring men to obtain permission to marry – there were complaints from parents unhappy about runaway daughters and maids. If some wives sold themselves to other soldiers, that did not seem to disqualify them for immediate marriage whenever their husbands died. All these policies, effective or not, were intended to allow officers and men to concentrate on war.

If life was so difficult in the army, why would anyone wish to enlist? Poverty, most of all – especially in areas that had been looted. Protection – from other armies and roving bandits. Escape from boredom – a desire to see the world beyond a village where fathers expected them to work hard at dull tasks. Unhappy love affairs – especially for boys who could not afford to marry or who imagined meeting exciting girls in exotic locations. There was also peer pressure. James Miller, in *Swords for Hire*, emphasises the value that Scottish clans placed on military experience, along with family traditions of overseas service. Many well-born Scots considered service abroad a rite of passage. For ordinary clansmen it was often 'go or be hanged': that is, life abroad was better than death in Scotland, and sometimes jail sentences were transportation to some disease-ridden colony in the tropics.

Military life was still rough. Cursing, fighting and drunkenness were proof of manhood, scars demonstrated disdain for pain and danger, and arrogance was a badge of honour – though lowly soldiers had better not insult officers. Officers and soldiers alike expected to benefit from opportunities to loot, especially if the communities were paying taxes or performing services for the enemy, or if the thefts would pre-empt the enemy from taking those resources themselves.

Rulers considered themselves above this kind of behaviour, though they understood that their wealth hardly came from voluntary contributions and they always insisted on their share of any loot. More so even than most of their aristocrats, they were blue-blooded snobs. They might acknowledge, reluctantly, that they and their subjects were all descendants of Adam, but they understood that their prestige rested on people believing that they were not only different, but superior. Therefore, kings required their courtiers, secular and religious, to have thirty-two quarterings of noble ancestry (seven generations), or to have a grandmother who had slept with a royal sybarite. Still, when pushed to it, monarchs would sell titles to those with the ambition to attend court, intermarry with self-made foreign dynasties, and give commissions and well-born brides to mercenary officers who understood that aristocratic manners consisted of self-confidence, a smattering of education and a refined sense for smelling out who counted. A bit of perfume helped, too.

Nobles considered their reputation more important than their lives. They were bound by customs which could range from chivalric to practical to risible: dressing properly, with wig, frockcoat and lace; speaking foreign languages well (especially French); dancing gracefully; appearing sexually attractive and somewhat aggressive (or more); and demonstrating mastery of swords and duelling pistols. This code of honour set them apart from the middle classes as firmly as from the peasants and artisans who filled the ranks of the common soldiery. Lynn, an expert on women in war, noted in *Battle* how important sexual pressure was in spurring young men into military service – young ladies spurned those who had not served, and

courts winked knowingly at liaisons between handsome veterans and their
pretty admirers. It was little different in the countryside.

There were many situations such as Grimmelhausen described so vividly
in *Simplicissimus*, a novel of the Thirty Years War, when his youthful hero
attempted to escape his kidnappers by passing himself off as a girl, only to
be discovered when the idle boys of the camp attempted a gang rape. Nobles
assumed that such women were their natural prey (and their attentions
may have been welcomed much in the way that young women today throw
themselves at politicians, athletes and rock stars), and commoners may
have relied on the power of unbridled masculinity. When all else failed,
or speed was of the essence, there was always force. One can imagine a
recruiter saying with a wink, 'all women love uniforms'.

The role of mercenaries changed between 1689 and 1717 – the era that
culminates in the War of the Spanish Succession (between France and
Spain against England, Holland and the German states) and the somewhat
detached Great Northern War (Sweden versus Russia and Saxony, with
Poland as a battleground). The new form of army – larger, better supplied,
better trained – was more likely to be paid and fed on time, but less likely
to have pretty girls in camp. Record-keeping improved, complicating the
practice of deserting one army, then enlisting in another.

This new army was distinguished by the use of the bayonet. This allowed
commanders to dispense almost entirely with the use of pikes to ward
off cavalry and to lead the charge into enemy formations. As the flintlock
musket replaced the matchlock, soldiers could fire faster, and wet and wind
had less effect. Artillery became more mobile and more dependable. All
these innovations required money. Commanders also provided uniforms
for their soldiers – making good money on the transaction – then did their
best to provide food and shelter. This reduced the need to send out foragers
who might spend more time robbing peasants than in rounding up chickens
and fodder. The result was what some historians called 'limited war'.

It would be more accurate to call it the era of limited results, because
all European armies were similarly recruited, trained and equipped; they
rarely clashed without the victor suffering such losses that it was difficult
to pursue the fleeing enemy and capture his fortifications and cities. Still,
though warfare was not limited in the ferocity of combat, after 1700 the
behaviour of the soldiery rarely descended to the level of earlier atrocities.

The long periods of peace that followed the end of the War of the Spanish Succession caused many to hope or even to believe that warfare was a barbaric practice of the past, one they would rarely see in the future. This was, after all, the dawn of the age of the Enlightenment, when men and women of education could create a more comfortable and progressive world for themselves and for those they governed.

In this orgy of self-congratulation, they often overlooked the importance of the army. Although the motives of the many foreign officers and men were more complex than a mere lust for money, we have to recognise that many were military contract employees whose loyalties and interests differed little from mercenaries.'

War as a Social Role

Historians have not completely overlooked mercenaries, but aside from those who specialise in the study of warfare, they have minimised their importance. This might be because contemporaries and modern writers alike have found that lives and scandals of the royals attracted readers, and that heroic deeds of military leaders caused hearts and breasts to flutter more than the anonymous suffering and dying of common soldiers.[2]

Political power was still exercised by the upper classes. Lords and knights provided armies with skilled leadership. Command came easily to them, trained as they were from childhood to boss servants around – facing death was a family tradition reinforced by ancestral portraits on their walls. They were often brave beyond reason, and loyal within the bounds of self-interest that extended to family members and friends. However, they demanded a voice on important issues, and then tended to insist on limiting their contributions strictly to contractual obligations. Rulers found this very frustrating.

Military service was a rite of passage for young males of this class. While they did not have to serve long, or even distinguish themselves in terms of courage and ability, they were expected to be willing to put their lives at risk. Bell summarises their roles in a chapter heading – 'Officers, Gentlemen, and Poets'. His example was Armand-Louis de Gontaut (1747–93), better known as Biron, or by his title – Duc de Lauzun. A French noble whose military career began in a nasty little colonial war in Corsica, where he distinguished himself mainly by seducing the wife of a prominent administrator, he became famous through raising a force of foreign volunteers (*Volontaires-etrangers de la Marine*) which he led in Senegal, then in the American War of Independence. These troops were mostly German, but Americans knew only that they served with Rochambeau's army in Rhode Island and later at the siege of Yorktown (where Biron supervised the British surrender). He cut a swathe through the ladies at Versailles, made the acquaintance of Voltaire, and rumour attached him romantically to Queen Marie-Antoinette. (We do not have to take this charge seriously. In *Citizens: A Chronicle of the French Revolution*, Simon Schama demonstrated how unsubstantiated pornography undermined the reputation of the rather dull royal family.) Like many an admirer of the American experiment in popular government, Biron lost his head over that concept – he supported the French Revolution enthusiastically, although later became a victim of the guillotine.

Biron was typical of many officers of the eighteenth century (Prussia excepted) in being a part-time warrior. Soldiers, too, were on active duty only during warm weather, usually being kept during the winter not in barracks, but quartered in private homes; they helped in planting and harvest.

There were some ghastly battles, but by and large generals tried to shield their soldiers from slaughter. It took too long to train men to waste them foolishly. Moreover, by the eighteenth century they tried to spare the citizenry. This gave rise to the concept beloved of historians: limited war. This, Bell notes, suited one of the dominant conceits of the aristocracy – self-restraint – perfectly. Slaughter was not only messy – it was boring. Lynn, in *The French Wars 1667–1714*, calls this 'war as process', a matter of wearing down opponents, in contrast to the dramatic Napoleonic 'war as event'.

Though fewer soldiers died in combat, disease still swept away many. The half-life of any unit on campaign is often estimated to have been about a year, meaning that within two years only 25 per cent would remain in the ranks, whether or not the unit had been in combat.

Lessons of the Battlefield

Bernard Lewis once remarked that the lessons of history are most quickly and thoroughly learned on the battlefield. Not instantly, of course. Great empires often compensate for defeat on one front by victories on another, or by girding up their loins and redoubling their efforts, or through the genius of a general or the folly of their enemies. Whenever a commander fails, fearful rulers and ambitious rivals blame his mistakes; only occasionally do they look for systemic failures such as the enemy having better weapons. Only a few dare ask why they themselves had not developed such weapons.

The most common response was to seek more central control. Rarely did anyone propose allowing *citizens* more opportunities to employ their talents and energies on behalf of the state – kings and courtiers believed that subjects lacked the ability to see what was best; they believed that commoners would always abuse freedom and, moreover, armed subjects would be dangerous. In addition, there was only so much room at the top, and if competent service were rewarded, the aristocracy would lose out too often. Lastly, everyone feared instability and unpredictability. It was best to stick with the familiar, even when familiar practices were no longer working.

As a result, traditional armies did not vanish immediately. In fact, under the right conditions – mountains, steppes and marshes – traditional forces were superior to Western armies. Not surprisingly, competent commanders often combined irregular and even feudal forces into their armies, just as non-Western rulers employed Western experts, officers and soldiers for appropriate tasks. Which commander would prove to be 'competent'? That was as difficult to foresee as which one would be 'lucky'.

Technology was not easily transferable. The skills needed to use the sword, spear and bow were easily acquired and while the first two weapons worked well under every extreme of weather, firearms did not perform well in rain or storms. Moreover, a state which could not make its own cannons and muskets was necessarily at the mercy of unpredictable commercial partners and access to international trade.

There was also class prejudice. As Buchanan noted in *Gunpowder, Explosives and the State*, gunpowder could only be made, mixed and employed properly by experts, and it was not a pleasant process. Nobles may have bathed little, but their tolerance for bad smells had its limits.

Horses smelled, too, but those were manly smells; though horses were subject to disease and panic, and made excellent targets, they were noble animals. Their advantages and faults could be predicted, a characteristic that commanders valued. The exception to trusting the tried and true was when commanders were at such a disadvantage that they would grasp at any hope whatsoever.

Nothing being less predictable and unsettling than battles, conservatives everywhere looked askance at the most visible representative of the modern world in military affairs – mercenary soldiers – and did as much as possible to disparage them or, when possible, to ignore them. Even the professional officer was often a foreigner, with strange habits, strange clothes and a strange religion; he may not even have spoken the language well, and he certainly had not mastered the genealogical minutiae that were so important in every court, or developed patience for the slow pace of civilised life or the connoisseur's appreciation of art, poetry, food and women. He often specialised in leading infantry.

The mercenary and the professional, the specialists in the art of war, however, did not go away. At least, not in Europe. Those who despised them would have to learn the harshest lessons of the battlefield – that war was no longer a part-time pastime.

European Armies in 1700

When the century began, almost all European armies were based on a combination of mercenaries and forced conscription. Conscription, of course, was unpopular, which is why princes wanted to round up ne'er-do-wells first. Such men were not only socially undesirable, but conscripting farmers and artisans would have hurt the state's economic base. The interest of the prince was to have as many taxpayers as possible, so he would limit the recruiting sergeants' natural inclination to enlist the closest sturdy farm boys, even though that was exactly what officers wanted. Instead, he encouraged his recruiters to go into neighbouring states, where there were always some young men ready to volunteer. It does not seem to have occurred to anyone that this practice of 'beggar-thy-neighbour' harmed everyone, or perhaps they just expected neighbours to cheat on any 'non-poaching' agreement.

Sometimes what seemed simple was not. Lynn notes in *Battle* that most of the soldiers in those regiments classified as 'German' were recruited in Bohemia and Moravia. Czechs, though their Hussite religion had been largely crushed in the seventeenth century, continued to perform as well as Hussite warriors in the past, particularly in employing artillery. Christopher Clark reports in *Iron Kingdom* that the Great Elector (Frederick William,

1620–88) reformed practices in Brandenburg-Prussia by assigning cantons specific numbers of recruits. Once the volunteers (some undoubtedly foreign recruits) were enrolled, then local communities would have to select men to fill out the quota: this was an incentive to recruit outsiders. Generous furloughs for planting and harvest prevented many involuntary enlistees from deserting. The Great Elector was much more rigorous in requiring military service from the nobility and gentry. This suggests that Prussia was not as absolute as legend had it, and that sharing responsibilities with local communities worked well. Still, recruiters were figures of terror at home and abroad. They were known to kidnap men, often after getting them drunk. Their obvious lack of morals made them dangerous to village maidens and honest matrons, whose boyfriends and sons could be saved from the draft only by sacrificing their virtue, and perhaps their possessions and cattle, too.

Still, as Dennis Showalter shows in *The Wars of Frederick the Great*, the stereotype of Prussian absolutism is exaggerated. At least, its unpopularity is. The total number of deaths and desertions in the army were not 20 per cent, as is often reported, but a little over 3 per cent. Training was more the responsibility of experienced comrades than tyrannical NCOs. Unit cohesion – that spirit common to athletic teams and workplace efforts – was more important than fear of punishment.

The Great Northern War (1700–21)

Augustus (1670–1733) of Saxony had started this conflict in the belief that he could easily acquire first Courland, then Swedish Livonia for himself. Those lands had once been part of the Polish–Lithuanian Commonwealth that he now reigned over as Augustus II, although he hardly ruled. His motive was cold-blooded opportunism – a combination of ambition and hypocrisy that came to characterise eighteenth-century politics. He had evinced the same lack of sincerity in his conversion to Roman Catholicism, which was necessary to be elected king of Poland; later, though he went through the formalities of worship, he found chasing skirts more exciting than hearing mass. He was not known as Augustus the Strong merely for his alleged feats of strength, but also for the incredible number of illegitimate children recorded by one of his administrators. Norman

Davies, in *God's Playground*, describes with relish the Saxon prodigy's exploits in Madrid and Venice, disguised as a matador and a monk, and his almost frenetic seductions of willing women. Jon White, in *Marshal of France*, cites contemporary wits as saying that he was a Lutheran by birth, a Muslim by appetite and a Catholic by ambition.

Augustus seemed to believe that no one could resist him, a delusion encouraged by the advisors and toadies surrounding him. He was at heart a bully and was never more so than when he tried to steal Livonia from the youthful and apparently frivolous new king of Sweden, Charles XII (1682–1718); to be certain of success, he had persuaded the king of Denmark and the tsar of Russia to join him in this international mugging. When Charles XII matured rapidly, beating all the armies opposed to him, Augustus sent a very attractive former mistress to seduce him (she even spoke fluent Swedish).[3] Augustus could not understand how his opponent could be both charismatic and asexual, or why he would be angry at being offered a handsome woman, or why the repeated efforts to buy him off with lands and money failed. It was typical of Augustus – he believed that everyone could be seduced or bribed.

His plan had been simple. Once he had an additional territorial base in Livonia, taxes and troops from there could help him overawe those great Polish and Lithuanian lords who resisted his plans to make himself one of the great monarchs of Europe. Poles saw through protestations that his policies were aimed at protecting their national interests and, consequently, fought only half-heartedly for him. Awkwardly for Charles XII, Poles had no interest in fighting for him, either. Both monarchs could hire troops in Poland, but neither could buy hearts.

Meanwhile, the Russian tsar, Peter (1672–1725), was occupying extensive parts of Livonia and moving into the eastern borderlands of Lithuania. Peter, whom later generations would call 'the Great' for expanding Russia's borders and modernising the state, was hiring as many foreign officers and troops as he could attract. This was not easy. First of all, Russia was far away; secondly, mercenaries could not safely travel through Livonia and those parts of Poland occupied by Charles XII's armies. Because mercenaries had little respect for Peter's oft-beaten armies, even the high wages seemed a poor payment for the risks involved. And lastly, because Russia was a vast, impoverished land promising hard duty and few comforts, they preferred employment closer to home – most often in Poland, where the king paid well.

Augustus, though almost invariably beaten, was able to raise army after army and still support Russian forces fighting on his behalf. To counter this, Charles XII placed a pretender, Stanislas Leszczyński (1677–1766), on the Polish throne; Stanislas raised armies as best his meagre resources allowed, but he could attract few Polish recruits, much less volunteers. As time passed, it became clear that though the Swedish king won every battle, he could not obtain a decisive victory – not even requisitioning everything he could from exhausted Poles and exasperated Saxons made those peoples give in. Repeatedly Charles defeated Peter's armies, but the tsar had what appeared to be an inexhaustible supply of stolid soldiery who died bravely in their places once they discovered that flight could not save them. Russian soldiers may not have understood much of the political intrigue on which the war was based (though rumour, speculation and propaganda certainly affected the attitudes of the men in the ranks), but their land was large, filled with swamps, forests and steppe, and they instinctively mistrusted foreigners. If Peter's soldiers worried that their hired officers might get them killed in some meaningless battle, they understood that Swedish and Polish overlords would likely make their miserable existence even worse. Better to fight for the tsar, who not only understood better what was going on, but who had protected Russia and the Orthodox Church from Roman Catholic Poles and Lithuanians, and also from Muslim Tatars – steppe warriors who were capturing Christians and selling them into slavery.

Charles, whose military genius allowed him to take on overwhelming numbers of enemies all at once, was not irrational in choosing war over peace. He could pay his soldiers only so long as they were occupying enemy lands. What would happen once he reduced the contributions he imposed on Denmark, Poland and Saxony, and after his enemies had rebuilt their armies? If he could capture Moscow, perhaps he could bring the Cossacks and the Turks into the war on his side. Only that way could he eliminate Russia as a dangerous rival.

Still, it may have been a strategic mistake for Charles to attack Russia from Poland instead of from Livonia. Even in 1708, when his forces were at their greatest, his army was too small to occupy Russia, his Cossack allies were undependable, Turkey was unwilling to join in the war and the Russian army was improving steadily. His invasion antagonised the maritime powers (England and Holland most importantly) who could have restrained Denmark from attacking his rear, costing his treasury important incomes and making it necessary later to import grain from Livonia. With a fraction of the troops needed to occupy Poland and Saxony, he could have secured Livonia.

Perhaps in the long run, Sweden could not have held its empire against the states allied against it, but Charles XII could have put off defeat for many years. To most historians the military catastrophe at Poltava in 1709 was the high point of the Great Northern War and led to the loss of the Swedish Empire. Surprisingly, the adherents of Charles XII and his detractors have not come to agreement on this matter. Nor are they likely to, not even in an era when there is nothing at stake except ego. Today most Swedes feel, in Michael Roberts's words, 'neither vainglory nor remorse' about the past. Sweden would not be the country it is today had the imperial era never existed, but there is no interest in reliving it.

Augustus II managed to return to Poland in 1710, but his Saxon troops soon accomplished the easy feat of provoking the populace. War-weary Poles put up with the now-overweight king's taxes and arrogance for five years, then almost (though not quite) chased him out of their country. It was not clear who, if anyone, could be elected king in his place, should the revolt actually succeed, but it did not matter long – Peter the Great invaded, crushed the rebels and put Augustus back on his overloaded throne. Henceforth, the Polish kingdom was a Russian protectorate in all but name, with the great lords and their private armies ruling their estates almost as independent states.

Davies, in *God's Playground*, notes that once Augustus withdrew all his Saxon forces from Poland, it was virtually impossible for him to govern effectively there. The Sejm – the two houses composing the Polish parliament, and the king – was surrounded by Russian troops. When Russian generals indicated that the king was to remain weak, the Polish knights, nobles and clergy silently agreed to cut the military budget. The foreign contingents of the royal army, small and dependent on the slender income of the crown estates, was henceforth staffed largely by Saxons. The numerous petty nobles, whose lives revolved around hunting and war, served largely in the private armies of the great lords; thus, Poland, the most highly militarised society in Europe, became the least able to defend itself.

Afterwards, Peter the Great extended his empire to the Black and Baltic seas, intimidating Swedes, Poles and Ottomans. However, just as it seemed as though there was no limit to his ability to seize more lands there, the Kazakhs invaded Kalmyk territories.[4] Peter, upon learning that destitute refugees were ready to serve him in return for protection, turned to the east. These years, according to Michael Khodarkovsky, in *Russia's Steppe Frontier*, were known among Kazakhs as the 'Great Calamity'.

Louis XIV's Wars of Aggression and Monetary Issues

The decades of conflict along the Rhine were started by French ministers who wanted to break the power of Spain, then were continued by Louis XIV (1638–1715) in the hope of acquiring German lands and perhaps even becoming Holy Roman emperor. For years it appeared that the 'Sun King', as Louis liked to be styled, would emerge victorious over enemies distracted by political turmoil and war. During Louis's reign the Great Condé (Louis de Bourbon, 1621–86) and Turenne (Henri de la Tour d'Auvergne, 1611–75) had brilliantly led the French armies, which were not only well armed and well supplied, but possessed more strong fortresses and many more regiments than their opponents. Military theories flourished, too – Prince Luxemburg (François Henri de Montmorency, 1628–95) had proposed reorganising the army into divisions and using independent advance units to clear the way for marching columns, but the times were not yet ready for such a reform. It took all the rulers of Germany, the Netherlands, England and Spain to hold Louis XIV off until 1700. Paying the soldiers of these armies was a challenge for each of the monarchs and their ministers.

Almost every state struggled to provide a stable coinage. This had been a problem ever since the Spanish conquered Mexico and Peru. The original bonanza had been gold, but it soon became silver. The Aztecs and Incas worked in silver, but they lacked the ability to extract it from ore, while the Spanish king's subjects from the Netherlands and Germany were able to produce bullion in great quantity. By the mid-1500s the Spanish opened the China market. There were no European products that the Chinese wanted, except novelties like clocks, but by sending silver from Mexico to Manila, they could purchase silks and other luxury items, then transport them home via Mexico, for sale in Europe at fantastic profit.

This trade in silver and oriental products quickly produced competitors and pirates – it being thought easier to steal these products than to buy them, which was especially true because French Protestants and Englishmen had no products that Asians wanted, or lacked the coerced labour that could produce them, hence trade with China was foreclosed to them. The Habsburg Empire further benefited from German and Bohemian mining operations.

It did not take long before these new supplies of silver contributed to price inflation. As the cost of goods and services increased, princes told their mint masters to stamp out more coins – which was only achievable by their putting less silver into each coin. This, of course, destabilised prices further. Copernicus (1473–1543) had observed that people tended to keep coins with high silver content and pass on debased coin. This was an early version of Gresham's Law – that bad money drives out good money. It was a principle that princes and princely advisors found difficult to grasp. Why, they asked, wouldn't people just demand the good money?

There was a three-fold answer. First, each state demanded that people accept its coins. Secondly, since there weren't enough good coins in circulation to sustain commerce, people either had to take the coins or do without. Lastly, though local commerce could operate on credit, mercenaries wanted hard cash. Princes, who had to deliver chests of coins to their generals, often sent debased copies of earlier coins. The mercenaries complained about the lower silver content, but since it was impossible to find a new employer instantly, if the difference between what they wanted and what was offered was not *too* great, they took the coins; and their employer saw to it that merchants and prostitutes accepted them, too. Awkwardly, these coins were then used to pay taxes.

Another problem came from 'clipping' – cutting the edges off coins. Lord Macaulay[5] described eloquently the troubles this gave the government of William III (1650–1702), which in the 1690s was fighting a desperate war in the Netherlands against Louis XIV. Clipping was a process of shaving off the edge of coins, each time reducing them in size, ultimately making the coins significantly smaller. Any government that continued to mint full-weight coins lost money each time it took in clipped coins in taxes, then had to buy silver on the inflated world market to mint new ones. Draconian penalties for clipping were ineffective – English juries did not consider the offence serious enough to justify harsh punishments.

One means of stopping this practice was a new process for milling coins that made each coin uniform in size and weight, fully rounded, with an inscription around the edge. However, sharp-eyed currency manipulators quickly shipped full-weight coins abroad, where they were melted down for the silver content; some bold thieves melted the coins down right at home. The English government was at its wit's end about how to provide coins to pay its troops and its other expenses.

Some proposals for reform, such as declaring that there should be fewer shillings to the pound, apparently assumed that the public and foreign customers were too stupid to notice; most proposals would have brought about destructive inflation. However, so many people benefited from the existing situation – most importantly bankers, who were money-changers – that getting legislation through Parliament was almost impossible. John Locke, the most famous political philosopher of the era, explained that something had to be done, and although no choice was perfect, taking the lesser evil – changing the currency – was the best long-term policy. Moreover, delay would only make matters worse. Ultimately, the Whig government of William III made its decision – old coins would be accepted for taxes on the basis of weight only until March 1696.

There was a monetary crisis, but once Parliament created new mints, public confidence slowly returned. British soldiers knew that they would be paid in good coins and, more important, foreign mercenaries became eager to accept English employment. Without this seemingly minor reform, William III might not have been able to force the French to accept the 1697 Peace of Ryswick, and later British campaigns in Germany and the Netherlands might have been impossible.

Troubles in Britain

The less we read about the past, the more easily we can persuade ourselves that there was a smooth flow of events; however, once we dig below the surface, we see that contemporaries were as concerned about now-forgotten crises and scandals as we are about our own. Each seemingly gentle stream had its rocks and rapids, most of which are remembered today only in local folklore. One such event was the Glencoe Massacre, the terrible culmination of a Scottish clan rivalry that almost toppled the English monarchy.

William III had seized power in 1688–9 in what his supporters called the Glorious Revolution, driving the Stuart king James II (1633–1701) into French exile, then involving England in Holland's war against Louis XIV – James's policies and his Catholicism had alarmed his Anglican and Presbyterian subjects, who worried that he was copying Louis's authoritarian ways. Although William seemed to have benefited from God's favour – the 'Protestant wind' that carried his army of Dutch, Danish and Huguenot soldiers to western England had also detained the Royal Navy in the Thames – this had not persuaded every Englishman and Scot that William and his wife (James's elder daughter, Mary, 1662–94) had a better claim on the throne than James's infant son, or even the exiled James II. Tories – as the politicians who lost power when James II fled to France were known – complained about William's Dutch ways and his difficulties in speaking English.[6] William had good reasons to expect Jacobites, as die-hard supporters of James II were known (Jacobus being the Latin form of James), to attempt a coup; even Tories who professed their loyalty to William and Mary might welcome a French invasion, much as Whigs had greeted the Dutch and their mercenaries. This was a most serious matter, since their overthrow would not only bring James II back to the throne, with vigorous and unchallengeable pro-Catholic, anti-Parliament policies, but it would lead to Louis XIV expanding his power over Germany, the Netherlands and Italy. Knowing how French troops had recently treated German Protestants in the Palatinate, Englishmen and Scots were unsure what the future held – some feared similar atrocities in their land, others hoped for them. As party lines formed, each began to think that striking first was essential.

At another time an event such as the Glencoe Massacre might have been dismissed as a primitive act of revenge, or representative of the ancient Lowlander–Highlander feud. In 1692, however, after redcoats had brought in the MacDonalds – staunch Catholics loyal to James II – as prisoners, it was too late to say that the MacDonald chief should have taken the oath of allegiance earlier rather than wait for permission from James II, by which time snow had made travel difficult, or that he should have gone to the right official to obtain the promised amnesty, or even that Campbells should not have been allowed to get near the MacDonalds. The number of men and women slaughtered in cold blood – less than eighty – was not large by continental standards, but was sufficient to besmirch the reputation of the Duke of Argyll, whose troops had murdered many of the victims. Certainly, William should have taken the public outrage over redcoats shooting civilians more seriously than he did. It did not matter that the king was in the Netherlands prosecuting a war – his government's silence was taken as approval.

In 1695 Tories and Jacobites sought to prosecute the soldiers as murderers. It was, as Macaulay admits, an awkward matter. As he said, it is terrible to burn down an entire town to hunt down bandits, but sometimes that has to be done, and matters of morality were not considered the same then as during the reign of Victoria. Holding troops liable for prosecution for following commands would have made them reluctant to obey any order by their officers and would have undermined all military discipline. In the end, practical men won the day – obedience to a foolish order may be a moral crime, but it was not a criminal act. Responsibility lay with the officers, not with the men.

Nevertheless, to placate the critics of the government, the king allowed a poor sergeant to be hanged. As soon as he dared, William pardoned the officers involved and then promoted them. Who actually knew the truth? There were plots against the king, but there were also informers who specialised in inventing plots that they would be then be rewarded for uncovering. Conspiracies and conspiracy theories were to be found in every country, but rarely more often than at this time. It is a wonder that rulers were not more paranoid than they were.

As it happened, Parliament, almost by accident, failed to renew the Censorship Act. Soon afterwards the first real newspaper appeared, and although publishers were extremely cautious about criticising the government, the principle of freedom of the press was established.

The Whig party retained power through William's reign. Tories protested the war, and Jacobites concocted plots that went as far as planning assassinations, but the deaths of Mary and subsequently the unhappy king did not produce the anticipated change of policy. Once Anne (1665–1714) became queen in 1702, she appointed Marlborough (John Churchill,

1650–1722) commander of the army in the Netherlands, and complaints diminished somewhat: Marlborough's past ties to the Tories persuaded them that he might be won over to their party again – and he did little to discourage this belief. In politics, as in command, he believed it was best to keep his plans to himself – even from the queen.

When the Habsburg emperor decided on Prince Eugene as his commander, and Queen Anne, despite her bouts of depression and indecision, retained Marlborough, the allies could prosecute the war against Louis XIV's famed marshals with a thoroughness hardly envisioned before.

One might well say that a new era of warfare had begun in 1683, when Christian armies, flush with the victory over the Turks at Vienna, became better organised and more professional, and that by 1717, with the end of the wars associated with Charles XII and Louis XIV, it had matured. Gone were the mutinous freelance units of the Thirty Years War. To keep mercenaries in check, however, employers had to pay them promptly and well. Raising the money would not be an easy task, but it was essential. For the soldiers, the prospect of permanent employment meant that they could not go on strike on the eve of battle, demanding their wages; commanders, in their turn, would have to pay the wages of fallen soldiers to their relatives and could not dismiss the troops when the war ended. Of course, governments found ways around this, such as putting soldiers on half-wages in peacetime.

Politics did not come to an end in 1717, and many people did not care – gin-soaked Britons mired in poverty hardly knew the difference between war and peace; brandy-swilling continentals were hardly better off. Everyone was poorly nourished, even the richest nobles and most corrupt clerics; those who did not suffer hunger were often overweight, and fresh vegetables were both seasonal and unfashionable. Epidemic diseases, most notably smallpox, swept away huge numbers; old age began with the loss of teeth, hearing and eyesight at ages considerably earlier than we experience today – fresh breath was so rare that it was worth remarking on. And the lice! Shaving the head or cropping the hair close, then wearing a wig that a servant could check for nits was the only defence – bathing was often impractical and clothes could not be washed regularly. In winter rooms were cold, or smoky and crowded. Privacy was not a common enough luxury to be appreciated, and toilet facilities were primitive. The pollution of city air and major rivers were to be expected wherever cities were simply expanded slums surrounding the churches, municipal buildings, palaces and noble residences. It was no surprise that London had experienced first the plague, then the great fire. This was the age of *The Beggar's Opera* by John Gay (1685–1732), *The Rape of the Lock* by Alexander Pope (1677–1744) and *Gulliver's Travels* by Jonathan Swift (1667–1745), none of whom had much good to say about the British public – or any other public. This was the beginning of the salon, the private drawing room that was more suited than the court for the educated, the notorious and the curious to gather for conversation and entertainment. The salon, open to talent as well to as those favoured by accident of birth, would give birth to the Enlightenment. These social gatherings, whether in London, Paris, Dresden or provincial towns eager to be known for their *bon ton*,[7] were managed by exceptional women who insisted on good manners and rationality, elegant style in speech, writing and clothing, and quickness of wit and tongue. Less ambitious women, if sufficiently attractive and lively, could meet exciting men, maybe even marry a rich one; actresses could advance their careers; and young men acquire patrons. The salons offered an alternative culture to a high society bored with deferring to royal etiquette and imbecility. Spas, such as Bath, permitted a similar experience during the months when cities were too uncomfortable, and, being less formal, were excellent places to introduce young women to society; if successful, they could be introduced to the king and other, more interesting men, then prepared in some salon for later seduction.

CHAPTER TWO

Christian Europe Presses the Islamic World

Vienna to Budapest

In 1683, after the Ottoman siege of Vienna was broken by an improbably broad Christian coalition, the Turks began their slow retreat back towards Constantinople (Istanbul came into official use much later). This story, told in my *Bayonets for Hire*, need not be repeated here, except to note that just as Grand Vizier Ahmed Köprülü's sappers and artillery were about to overwhelm the exhausted defenders of the Austrian capital, King Jan Sobieski (1629–96) brought a battle-tested army from Poland, with Lithuanian reinforcements following behind; they joined Catholic and Protestant Germans led by Charles of Lorraine. Monarchs who did not participate paused in their own wars so as to not distract the Holy Roman emperor and his allies. Köprülü apparently did not think that such disparate forces – which had never fought together before – would even be able to reach Vienna. Sobieski, however, knew his opponent well and correctly judged that the grand vizier would not anticipate a daring night march over the rugged hill country of the Vienna Woods, nor that the Christians would follow up the victory by pursuing him into Hungary.

Köprülü paid for his military failures in the traditional Ottoman manner – strangulation with a silken cord. Perhaps nothing better marked the differences between the two systems of belief as this. Condemning an unsuccessful general to death was not unknown in the Christian world, but it was not systematic. The sultans believed that such punishment put a ramrod up the vizers' backs. This was a metaphor less vivid than the regional specialty of a stake through the anus into the abdomen and out one shoulder, then being hung on public display, to wriggle for hours or days until death came, but it reminds us that people took their politics and religion seriously in those days.

In 1686 the Christians captured Budapest, then pressed south under the leadership of Ludwig of Baden (Türkenlouis, 1655–1707) and Eugene of Savoy (1663–1736). With uprisings among the sultan's Christian subjects assisting the advance, it seemed as though the Austrian army might sweep right to the gates of Constantinople. At the same moment the Russian army was pressing south towards the Black Sea, and Venetian fleets were capturing bases along the Adriatic Sea, then advancing into Greece. Not joining the offensive was Louis XIV, who had hoped to be called to save Christendom (and be rewarded with lands and titles, perhaps even that of Holy Roman emperor); instead, he moved to interrupt it by crossing the Rhine to ravage German lands. The emperor, Leopold (1640–1705), had to break off the Balkan campaign and transfer much of his army to the Rhine. This disrupted the Christian offensive and gave the Ottomans time to recover.

In 1690 an Ottoman army retook Belgrade (Beograd) and, following the designs of a Venetian engineer, converted it into a modern fortress; its location at the junction of the Sava and Danube rivers, a point where the Danube shifted its flow from southwards towards the east, made it the most strategic position in the Balkans. All that the Austrians could do to limit attacks into Hungary was to build an impressive fortress at Petrovaradin (Peterwardein) just to the north.

Rhoads Murphey reminds us in *Ottoman Warfare, 1500–1700* that Westerners have traditionally misunderstood the Turkish state, inaccurately believing that it was weaker than it was. The surprise was not in the temporary setbacks, he said, but in historians believing that such reverses were connected to Islamic beliefs and Turkish social practices. The Ottomans had delivered peace, stability, religious toleration, prosperity and good government, foundations which allowed for speedy revivals after seemingly terrible defeats. Hence, while the 1699 Treaty of Karlowitz, which surrendered Hungary and Croatia, can be seen in the long run as the beginning of Ottoman decline, that was not apparent at the time.

New Wars to the North, a Truce in the Balkans

In 1700, when Augustus the Strong invaded Livonia, beginning the Great Northern War, he took Poland and Saxony out of the Balkan wars almost completely. When the War of the Spanish Succession broke out the next year, Christian hopes for victory in the Balkans disappeared. Austria could not send troops south, the subject peoples were left to their own devices, and the Turks breathed sighs of relief.

Eugene of Savoy, the 'little Capuchin' who had crushed Ottoman armies, now led the Habsburg forces against Louis XIV's seemingly invincible armies. Italian by ancestry, French by birth and upbringing, the beneficiary of military reforms instituted by Raimondo Montecuccoli (1609–80), he became the greatest of all of Austria's generals. Not an intellectual himself – merely an inspired leader of men who understood the importance of manoeuvre – nor physically impressive, he could nevertheless persuade the emperor, the bureaucrats of the War Council in Vienna and his officers to follow his recommendations. His love of combat gave him an important advantage over cautious opponents, and a decisive one over poor generals. His troops adored him. Not only did he care for them well, but when they saw him galloping across the battlefield, his red cloak drawing enemy fire that failed to down him, they knew that victory was certain.

Most of Prince Eugene's men were mercenaries, recruits from the German lands, but some from Italy and Croatia; and a smattering of the refuse of all Europe. He dressed them in heavy grey cloaks that were too heavy and too hot for summer marching, but warded off the cold rains of spring and autumn; they also provided some protection against spent bullets and weak sword thrusts. Most important, they made his men look like soldiers.

The emperor appreciated battlefield victories, but he was frustrated by repeated revolts in his newly acquired Hungarian lands. Those were Leopold's own fault. Had he not attempted to force Roman Catholicism onto his new subjects, he might have been able to implement programmes with more potential for taming the tradition-minded Magyar lords – such as freeing their serfs, a step that would have left them without dependable labour at the same time that it would have won him popular loyalty. However, it was impossible for Leopold to think in such revolutionary terms, and in any case he was not known for thinking much at all. Although the emperor was not far-sighted enough to realise the advantages of free labour or freedom of religion, he did give lands to refugee Serbs, Orthodox believers who settled on the southern frontiers and held them against Turkish attacks. When Hungarian nobles made, in William McNeill's words, 'a sulky retreat into an archaic localism', Leopold offered some concessions, most importantly abandoning efforts to integrate Hungary into Austria. With Hungary a separate kingdom, the reforms that Leopold's administrators proposed were piecemeal efforts; the result was the patchwork state we have come to identify with later Habsburg inefficiency.

In *The Habsburg Monarchy*, Charles Ingrao says that colonisation in the lands gained by the Treaty of Karlowitz, combined with refugees from the Ottoman lands, redistributed the population of the borderlands. Germans, French and Italians took up lands, as did Magyars, Slovaks, Ruthenes, Serbs, Romanians and Bulgarians. For the short term, the project was a great success. McNeill, in *Europe's Steppe Frontier*, saw it differently – many Magyars still preferred Turkish rule, and many regions had suffered population losses. Moreover, traditional commercial networks were now disrupted. Grain was formerly sent to Constantinople, but now having no market, farmers were turning to herding: an additional advantage to raising cattle and sheep was that in time of war the animals could be driven into hiding. This created a military frontier zone where, once the fields were burned, neither Christian nor Turk could find food or fodder.

In contrast, the northern Hungarian lands, where swamps had spread during the era of depopulation, became the breadbasket that fed Austrian armies. By relieving commanders of dependence on supplies brought from farther up the Danube, this made campaigns into Moldavia and Wallachia more practical. Once Transylvania was no longer a rebel stronghold, Habsburg control of Slovakia became more certain.

The Ottoman Revival

With Austria fully committed to the War of the Spanish Succession and Peter the Great of Russia fighting Charles XII of Sweden, the Ottomans had a full decade to rest and reorganise. They might have remained at peace even longer if Peter's victory at Poltava in 1709 had not destroyed Charles's army, allowing Peter to then choose where to attack next – and he looked south, towards the Black Sea.

Turkish intervention before Poltava, Charles had tried to tell the sultan, could have produced a very different outcome to the Great Northern War. After the injured Swedish king took refuge in the Ottoman domains, he pleaded in vain for troops to resume the contest; he was certain that his genius and that of his surviving officers could make any troops into an effective army – after all, only his elite units had been composed of native Swedes. Improbable as that might sound today, Charles's contemporaries had learned by harsh experience that it was a mistake to underestimate him. One might well wonder if, under the king's leadership, the Ottoman army could have recovered lands that had been lost earlier. However, neither the sultan nor the grand vizier seized the moment; the former was essentially ignorant of politics and war, the latter viewed peace as both necessary and desirable – even that false peace that precedes an attack by neighbours. Thus the Turks lost the services of a military genius. Or such is the viewpoint of many historians. (McNeill, in *Europe's Steppe Frontier*, prefers an alternative explanation – that the Turks saw no point in sacrificing troops and money to gain what was still an almost empty stretch of grassland.)

The argument that Turks needed an extraordinary commander to make up for their deficiencies in weaponry and organisation was partly refuted in 1711 when an Ottoman grand vizier of modest ability faced the Russian tsar in Moldavia. Peter had expected an easy victory, but found his large army utterly incapable of warding off the swarms of Turkish light cavalry that surrounded it in the marshes of the Pruth River. With supplies being swiftly eaten up and no good water available, with neither retreat nor advance possible, and his camp under artillery fire, Peter asked for terms. Fortunately for Peter, Charles XII was not there to finish his army off. Instead, the grand vizier accepted a large bribe that included jewels belonging to Peter's wife. It probably did not matter that Charles XII had returned to Sweden. What the Ottomans needed were battlefield successes that could be turned into diplomatic victories – as this treaty appeared to be. Charles XII, who was a genius in commanding an army, never seemed to know when enough was enough. The grand vizier understood that the Swedish king would have dragged the Ottoman Empire into a long war to destroy Russia, a result that was unlikely to be achieved no matter how many resources the sultan wasted in its pursuit.

The tsar's surrender was humiliating, but he escaped with his life and most of his army. He abandoned his dream of acquiring a port on the Black Sea, returning Azov to the sultan, then turned his attention back to Charles XII. The Swedish king was home once again, undaunted and eager to win back everything he had lost, no matter that his resources were almost exhausted. This was not a situation the tsar could ignore, so he honoured his treaty with the sultan.

Four years later, in 1715, the Ottoman army recaptured the Morea from Venice. This important territory, practically an island, had once been home to Sparta and the Olympic games. Its harbour at Navarino had offered refuge to merchant ships since the days of Odysseus, and it had been the last great Venetian outpost in the east. Venice, once an important commercial and military power, saw its importance shrink; its rival, Ragusa (Dubrovnik), which had better relations with the Turks, became a more serious commercial rival. Every sign indicated that the 1683 Christian victory at Vienna had resulted from a lucky combination of events which would never be repeated – the Ottomans were once again the dominant power in the Balkans.

This was a significant change from the situation six years earlier. Until 1709 the Austrians had hoped for a great Christian alliance that would drive the Turks out of Europe; however, before Peter's offensive into Moldavia turned into a disaster, Joseph I (1678–1711) feared the tsar would advance all the way to Constantinople. The emperor, whose Austrian troops were so committed to the French war (discussed in Chapter Three) that there were none available to besiege even weakly garrisoned Ottoman fortresses, seems to have concluded that the sultan was a safer neighbour than the tsar. In any case, Peter's defeat removed all worries that the Balkan lands would be ruled by an Orthodox Christian rival who might be more dangerous than the traditional Muslim foe. Only after 1713, when the aged Louis XIV agreed to peace, first with Great Britain and Holland, then the next year with the Holy Roman Empire, could Emperor Charles VI (1685–1740) turn his attention southwards again. The end of the War of the Spanish Succession had released masses of mercenaries back on the market, and Charles no longer had to watch his back for the customary swift French stab – that nation had been reduced to bankruptcy and starvation several years before. On the other hand, northern European rulers were still occupied with Charles XII of Sweden, who was miraculously holding out against all of them – and even taking the offensive.

Charles VI, understanding that his subjects were exhausted and the conflict with his dynastic rival in Spain was not over, was reluctant to approve a Balkan campaign without allies – and none were to be found. Nevertheless, the issue was fundamental – the Turks intended to retake Hungary, and, knowing this, Charles had ended the French war before winning a total victory and ordered Prince Eugene to hurry home.

The Austrian Army Captures Belgrade

The Turks opened the war in 1716 with the new grand vizier marching up the Danube to attack Petrovaradin. Prince Eugene had been planning to move south in any case, but he now had an incentive to hurry – the great fortress was defended by locally recruited Serbs, with only a handful of trained professionals.

When Prince Eugene approached Petrovaradin in August, he had forty thousand effective troops from Austria, Germany, Croatia and Serbia to face one hundred thousand Turks and their allies. The numbers are unreliable – in addition to being estimates and including support forces, his originally large army had been reduced day-by-day by heat, exhaustion, disease and combat.

Eugene's first goal was to defend Petrovaradin, his second to capture Belgrade. Both fortresses sat on high bluffs overlooking the Danube and were the most strategic points along the entire river; he knew that Belgrade was impressively fortified and could not be taken easily, but he had been with the army that had accomplished that feat in 1688.

When Eugene approached Petrovaradin with a small advance force, he found that the grand vizier had already begun to wear down the fortress walls on the land side; the bridges across the Danube, however, remained in Christian hands. Leaving his army encamped securely slightly upstream, he made a personal reconnaissance of the situation and learned that there was no time to be lost – the grand vizier, having decided that Eugene's army was too small to be a danger, had announced his intention to storm the fortress the next day.

That very night Eugene led his army across the bridges into Petrovaradin, his arrival shielded by a snowfall, something very rare for an early August day in the Balkans. Eugene did not allow his opponent time to reassess the situation, but ordered his men to assault the Turkish lines immediately. The grand vizier, believing that he was facing only a sally by the garrison, concluded that sending his janissaries forward to strike the Christians before they could all clear the gates would make him master of the fortress by evening. Indeed, it appeared for a moment that the Turkish assault would break the lines, but Eugene calmly sent troops to the centre to shore it up, then led his cavalry on a devastating charge into the flank of the Ottoman infantry. The light Turkish horsemen sent to intercept him were unequal to the task, and when they fell back, their Tatar auxiliaries rode quietly away. That afternoon Eugene's men, supported by cannon fire from boats on the Danube, stormed the incompletely fortified Ottoman camp. Only half the Ottoman army managed to escape to Belgrade.

The grand vizier soon received a death sentence from the sultan, and after the ritual strangulation, his body was buried with honour in the Belgrade fortress, which was still one of the strongest in all Europe. Eugene's army, reduced in numbers by casualties and disease, was not up to the task of following up its victory.

There were several eyewitness accounts of the next year's campaign, but none more interesting than that of the son of Augustus the Strong, Maurice de Saxe (1696–1750) – *Memoirs on the Art of War*. Christians who did not understand fully what difficulties were involved in besieging the great fortress were enthusiastic about the prospects for capturing it. Volunteers flooded in from great noble families; even Maximilian II Emanuel of Bavaria (1662–1726) sent his heir, Charles Albert (1697–1745), and a younger son, with 5,000 men; 6,000 Saxons also appeared, with 2,300 from Hesse-Kassel, and more from minor states. French and Britons came in smaller numbers, but everyone saw the potential for earning fame while experiencing a historic moment.

Maurice, who had been too young to be given a command, kept close to Prince Eugene and hence not only saw what happened, but heard when decisions were made. Eugene had barely laid out his siege lines facing the fortress when a huge Turkish army appeared, perhaps led by the grand vizier in person. Calmly, Eugene drew up a second line of fortifications to ward off his new enemy, then continued the siege in spite of Turkish cannons firing down on his men from high ground. After two months, however, when appalling sanitary conditions threatened to reduce his men to invalids, Eugene chose to strike at the Turkish emplacements to his rear while he still had enough healthy troops to fight.

Taking advantage of the morning mist, Eugene sent his infantry towards the Ottoman trenches. Slowly, firing steadily, they moved forward, taking one entrenchment after another with the bayonet. De Saxe remembered watching two regiments – Lorraine (Austrian) and Neuburg (Teutonic Knights, and the home of the emperor's mother) – become isolated from the rest of the infantry. When Prince Eugene saw horsemen moving towards those units, he asked de Saxe if he could tell who they were. Informed that they were Turks, Eugene was alarmed. De Saxe did not see the danger himself, but he rode over as ordered to warn the commanders. He arrived too late. Although the units had changed face and fired a volley at thirty paces into the charging Turks, they were overrun and slaughtered almost to a man.

Prince Eugene, despite having only his bodyguard around him, rode to the rescue and drove the Turks away, but when they examined the battlefield later, they found that only thirty-two Turks had fallen here. This skirmish, though costly, was only a temporary setback – the Bavarian infantry had continued the advance with cavalry support until they had taken the gun emplacements, after which the Turkish army fled. Two days later Belgrade surrendered.

In de Saxe's opinion, the Turks were defeated because, 'it is neither in courage, numbers, nor riches, but in discipline and order, that they are defective'. There was also the matter of leadership, a quality that Eugene possessed like few contemporaries. Maurice was so eager to emulate him, that when at the age of twelve, he had joined the prince's entourage in the campaigns in the Low Countries, Eugene had kept him close by so that he would not dash off in some mad heroic gesture and get himself killed. The two made a nice contrast of personalities and physical types – Eugene was slightly built, but energetic, clad simply to emphasise his clerical status, while Maurice was strong and athletic, a lover of women and life. They were both excellent warriors, but it was Eugene whom future ages would celebrate in song as *der edle Ritter* (the noble knight).

Among the war booty was an Arabian stallion, Belgrade Turk, that its new owner used to start a thoroughbred bloodline. James Edward Oglethorpe

(1696–1785), later the founder of the American colony of Georgia, never forgot the experience of being one of Prince Eugene's aides-de-camp. Uncle Toby, one of the most memorable figures in Laurence Sterne's 1760 novel *Tristam Shandy*, reminisced at length about an unfortunate acquaintance who had got to Belgrade just in time to participate in the fight, then had his fortunes go irretrievably bad.

The same may be said about Austria. Prince Eugene recommended that Leopold offer peace in return for possession of the Banat, the rich lands just north of Belgrade on the opposite bank of the Danube. More territory, he said, would be more trouble than it was worth – so much of the Balkans had been depopulated or impoverished by war that the remaining people could hardly support the garrisons necessary to protect them. Few could then imagine that Austria's road also henceforth led downwards – there seemed to be little risk in allowing the sultan to hang onto these lands for a few more years.

But what choices were there? There was always Russia. Should the Ottoman Empire actually collapse, not only would there be the expensive proposition of bringing order to the Balkans, but the new territories would have to be defended against the tsar. On the other hand, the newly enlarged Russian state was unstable. There could always be a new 'Time of Troubles', when a dispute over the succession would again lead to civil war and foreign invasions, and certainly there were problems on the steppe. If Russia ceased to be a player in regional politics, the sultan would turn his full attention to Austria.

Beyond the Russian Frontier

Michael Khodarovsky, in *Russia's Steppe Frontier*, noted how Ivan's conquest of Kazan and Astrakhan in the 1550s had upset the traditional balance of power in the region, leaving the situation fluid for years to come. The steppe was not empty, he said, disagreeing with McNeill's *Europe's Steppe Frontier*; rather, he argued that the vast grassland was filled with nomadic peoples. Whereas McNeill emphasised technological innovations in agriculture, Khodarovsky stressed the protection that tsars could provide to farmers who moved onto that great prairie. He said that Moscow's role as protector of Russian Orthodox peoples changed in the eighteenth century, when

Muslims and pagans crossed the lines, often becoming Christians, to participate in the more vibrant Russian economy. If Western Europeans thought Russia poor, steppe peoples considered it incredibly wealthy.

Russia was expanding eastwards. Tsarist expeditions reached Lake Baikal around 1600, the Amur River shortly afterwards. When the explorers ran into Manchurian troops, they pulled back; outnumbered and outgunned, they saw that this was not the moment to provoke a confrontation. In 1639 Russian explorers reached the Pacific Ocean, and in 1728 they built sailing ships that soon reached Alaska; fur trading soon became a profitable business.

To a certain extent eastward exploration and conquest reflected an effort to deal with a serious problem in the southern borderlands – what to do with the Cossacks. In the 1600s the Ukrainian horsemen had been sufficiently powerful to defy both Moscow and Poland–Lithuania, but a century later most had been reduced to auxiliaries of the tsar's Western-style armies. They had traditionally lived by raiding Tatar lands, but once Russia had established itself on the Black Sea and made peace with that enemy, the Cossacks were as much a problem as an asset. Tsars and tsarinas had to divert Cossack energies to other wars in Europe, or to the conquest of Siberia.

Cossacks were frontiersmen, but Khodarkovsky warns us that the common comparison of the American frontier experience with Russia's is fundamentally misleading. If the American frontier created independent men and women, that of Russia expanded serfdom. There was no Bartolemé de las Casas or Edmund Burke to protest government mistakes and misdeeds, but there were brutal and corrupt governors aplenty. It could not be otherwise. The frontier was an open space where no man or government ruled until after its military conquest. Then, far from Moscow and St Petersburg, tsarist officials, without traditions of constitutional government and free enterprise to fall back on in lieu of imperial instructions, found themselves challenged by problems that arose from the region's vastness, its multiplicity of ethnicities and the climate.

As Russian forces advanced into Kazakhstan and Siberia, tsarist officials recruited leaders from the native peoples, using a combination of economic incentives, commercial enterprises, and military and political pressure. This did not always work. Native peoples looked for new ways to defend themselves, most often not against Russians, but against those displaced by the Russian advance. Some turned to European weapons and European instructors.

Pressing on these same peoples, but from the east, were the Chinese. From 1720 on, using matchlocks and better organised armies, Chinese emperors sent armies westwards along the Silk Road and into Tibet. Numbers, equipment and epidemic diseases overwhelmed the disorganised resistance of steppe tribes and mountain peoples alike, with one exception – the Dsungars (Western Mongols), whose lands lay just south of Lake Baikal. Once the Dsungars learned to employ Western firearms, they were able to turn back all invading armies. However, getting around their enemies' firearms embargo was a difficult matter, because they had no way to transfer gold to Western merchants. Their solution was to hire a Swedish artillery officer to manufacture muskets. Johan Renat (1682– 1744), who had been captured in the battle of Poltava and sent to Siberia to draw maps for the imperial army, worked for the Dsungars from 1716 to 1733. His career was adventurous almost beyond belief – his parents were Viennese Jews who had converted to Lutheranism, a decision which must have aided him in enlisting in the Swedish army. In Central Asia he met and married a Swedish war widow who was helping native peoples develop their textile industry. When he returned to Stockholm, he rejoined the Swedish army, but he could not find anyone who was interested in detailed maps of lands beyond the eastern Russian frontier. Sweden had an interest in Russia, but only in those regions closest at hand.

Siberia, vast as it was, was a somewhat porous prison. Those fleeing tsarist armies could find help from others who hated the tsar, but we know little more about the Dsungars and other peoples caught in this turmoil. Reliable information was not even reaching the capitals of Russia or China, much less the West. We do know that when the Dsungars occupied Tibet in 1717, they behaved so badly that the Tibetans called on the Chinese emperor to rescue them.

One might wonder if the Dsungars should not have made a closer relationship with the tsar. After all, Russia was not the only expanding power in Central Asia, and while they were able to turn back the Russians, thanks to their swarms of light cavalry, they were not equally successful at dealing with Chinese armies. Manchu cavalry, working together with Chinese infantry along a series of fortified posts, eventually wore the Dsungars down.[1] Once the Chinese emperor brought the Dsungars inside his sphere of influence, he sent armies farther west towards Turkestan; by 1750 China had established itself deep in inner Asia, which encouraged him to look at other frontiers.

In 1765 Chinese armies invaded Burma to resolve a border dispute. This quickly became a desperate conflict with peoples accustomed to violence and warfare – the difficulties should have been no surprise, since such unrest was behind the border problems. Peace came in 1769 after the surrender of the surrounded Chinese army.

Afterwards China began that pull-back inside traditional boundaries that has lasted into modern times, causing many contemporary Europeans to mistake China's attitude for Korea's – that of a hermit kingdom. It was a historic choice, one that was not clearly a mistake until the middle of the nineteenth century (and not recognised as such by the imperial family even then). China had soldiers, but did not honour them; when centrifugal forces appeared, unity became difficult to maintain.

China's moment of expansion set off a chain reaction to the south – the Burmese invaded Siam (Thailand) and the Malay peninsula, spreading political chaos to a larger region. New states were on the march, older ones were giving way. Each hired whatever soldiers were available. Rulers might not have wished to do so, but the instinct for survival pushed old prejudices and morals aside.

Mameluke Recovery

The Ottoman sultan Selim I (1470–1520) had smashed the Mameluke army in Syria in 1516, eliminated its last organised resistance in Egypt within two years and later slaughtered rebellious units that had enrolled in his army. It seemed as though those famed slave cavalrymen were finished. However, Selim's successors discovered that the southern frontier of Egypt was difficult to protect, and they lacked the will or incentive to drive into the Ethiopian highlands, the wilds of Somalia or the deserts around Darfur to finish off mobile enemies. The solution was to seek out surviving Mamelukes and put them in charge of the Upper Nile frontier.

After this the Mamelukes revived quickly, once again buying Circassian slaves from the Caucasus Mountains and training them as warriors. They chafed under Ottoman restrictions that kept their numbers small, but they understood that time was on their side, and that one day Ottoman attention would be diverted. By the time the sultan or grand vizier noticed, they would be the major power in Egypt once again.

Working with Ottoman forces, in 1586 they commissioned a corsair (i.e. a Muslim pirate) named Ali Bey to sail out into the Red Sea, then follow the coast as far as Mombassa, destroying Portuguese settlements as he progressed. In 1589 Ali Bey made a second plundering expedition, only to be trapped in Mombassa by a Portuguese fleet dispatched from India. In desperation he made contact with a local Bantu tribe called the Zimba, who were widely feared as fierce warriors and reputed to be cannibals; most likely, they were Galla, Zimba being a synonym for man-eaters used all over the region. He hired their services, only to regret it almost instantly – the Zimba attacked the Muslim sailors, then ate them; they captured Ali Bey, but he somehow survived. The Portuguese smashed the Zimba shortly afterwards, practically annihilating them.

However, the Portuguese oceanic empire could not be reconstituted. In coming decades, Dutch, then English and French competition would shove the Portuguese aside. By 1700 the former Ottoman and Portuguese authority in the Indian Ocean were but memories. Ports were shared by Europeans and Muslims for trade in African products – mainly human beings who were becoming more prized across both the Atlantic and Indian oceans.

North Africa

The Ottomans and Portuguese also collided in Morocco, and the Ottomans and Spaniards in Algeria – both wars largely prompted by piracy. While modern readers might wonder why Voltaire included a story about piracy in *Candide*, readers in 1759 understood. In his fictional account – Voltaire was better known then as a historian than as a satiric novelist – an old woman told how, when she was a young princess (the daughter of the pope, no less), her ship – a vessel belonging to the papacy – was captured by Moors. The soldiers protected themselves 'like true soldiers of the pope' by throwing themselves on their knees and begging for last rites. The Moors stripped everyone bare, then stuck their fingers into places suitable only for bodily functions and reproduction, explaining that everyone does this, even the Christian pirates, to all prisoners, male and female alike. It was a ritual of the law of nations. The pirates then raped all the women, which was not so bad, Voltaire suggested, though the narrator had the honour done by a very ugly Negro. (Very little political correctness existed in eighteenth-century France, and Voltaire rarely paid much attention to it.) Much worse awaited the prisoners in Morocco, where fifty civil wars raged at once, Blacks against Blacks, Browns against Browns and Mulattos against Mulattos. The captives were all slaughtered, too, the princess excepted, she being left for dead in a process that had taken hours and was interrupted only for the five appointed times for prayer. Even though apparently dead, the princess still retained her beauty, which had been such that her maids sighed in envy at seeing her undressed (and all the courtiers had longed to be in their places); she was awakened by a eunuch's efforts at rape – she remembered his saying, 'O che sciagura d'essere senza coglioni!' Obviously, that Muslim slave had an Italian origin – which would not have surprised Voltaire's readers, who were not only familiar with how Muslims dealt with prisoners, but also with their own practice of making certain that young choir boys did not lose their beautiful high notes.

Still, piracy was in decline. In its place came trade. Europeans found the commerce with the Ottoman Empire so profitable that they were willing to risk being robbed again and again. As for the Ottomans, they discovered that buying over-priced European products was better than hoping something useful could be stolen on the high seas. Hence, the sultan restrained the North African pirates as best he could. The détente would not break down until the French Revolution.

Had there been greater stability in Algeria and Morocco, peaceful intercourse might have become the universal rule. But the frequent changes at the top of the many states were accompanied by freebooters sailing out onto the Mediterranean and Atlantic, even as far as Iceland. When the greatest ruler of the era, Mohammed III (1710–90) of Morocco, was unable to afford foreign fighters, his military options were limited. As a result, his Alawite regime emphasised negotiation with rivals, the army's main role being to assure that talks did not slow down unduly. This powerful Berber king managed to balance the various pressures – military, religious and economic – in such ways as to pass a strong Moroccan kingdom down to his successors. By emphasising Arab language and culture, he neutralised the influence of potential rivals, both local Berbers and the neighbouring Ottoman Turks, and brought Morocco into greater contact with the larger Islamic world.

Limits of the Gunpowder Revolution

Christian and Islamic navies fought for control of the trade with India and the Spice Islands, but farther east they encountered states too powerful to be intimidated and too proud and stable to be impressed. They exerted some influence through trade, but without making immediate changes in culture or policies.

China and Japan had adopted Western weapons momentarily, during periods of instability – but only then. As Chase points out in *Firearms: A Global History*, guns were not suitable for all conditions. Once order was restored, the authorities disarmed the common people, taking not only firearms, but also swords – in Japan melting them down to make statues of the Buddha. The Samurai were allowed to retain their swords, but they lost their castles. Still, this was a long way from the conventional belief that the Shogun eliminated all firearms. Muskets and cannons still existed, but the country was so pacified that there was no need to use them, much less keep up with developments elsewhere in the world.

The final step in this process of pacification was to isolate themselves, not only from diplomatic and commercial contacts, but from all Western influence, effectively cutting the people off from all but minimum contact with the outside world. Geoffrey Parker, in *The Military Revolution*, notes that this was an effective policy for the centuries of isolation, but not after Westerners could reach them. When sailing ships could more easily carry guns and merchandise half-way around the world, it would become increasingly difficult for governments to tell outsiders to just go away.

There are lessons here. First, to end the misuse of firearms a government has to be strong enough to take weapons from the entire population, while retaining sufficient weaponry to coerce everyone into obedience. Second, a government cannot stop with seizing weapons, but has to prevent the population from becoming infected with dangerous ideas. It may be that change itself has to stop, and progress cannot be made without change. There is room for an important political debate here.

When a choice has to be made between stability and change, most people opt for stability. This gives authoritarian rulers, aristocracies and religious elites every advantage. It is why Karl Marx and Friedrich Engels, looking at British rule in India and deploring its injustices, nevertheless said that stern measures were necessary to break the hold that class, religion and superstition had on the entire population. Inertia was more than a principle of physics – it was a human characteristic; standing still had to be replaced by forward motion, and the most difficult part of getting anything moving is that first push. If violence was needed, so be it.

What could the West learn from the East? Almost nothing, it seemed.[2] As Voltaire wrote in an article for the *Encyclopedia*, 'If you have nothing to tell us except that one barbarian succeeded another on the banks of the Oxus and Jaxartes, what is that to us?'

What was it? It was part of a process of sweeping change that was blowing east from Europe. Europeans were still far distant from most Asians, but they were setting peoples in motion. Soon their ships would be approaching the shores of India and China.

CHAPTER THREE

War in Western Europe, 1700–1717

The Balance of Power is Upset

Until 1700 it appeared that a Habsburg would inherit the Spanish crown when the physically degenerate and impotent forty-year-old Carlos II died. His empire consisted not only of Spain and its worldwide empire, but also of Naples and Sicily and other Italian states. If those lands fell to the Austrian emperor or his brother, the Balkan War would be given new momentum, and the line of the Rhine could be held against France more easily. However, when the most likely candidate– the seven-year-old son of Max Emanuel of Bavaria – died, perhaps of poison, Louis XIV was able to persuade the almost blind, deaf, toothless and bald Spanish ruler to name Louis's grandson, Philippe (Filipe V, 1683–1746) as his heir. Although Carlos was demonstrably mentally unsound – the details are almost too bizarre to recount – many Spaniards preferred him to the prospect of arrogant Frenchmen telling them what to do. Worse, Louis XIV's neighbours rightly feared this would upset the balance of power, perhaps making the Sun King dominant over Western Europe. Protestants, in particular, worried that the Sun King's Catholic fanaticism would lead to their destruction.

In Britain this led to a further development of the two-party system.[1] According to Brendan Simms, in *Three Victories and a Defeat*, the principal issue was not religion – one traditional explanation of the reasons for choosing one party over the other – nor even the hope of getting office through influence. Instead, the main issue was foreign policy. That is, those who called themselves Whigs saw Britain's greatest danger in some great continental power occupying the Channel coast; hence, they were willing to send troops to oppose the French in the Low Countries or even to accept a Dutch king. That conglomeration of personal and class interests known as Tories preferred to rely on the navy, on commerce and on colonies. For the moment, the Whigs were dominant. They were reluctant to entrust command to Marlborough, who insisted on remaining in contact with Tory friends in France, but his wife persuaded Queen Anne that there was no danger.

It was an odd situation. Anne's father, James II, had traded, it was said, three crowns for a mass; he was not a bad man or stupid, but he possessed an overabundance of the Stuart traits of bad judgement and stubbornness. Anne quarrelled bitterly with her sister and brother-in-law, Mary II and William III, then through their early deaths found herself queen. A tragic figure who had seventeen pregnancies, but lost all her children at birth or to illness, and then her husband, she was seen as a caretaker until her half-brother in France saw fit to abandon Catholicism and become her heir; if James Stuart refused to become a Protestant, the next in line of succession was George of Hanover (1660–1727), a man Anne hated for having refused to marry her. Often drunk, grossly overweight and eventually friendless, Anne became living proof that Britain needed a monarch more than it required a ruler. For critical years the duchess of Marlborough bullied her into behaving, which meant leaving policy decisions to her Whig advisors.

The coalition opposed to Louis XIV reconstituted itself, though Max Emanuel of Bavaria, identified by his Turkish foes as the 'blue king', lost patience with waiting for the imperial crown to come to him – he allied himself with France, hoping that victory would bring him extensive new lands in Germany and the Low Countries. With Spain, France and Bavaria now allies, the British, Dutch and German coalition seemed overmatched.

It was now impossible for the Habsburg emperor to continue the war with the Ottomans or to do anything about the Swedish advances in the east. All resources had to be committed to defeating the Bourbons. The emperor, Leopold, sent Eugene of Savoy into Italy, and his own brother Joseph (1678–1711) to Spain to rally the forces that hated the prospect of proud Spaniards bowing to Paris; unfortunately, those who rallied to him felt the same way about Madrid. Every faction tried to raise an army.

This made it a great moment to be a mercenary. Everyone from Russia to Spain, from Sweden to Italy, was hiring troops, and experienced officers were in high demand. Rulers strained every resource to raise the necessary funds – increasing taxes, borrowing money and debasing the currency.

Others profited from the situation – by renting out his armies, the duke of Württemberg was able to defend his lands against Louis XIV and make money, too.

European armies were evolving steadily in technology and tactics, but doing so unevenly. There was a negative side to size, in that when improvements in weaponry were available, rulers with large armies found it too expensive to replace outmoded muskets and cannons. Nobody wanted to make half a change – storing multiple replacement parts, many sizes of cannon balls, and other supplies was too great a problem. As a result, the most significant changes came not in weaponry, but in the form of improved drill and management.

Armies had been good before, but in this period they became much better – it appeared for a moment that no one could stand up to the forces of France or Sweden, which were allied to the extent that their geographical division allowed. To a considerable degree, this new superiority came from better command and control, especially in combined arms, but also from accumulated experience disseminated in memoirs and manuals. As officers and men better understood what they were doing and what was possible, they were encouraged to attempt the impossible, and often they achieved it. Well-drilled and motivated units could defeat far more numerous enemies, even when possessing little more than their bayonets. The career of Charles XII of Sweden showed what an inspired leader and enthusiastic soldiers could achieve; good leadership could do wonders even with mediocre troops. This was demonstrated repeatedly in Western Europe, too, in the great battles of the War of the Spanish Succession.

The decisive battle of this latter conflict was fought in Bavaria in 1704, between two villages just north of the Danube River – Blenheim and Höchstädt. This war had opened with campaigns in Italy (Prince Eugene) and the Netherlands (Marlborough), then the English duke had slipped away from his French opponent to bring the coalition troops south into Bavaria. He had cleverly disguised his plans until he was too far along the route to be stopped, and meanwhile Prince Eugene had crossed the Alps to join him. The French did not worry excessively – Marlborough's army was new, essentially untried, and no one with experience expected much of it. In those days Englishmen were reputed to be too excitable and too little inclined to accept discipline to be good soldiers; and their Dutch and

German allies were too respectful of their French opponents to do more than manoeuvre from one entrenchment to another. Marlborough was ready to break with every expectation – he was determined to challenge the French in the field and beat them.

The army marched, as the proverb goes, on its stomach. Or, as one writer suggested, it wriggled slowly forward – a word which better describes the progress of long columns of men, horses, cannons and supply wagons. Van Creveld tells us in *Supplying War* how Marlborough's agents (the Medina brothers – forerunners of today's Halliburton and Root) had made arrangements days ahead of his army's march from the Low Countries into Bavaria. The troops would be awakened at dawn, fed, then put on the road – cavalry and artillery first, then the troops marching – often singing and waving at pretty girls – then the rest of the 'impedimenta'. The cooks, who had somehow got underway early, would reach the site of the next camp, twelve or fourteen miles away, early enough that when the troops arrived, the mid-day meal was ready. The soldiers set up the tents, then lounged around until supper. Presumably there was time for infantry drill, but not cavalry exercises – the horses needed time to rest and to graze.

Marlborough's officers visited communities along the route, offering to buy supplies; should towns and villages be reluctant to co-operate or asked high prices, the officers reminded them that Marlborough's politeness had its limits – he was going to feed his men somehow, and that if the village elders would not sell, he would confiscate what he needed. Once he reached Bavaria, he sent out flying columns to collect or destroy all the foodstuffs they could find, at one stroke feeding his men and starving the enemy. The Bavarians and French took the bait – to protect what remained of the Bavarian economy, they came close enough for Marlborough and Eugene to strike.

Not many observers gave the coalition much hope – far from its bases, its supply route in danger, many of the troops untested (especially the British contingents), and French confidence multiplying the worth of their experienced formations, they expected Eugene and Marlborough to be cautious. As the French and Bavarians moved towards the enemy on the north bank of the Danube, they were more concerned that the coalition army would escape than that it would risk a pitched battle. When the

French commander set up his final camp along a ridge that led towards the river, he was not worried about a surprise attack; although he was almost blind, he had been told that his regiments were well placed for falling into line in a hurry, and the two armies were still far apart. But Marlborough and Eugene made a night march, crossed a formidable swamp under the guns of the French regiments, formed their ranks and attacked uphill. At the end of the day the French army was largely destroyed or captured, and the Bavarians were in flight.

After that it was no longer a matter of survival for Britain and Austria, but of whether they could defeat France. The first battleground was not across the Rhine – that had been tried before, without success – too many fortresses there. This time they would strike at southern France through Italy, hoping to reach Spain, where they could root out the Bourbon king in favour of the new Habsburg candidate, Archduke Charles (1685–1740, Carlos III, later Charles VI of Austria), who was popular only in Catalonia – a province that looked back longingly to its ancient independence as the kingdom of Aragon; it was awkward that Charles claimed to be king of all Spain, because victory would have reimposed Castilian rule over the Catalans. This spoke against the chances for a coalition victory. A British army had marched from Portugal to Madrid, but was unable to maintain itself in the Spanish capital. Slowly the Bourbons gained the upper hand.

Although Eugene did not enjoy the success in southern France he had hoped for, he was very pleased with the support he received from the new emperor – Joseph, who had hurried from Spain after his brother's death in 1705, thought independently, rebuffing efforts by the pope and Jesuits to dictate his policy, ignoring the flattery of courtiers and not succumbing to despair when faced by setbacks, rebellions and disappointments. Joseph's greatest contribution to the allied victory was his willingness to take up the additional war in Italy that stretched Austrian resources, but tied down large numbers of Spanish and French troops.

The plan had been for Eugene to capture Toulon as a base, then carry the war into Catalonia. But he lacked enthusiasm for the venture, preferring to take Naples, because that kingdom had been promised to the emperor in a secret treaty, while there was little hope of crossing southern France. He nevertheless advanced as far as Toulon, where French and Bavarian soldiers pressed into his army after Blenheim deserted in droves. The desertions may have been a protest against the hard black bread his cooks offered, and from disgust with the local wine, but on the whole Eugene's Germans were as destructive by land as the English and Dutch were from the sea; this won him no friends among the local population.

To meet the Austrian challenge, Louis XIV transferred his finest field marshal, Vendôme, from Spain with instructions to hold Savoy and recover Lombardy.[2] It was a golden moment for mercenaries, whose services were called upon by so many princes, and especially for Italians, who had been excellent mercenaries since the Renaissance. Vendôme was a no-nonsense commander whose rude manners made him many enemies at court. Although Nancy Mitford, in *The Sun King*, cattily remarked that Vendôme's nose had been eaten away by syphilis, making him look like 'an old, fat, dirty, diseased woman', his portrait belies such a description. Voltaire was willing to overlook the marshal's physical faults, condemning only his clothing. The marshal's courage and competence counted more, and his troops loved him.

Marlborough had drawn up plans to join Eugene in Italy, recruiting Huguenots to replace his sturdy Dutch troops, the intent being to have native Frenchmen with him when they entered Louis's kingdom, but when Vendôme defeated Eugene at the battle of Cassino, that plan had to be abandoned. Louis XIV took advantage of the improved situation in Catalonia and Italy to send Marshal François de Neufville, duc de Villeroy (1644–1730), north with a massive army of the best French and Bavarian regiments. This deterred Marlborough from making a long march south, one that would take him across the Alps. Without question, he had to give priority to defending the Low Countries – if the Dutch collapsed, so would the entire coalition facing the French.

Marlborough met Villeroy on the Belgian plain at Ramillies in May of 1706. Lining up his men in the traditional formation of infantry in the centre, cavalry on each wing, Marlborough's dispositions were copied by his French opponent. Then Marlborough, by a feint on the right, distracted Villeroy's attention from the movement of his cavalry to the left and his reinforcing the infantry in the centre. The cavalry engagement was the greatest in memory, with Danes led by the duke of Württemberg flanking the French position; as the surviving French cavalry units fled, Marlborough realigned his forces so as to come upon the rattled infantry simultaneously from the front and rear. The French foot came to the logical decision – that nothing was to be gained by fighting to the last; the entire French army dissolved in a wild flight to the rear.

Oudenarde

Louis XIV was not ready to admit the war was lost. He knew that his enemies were a coalition, and a coalition could come apart after a single defeat. He came to believe that Marshal Vendôme was again the answer to his many prayers, which certainly became more numerous as his religious fanaticism increased. Although the marshal's immoral behaviour and language distressed the Sun King, Vendôme had beaten Eugene in Italy; perhaps he could do the same with Marlborough, causing his fragile political backing at home to come apart and the coalition to dissolve.

Earlier, Vendôme had worked wonders in Spain, where Bourbon hopes faded after he had been sent to Italy. But there, too, the situation now looked better for Louis XIV. The French army led by the duke of Berwick (the son of Marlborough's sister and James II) was only 25,000 strong, about half French and half Spanish, but it contained an excellent striking force of Irish infantry. In April 1707, it fought a battle at Almansa that determined the fate of the central plateau.

The British–Portuguese army had been commanded by the marquis de Ruvigny (1648–1720); Ruvigny had learned his tradecraft under Louis's greatest commander, Turenne, but, being a Huguenot, went into exile when Louis XIV revoked the Edict of Nantes – effectively stripping the Protestants of long-held rights. This battle, as numerous historians have remarked, made Almansa unique for having the French army commanded by an Englishman and the English army commanded by a Frenchman.

Ruvigny had served William III in Ireland, the Habsburgs in Italy, and after 1704 commanded the English forces in Spain. His army contained English, Portuguese, Dutch and Huguenot units, perhaps a total of 22,000 men. He chose to strike at the centre of Berwick's force, then committed his reserves too early. This left him open to a counter-strike by Berwick's cavalry, which quickly routed his forces. About a quarter of Ruvigny's men escaped, an equal number died and the rest became prisoners.

These victories proved that France was far from finished. Its resources were great and its king still confident that the coalition against him would break apart. In 1708 Louis XIV ordered Vendôme north, stripping many garrisons of soldiers to provide him an army; the king had built a formidable barrier of fortresses, but he could not both garrison them properly and provide enough troops for Vendôme. Though the fortresses were now at risk, the field marshal had an army he could lead into Flanders, and reinforcements were on the way.

The aged Sun King then made a terrible decision – to give overall command to his grandson, Louis, duke of Bourgogne (Burgundy, 1682–1712). To say that Bourgogne was an idiot insults idiots – he was a religious fanatic who would have preferred to make an alliance with Austria against all Protestants; he also believed that his grandfather was too strong and should share power with the nobility and the provinces. His duty was to guide the strategy of the campaign, with Vendôme only making recommendations on tactics. To make matters worse, Louis XIV insisted on reviewing every important decision personally. At one point this resulted in changing the direction of the invasion of the Low Countries from the west to Flanders, causing the delay of a month that allowed Eugene to start his forces on the march northwards, hoping to join Marlborough before Vendôme could force a decisive battle.

Some historians have looked upon these marches and countermarches as a gigantic board game – Marlborough moves his pieces here, Vendôme counters there, they roll the dice and pieces are removed from the board. Of course, there were no pieces, just soldiers, horses, camp followers, wagon drivers, bakers, prostitutes, priests, mayors and city councils. Worst off may have been the peasants holding paper promises to pay for confiscated animals, fodder and seed corn.

Eugene's march north in that summer may have been as much to move his supply base out of Italy for a while as to make possible another Blenheim. An army on the move could collect supplies from untouched regions, while a static one exhausted the food and fodder wherever it was stationed. Van Creveld cites Marshal de Saxe's *Memoirs* on his adaptation of this system: first his officers distributed circulars to the inhabitants, listing what contributions were expected, then sent twenty or thirty men to collect the food from local magistrates; if the magistrate failed in his duties, the soldiers would loot his house or burn it down. Nothing personal, as was said in *The Godfather*, just business.

Still, there was some potential for another decisive battle – if Marlborough and Eugene could join forces again, they would outnumber Vendôme. However, because the Austrian army had to cross the Alps, then circle around France, while Vendôme's reinforcements were marching straight north, the best Eugene could do was to hurry ahead of his main forces to buck up the spirits of his friend. Marlborough, he found, was ill and despondent – the French armies, vastly outnumbering his, had been driving him steadily back. Eugene realised that his Austrians would not arrive soon enough to prevent key fortresses from falling, but if Marlborough forced a fight with the troops on hand, he stood a chance of beating Vendôme before reinforcements arrived.

They decided to intercept the French at Oudenarde – a march that required their troops to cover fifty miles in two days! The Dutch were reluctant to go on the offensive, but finally agreed, and once that was decided, the Germans came along, too. Winston Churchill remarked on the extraordinary enthusiasm of the common soldiers, something, he notes, that was very rare in that age: they went forward almost at a run, pushing the wagons of the well-born 'supernumeraries' (nobles who wanted to be associated with the war, but had no responsibilities except to observe) out of the way, then stealing their possessions before hurriedly rejoining their place in the march. The first coalition units had crossed the Scheldt before Vendôme knew they were on the way; however, the French marshal reacted swiftly, sending Swiss units to hold a hill from which they could fire on the coalition army as it assembled. Bourgogne, thinking that taking up such a forward position was too risky, instructed the marshal to withdraw to a defensive line on a height farther back; the royal grandson's orders, however, did not reach Vendôme, who was leading an infantry charge. The French were thus left with one inexperienced commander well to the rear, out of touch, and the veteran immersed in the fight, equally unable to get an overview of the battle. The result was confusion: 95,000 French versus 80,000 British, Dutch and Germans, their numbers as uncertain as their commanders' knowledge of what was going on.

The battle was close-run. Vendôme stood on the left, directly in front of Bourgogne's idle units, and pressed the coalition forces hard – the son of the elector of Hanover, later to become King George II, had his horse shot from under him in a charge. The rest of the French army stretched out to the right.

Meanwhile, Marlborough had been placing units into the line as they came up, then assigned Eugene the endangered right wing of the lengthening front so that he himself could direct the attack on the left, where French troops were drawing out the line, threatening to come around his flank. Despite his desperate situation, Marlborough twice shifted troops to Eugene, repaying his debt from Blenheim, where Eugene had done the same for him; if the bridges had not collapsed, Marlborough would have been ready for the march around the French right earlier. As it was, as soon as the Dutch regiments were in position, he sent his men against the French with a vengeance. Too late Bourgogne sent his cavalry forward on the right. The effort failed. The French position was collapsing when dark made further fighting impossible.

Saint-Simon said that Vendôme's position would have been in even greater danger if an allied dispatch rider had not mistaken the crimson uniforms of the royal household troops for British redcoats; reading the message and learning that they were about to be outflanked, they fled immediately.

Vendôme then ordered a retreat, abandoning the units still in contact with the allied coalition, and escaped. Marlborough complained that one more hour of daylight would have won the war – but it was just too dangerous to have coalition forces blundering around in a night-time pursuit of an enemy that could have rallied. Winston Churchill reports that Marlborough had Huguenot officers calling into the darkness, 'A moi, Picardie' and so forth, summoning seven thousand dispersed soldiers from famous regiments to come forth, to be captured.

Total losses: the coalition suffered perhaps three thousand, maybe five thousand dead, wounded and prisoner – the French five times that many.

Louis decided that a change of locale might be good for Vendôme and the morale of his army as well – he sent him back to Spain to save his grandson's deteriorating situation. Vendôme did extremely well there, winning victories at Brihuega and Villaviciosa that doomed the Habsburg hopes of recovering their ancestral kingdom and its worldwide possessions.[3] The French armies in the north fell back on the border fortresses.

Malplaquet

The French fortresses made it impossible for Marlborough and Eugene to march immediately on Paris. First Marlborough and Eugene had to capture Lille, and by the time they had accomplished that, with appalling loss of life on both sides, winter had come. The campaign had been brilliant, though marked by oddities such as Marlborough – unable to provide food for his men, being in effect besieged while conducting the siege – giving his men money instead of bread. It may have been the only time in the history of warfare that troops grumbled about being paid. What was there to buy?

Louis XIV was now ready to sign a humiliating peace – there was a near famine in Versailles, the result of an autumn frost that was later and colder than anyone could remember, and a spring frost that killed the emerging wheat. The same bitter cold, fifteen hundred miles to the east in the Ukraine, was destroying the Swedish army of Charles XII – but the allies overreached themselves, demanding that the French king assist in driving his grandson from the Spanish throne. This may have been a misunderstanding, in that the allies only wanted the French to cease assisting Spain, but it might have been a deliberate misunderstanding. Louis XIV used the demand to rouse public opinion against the allies' arrogance, thereby managing to prevent public demonstrations against the war. Still, it was obvious to everyone that the campaign of 1709 would be decisive – the allies were now inside the ring of French fortresses. One more blow by the allies might cause a total collapse of Louis XIV's army, but defeat could bring the coalition down.

Marshal Villars[4] had only 80,000 French, Bavarian, Swiss and Irish soldiers to face the 110,000 troops of the allies, but he was a forceful, independent-minded commander who habitually ignored the detailed royal instructions that had caused his predecessors to miss opportunities. Ordered to protect the minor fortress at Mons, Villars placed his men – many of them fresh recruits – in strongly fortified positions, some in dense woods, across the allies' path and dared them to attack. The British and Austrians did so on 11 September 1709.

Prince Eugene took the right wing, Marlborough the left. Prayers were said – many prayers, in diverse tongues – and brandy distributed. Fog delayed the attack, which began on the right. Marlborough's plan had been to assault both wings so strongly that Villars would have to shift troops from his centre, after which the British infantry, held in reserve, would roll over the weakly defended French entrenchments. However, the French were ready to fight. Voltaire, who interviewed Villars later, was told that soldiers who had not been fed for a day threw away their bread to hurry into the battle.

The advancing Dutch and Scots were shot to pieces; twice they reformed and went forward again, but were barely more successful than on the other wing – the attacks were disasters. The French, dug in along the curving edges of the woods, fired into the exposed flanks of the regiments marching by in beautifully dressed ranks. Nevertheless, Marlborough persisted and, by mid-day, as the forces on the wings had advanced almost to the point that they could close in on the centre, Villars launched a counterattack. At this moment the French luck ran out – the commander and almost his entire staff were hit by artillery, Villars suffering a crushed leg. Once the Austrian infantry swept over the French lines, Marlborough sent the British infantry forward. As expected, it stormed through the collapsing French positions.

Villars recovered sufficiently to demand a chair be brought, from which he continued to direct his forces, cursing at the duke of Bourgogne, who was again watching the combat at a distance without sending his troops forward. When a surgeon advised cutting the leg off, Villars promised he would shoot him if he tried! (The surgeon was probably correct, in that the field marshal had to wear a heavy brace for the rest of his life.) It probably did not matter – the battle had now reached that point described by Tolstoy where the combatants took command, so committed to killing and dying that it hardly mattered what orders were issued.

On the other hand (there is always an 'on the other hand'), Marlborough's cavalry was on the point of being routed when he sent a message to Prince Eugene – the imperial cavalry appeared and swept the French from the field. Eugene, though struck in the head by a musket ball, shook off the blow and continued the fight – like many cavalrymen, he wore an iron plate inside his hat and so was not badly injured. By the end of the day Marlborough and Eugene had defeated both the French infantry and cavalry and captured every stronghold, but Villars's army had maintained its order and marched away. The battlefield was piled with dead and wounded – a sight so terrible that even men accustomed to slaughter blanched. Marlborough and

Eugene had lost as many as 24,000 men! This was perhaps twice as many as Villars. Figures are almost impossible to trust, and, without question, many wounded Frenchmen were bayoneted by the victors – just as they had bayoneted allied wounded earlier in the engagement. Blood lust had risen to a level no one had ever seen. In Winston's Churchill's words, 'the soldiers of every nation, national and mercenary alike' had fought 'with a ferocity hitherto unknown to the age'. They were now satiated. That was also true of the commanders and the politicians. Wolf notes that eighty Dutch regiments had marched into battle, but afterwards there were only eighteen. Under the circumstances, it was impossible for the allies to push south to Paris, and equally impossible to keep such an army in the field longer. The time had come to negotiate a peace.

Brauer and van Tuyll, authors of *Castles, Battles and Bombs*, reflect on the changed situation. The increased expenses for the larger armies, the fear of losing valuable trained men and expensive equipment, had turned campaigns into manoeuvres for slight advantages. But one man was a great exception – Marlborough, whose four great battles cost almost as much in blood as historians have shed in ink. He was either, the authors posit with a twinkle in their eyes, a daring general frustrated by cowardly Dutch allies or a calculating leader working with sensible Dutch leaders. They suggest that Marlborough's decisions to fight were made primarily to take advantage of moments when he could surprise his opponents. If the Dutch put greater value on their own troops than he, that is understandable – they understood that one lost battle could cost them their independence. Caution made as much sense for them as rashness did for Marlborough.

Parker reminds us in *The Military Revolution* that Marlborough conducted thirty sieges over ten campaigns; his five great battles were exceptions that reflected the fact that his French opponents had the resources for a war of attrition and would have been foolish to offer battle except under the most favourable circumstances. Marlborough, being weaker, had to take greater risks. Marlborough's genius lay not only in his ability to defeat capable French field marshals, but in keeping a coalition in being and persuading his partners to accept high causalities. That is, he had to persuade rulers and generals that the benefits from a victory were worth the cost of pitched battle, even worth risking a decisive defeat.

Black, in *European Warfare, 1660–1815*, says that the high casualties of
Malplaquet refute the idea that this was an era of 'limited war'. Some might
say that this comment was slightly off the point, limited war meaning
that civilians were less traumatised than in the seventeenth century. Of
course, civilians in the way of foraging armies would hardly be consoled
by comparing their lot favourably to what their great-grandparents
had suffered in the Thirty Years War. Redlich, in *The German Military
Enterpriser and his Work Force*, volume II, says that prior to the early 1700s
the death rate among soldiers was about that of women in childbirth.
Now efforts were made to improve the circumstances of military life –
new barracks, better food, regular pay, provision for those permanently
disabled and pensions for widows and orphans – but with mixed results.
Whether in combat or not, men died of disease, drink and dissipation,
with foolishness taking away more than a few. While individuals might
later dwell over memorable moments and the exploits and follies of old
comrades, few waxed nostalgic about army life in general. As for battle, it
was best witnessed from afar. Close up it was all terror and blood until the
end, when the exhilaration of knowing one would live would be combined
with the adrenalin rush of combat – often leading to retaliatory murders
of enemy troops who had not managed to flee.

Maurice de Saxe was a youthful witness to these desperate combats in
the Low Countries. He had always been kept well to the rear by Prince
Eugene, who had taken him as an aide as a favour to Maurice's father, the
elector of Saxony, but he had been close enough to the slaughter to see that
this was no way to fight a war.

De Saxe was, consequently, a cautious commander. It was not that he
was afraid of combat – his fight at Fontenoy demonstrated that – but he
believed that a good commander could attain his goals without excessive
bloodshed. In this he foreshadowed Clausewitz's dictum that war must
have a political objective and not become an end in itself. Brauer and van
Tuyll praise de Saxe in *Castles, Battles and Bombs*, noting his comment
that it took four years to train a good infantry battalion. By this, de Saxe
implied that a unit that could outmanoeuvre and outfight several times its
number of poorly trained formations should not be sent needlessly into a
fight. His insistence that quality was more important than quantity fitted
well with the financial situation of his employer, Louis XV, who could not

raise armies equal to all his enemies combined. Even France, as rich and populous as it was, could not afford everything its generals wanted.

Villars, the hero of Malplaquet, did not allow his shattered leg to deter him from marrying a handsome but flighty young woman who cuckolded him at every opportunity. In 1712 he finally won a battle against Eugene; his subsequent offensive into Germany persuaded the Austrians that the time to make peace had come. Britain was already out of the fight, despite maintaining its army in the field. Queen Anne had removed Marlborough from command after quarrelling with his overbearing wife and instructed the next commander of the army, the duke of Ormonde, to avoid combat or sieges without specific instructions.

When the Dutch signed an unfavourable treaty without consulting their British ally, the dyspeptic satirist Jonathan Swift wrote a biting political tract entitled 'The Conduct of the Allies', noting that 'Ten glorious Campaigns are passed, and now at last, like the sick man, we are just expiring with all sorts of good Symptoms.' The debt had reached one-quarter of the total value of the realm. How would they ever pay it? If Britain was unable to continue the war, he wrote, it would be better to make peace.

The pamphlet has been widely credited with saving the ministry and bringing about peace, but two years later the Tories fell anyway. Swift retired to Dublin to work on his masterpiece, *Gulliver's Travels*.

By 1713 the allies were exhausted, both in military and financial terms, and France was starving. Louis XIV, nevertheless, had held out for better peace terms, which he finally obtained. Queen Anne died the next year. The last reigning Stuart, whose unhappy life was one tragedy after another, she took refuge in chocolate, a luxury that almost only she could afford in such volume. This, together with gout, bloated her body so greatly that when she died at the age of forty-nine, she could barely be fitted into a specially made, almost-square coffin.[5] Her physical degeneration almost became a metaphor for British politics.

There were uprisings in the Italian peninsula, but all failed. The war had brought little more than a reshuffling of the bedrooms in the spacious palaces of the petty duchies there. Spain remained ensconced in Sicily, but Habsburgs took over Milan, Naples and Sardinia; the Bourbons subsequently came back in Naples, after which the Habsburgs claimed Florence. In fact, the resistance to the new dynasties may have been as much against the newcomers' efforts to institute 'reforms' as to the newcomers themselves.

As a result of local resistance, the new rulers sought both to reduce their identification with the heads of their dynasty and to install in every possible office foreigners who would obey orders without much question or inefficiency. Faced with cries of 'Barbarians, go home!', the new rulers hired foreign mercenaries to intimidate the populace and put down insurgents whenever they rose up.

The failure of revolutions never seemed to dampen the ardour of patriots, religious fanatics and malcontents. Every king understood what it meant to say that 'uneasy rests the head that wears the crown', but most understood that popular enthusiasm rarely lasted beyond the lynching or beheading of the ringleaders. The problem was hanging on until the rebels could be delivered to the hangman or the executioner. That was where the mercenary proved his real worth.

Peace

The British tired of the war just as Queen Anne's and Marlborough's health failed. Most of all, the subsidies to Dutch and German allies had become a crushing burden on the taxpayers. This brought Tories into ascendance with a programme that, according to Brendan Simms in *Three Victories and a Defeat*, emphasised naval power, commerce and acquiring colonies; these policies contrasted strongly with the Whig emphasis on keeping dangerous continental enemies from acquiring a base on the Channel whence an invasion of England could be launched.

France was tired, too. When the duke of Bourgogne and his wife died of smallpox in 1712, their eldest son became dauphin, but promptly died of measles. Therefore, when Louis XIV finally died in 1715, the crown went to the five-year-old Louis XV (1710–74). The regent's best decision – to get along with France's former enemies – required joining them in forcing Spain to make peace too; his efforts to end Charles XII's war with Denmark were less important in making peace than the Swedish king's sudden and somewhat mysterious death while reconnoitring enemy positions. Then it was necessary to persuade the Russian army to return home – after occupying Poland, it had penetrated as deep into Germany as Mecklenburg.

For years after the conclusion of the War of the Spanish Succession there was no cause worth risking an army for. Moreover, no continental king was in a position to raise a great army; each found it hard to pay the interest on his accumulated debt. Spain was the great loser – it ceded Italian lands and the Spanish Netherlands to Charles VI of Austria, Gibraltar to Great Britain, and Milan to Savoy. France gave up huge but as yet undeveloped parts of North America to Great Britain. Yet English Whigs were outraged – believing that they could have gained more. However, the Tories were now in power, and they wanted peace.

Whigs saw that only Great Britain had the resources to continue the war – thanks to trade with European allies and exploitation of newly acquired colonies and trade concessions, British governments enjoyed incomes that could not be equalled by continental powers – and believed they should seize the moment. Holland, once the principal trade competitor, was now reduced to a grudging minor ally. It was an unparalleled opportunity to make money, but the politicians shrank back from wars without allies.

Great Britain also now had a new monarch – George I of Hanover. Henceforth Britain was a continental power, with German possessions that war might put at risk. The Stuart claimant, James Francis Edward (1688–1768, the 'Old Pretender'), had missed his chance by not converting to the Church of England; that would have got him around a succession law that barred all Catholics from the throne, but he was too honest to compromise his beliefs in any way. George, whose aged mother was the granddaughter of James I, was the only Protestant with a claim to Stuart ancestry and whose lands would be useful in continental politics; still, he owed his selection to renewed Whig activity, and to the Tories being divided between practicality and pro-Stuart sentiments.

While most Englishmen and Scots accepted their new monarch, however grudgingly and despite complaints that he spoke almost no English, a few decided that action was required – if Parliament would not act to prevent the harm to national interests, armed men must.

1715

The economic situation in Scotland was bleak in 1715, the year of the great Jacobite rising. In a sense, prosperity had never returned after the Civil War six decades earlier. But also, except in having people who were by turns quick-witted, stubborn, brave, quarrelsome, intelligent and opinionated, Scotland was by nature poor. Resistance to William of Orange had been crushed or corrupted, after which came the collapse of the poorly planned schemes for overseas investment. The Darien Plan – trade on the isthmus of Panama, in Africa and the Indies – cost the Scots, according to Szechi, in 1715: *The Great Jacobite Rebellion*, a quarter of their liquid capital. Smuggling to North American colonies could not make this up, given the economy's dependence on small, rocky farms and grazing.

In 1707 the creation of the United Kingdom had opened some opportunities in England that ambitious Scots had seized avidly. Still, significant change takes time. Meanwhile, Scots remained badly divided – clan against clan, Highlander against Lowlander, Presbyterian versus Episcopalian (with Catholics watching on) – and resentment grew against the more prosperous nation to the south. It was widely felt, without logic entering into the matter much, that bringing the 'king across the sea' to the throne would make everything better, but most specifically he would eliminate the 'penal laws' that disqualified Catholics from public office.

James Stuart was the famous 'warming-pan baby' whose birth had set in motion those events of 1688 that Protestants called the 'Glorious Revolution'; that is, Protestants had been willing to tolerate having an aged Catholic monarch (James II) for a few years, but they would not risk having a Catholic heir who in the next half-century might overthrow the Protestant settlement.

George I was not a popular choice even in England. Jacobites plotted uprisings in England, Ireland and Scotland, all to be supported by a landing of armed exiles and French troops.

If public opinion in Scotland had been united, the plan might have succeeded. However, there was not sufficient support to guarantee victory – both England and Scotland were war-weary, and there was not much enthusiasm even in Ireland, where the spirit of rebellion was seemingly breathed in with every child's first cry of protest against the unfairness of life. Highlanders, largely Catholic, were enthusiastic but unrealistic. Lowland Scots, largely Episcopalians, did not favour Irish independence or the restoration of Roman Catholicism, which were the ultimate goals of the most radical rebels. Nobody seemed to support official toleration, the one policy that had a chance of bringing about peace – except the exiled king himself. This dull Stuart prince was a moderate – James did not feel himself compelled to force his personal beliefs on his subjects. This disconcerted many of his supporters who saw little point to risking their lives for a prince lacking in charisma who might extend toleration to their rivals in religion and politics; and his protestations did not persuade Protestants.

Nor did the French support the enterprise. Neither Louis XIV in his last days nor the regent for his great-grandson[6] wanted any legitimate dynasty overthrown – or even a semi-legitimate one: memories of the Fronde were still fresh – though only a few ageing Parisians had witnessed that civil war personally, everyone had heard stories of what happened when foreign troops and rebels took over the nation. There was, of course, the lure of hampering British foreign policy – no patriotic Frenchman could wish the ancestral enemy well – but revenge took second place to avoiding another twenty-five-year war.

Despite all this, many Scots were ready to rise. Some had lost contact with reality, perhaps, but they were not the first revolutionaries to do so, and if challenged on the practicality of their mad adventure, they could point to rebels who had managed to seize power when their opponents failed to respond appropriately. Given the fluid situation in England, perhaps all the pieces in the puzzle would fall into place. Moreover, there was the matter of honour.

The conspirators estimated that they could raise a force of twenty thousand exiles (and an equal number of Irish who wished to return to their homeland), and they hoped that once they had obtained an initial victory, French soldiers would join them. That would be a sufficient army to overcome what remained of Marlborough's now demobilised forces; moreover, the duke being too ill to take the field personally, the English army might be badly led. The reality was otherwise – there were never that many exiles who could bear arms, and the regent in Paris went no further than to acknowledge the traditional friendship with the Scots. Highlanders may have been ready to fight, but unless they were paid, they would have to plunder the countryside, driving the Lowlanders into the arms of the Hanoverians. Military supplies – necessary to arm insurrectionists – were too bulky to hide from government officers and, hence, were available only in small amounts. The only sensible point on which all Jacobites could agree, both in England and Scotland, was that no uprising was likely to succeed without the assistance of foreign soldiers.

The question was, who would hire out such a force? Sweden, France and Spain all came into consideration; however, as one of the participants, James Keith, remembered the situation, those nations gave little more than encouragement.[7] The French were determined to honour the peace terms that had ended the long war, which precluded the open support necessary to arm either a sufficient number of exiles or potential rebels in Scotland. Under-the-table support was there, of course, but it was so small that it could be plausibly denied. Keith was in a position to know. So were the authorities in London and Edinburgh.

In September the earl of Mar (John Erskine, 1675–1732), whose personal quarrels with the Whig ministers had cost him his position as secretary of state for Scotland, called on the clans to overthrow the Hanoverian dynasty. Mar, whose debts could be erased only by a revolution, argued passionately that only a male Stuart should be monarch of the United Kingdom. He rallied some two thousand Highlanders to his army and had some initial successes, though in terms of forming a substantial army there were not exactly reverses, but certainly no steps foward. When opposing armies took the field, there were more Scottish Whigs (Campbells, Frasers, Grants, Munros, Gunns and Rosses) in arms than Jacobites. The Whig commander, Argyll,[8] had 3,700 soldiers, 2,000–3,000 militiamen and 3,000 clansmen; holding more of the forts, he had more arms and supplies.

Through the campaign of both Mar and Argyll, the numbers in the armies rose and fell with bewildering rapidity, and if one added in men who were coerced to serve, then left as quickly as they could, the total number of Scots in each army would be perhaps twice as many. Meanwhile, the army of Lowland Jacobites grew slowly to eight thousand foot and one thousand horse, subsequently marching into England to support the expected Jacobite rising.

The Hanoverian government was able to meet this threat by raising new regiments of unemployed veterans from Marlborough's armies, men who required little instruction in the intricate drills of infantry warfare. There were also many half-pay officers willing to come out of retirement, eager to prove their worth and perhaps gain a permanent position in the army or obtain lands confiscated from rebels.

In contrast, the Jacobites could recruit few experienced soldiers; instead, they had a combination of enthusiastic but undisciplined volunteers and men who were forced to serve. Officers from foreign armies hurried home, but when they tried literally to 'whip' these men into shape, the men deserted. The officers of the southern army might have benefited from waiting until the troops were trained or even by going to the assistance of Mar, but they believed that the situation in England could be exploited only if they struck quickly. Soon, dispirited by the failure of English Jacobites to appear and surrounded by a smaller but more efficient government army, they surrendered.

Mar's army, meanwhile, had swollen to eight thousand men, but he knew that his untrained men would perform poorly on the battlefield. Only upon hearing that six thousand Dutch and Swiss troops had landed in England, did he decide to march against Argyll. The alternatives, to delay or to await James's arrival, were to risk being totally overwhelmed.

The two armies collided accidentally in mid-November at Sheriffmuir, each on the march, each unaware of the other's presence. As Mar was moving south, his army divided into several parallel columns, he observed scouts on a hill ahead of him. Ordering some cavalrymen to drive the observers away, he continued forward without forming a line of battle. When the advanced force reached the summit, they were startled to see Argyll's army almost on them. With retreat impossible, battle was joined. Mar began feeding his oncoming units awkwardly into the developing combat. Argyll being almost as surprised as Mar, there was no way for either commander to exercise control. The only exception to chaos on the main battlefield was Argyll's infantry standing fast, and some Jacobite cavalry successes.

Each side was victorious on parts of the battlefield, but when Mar's enthusiastic horsemen dashed off in pursuit of fugitives, he had no means to rescue his Highlanders, whose wild charges had been broken by sustained volleys of musket fire. At the end of the day Argyll held the field, but Mar still had more men. The numbers of killed and wounded, like the size of

the armies, is not clear, but Mar was psychologically beaten. Seeing that
Argyll's army remained intact and would soon be reinforced, Mar ordered
a retreat. His army quickly began to melt away.

A month later, on 22 December, James Stuart landed in Scotland,
sea-sick and almost alone. The handful of supporters who met him were
enthusiastic, but disappointed that he had brought no army, then even more
disappointed to learn that he had the personality of a dead fish. James, for
his part, was shocked by the disorderly mob that passed for his army –
and, like his father before him, he let his feelings show. All he could do
was retreat northwards, burning towns and crofts behind him – but hardly
slowing Argyll's advance. In February James Stuart and Mar boarded a ship
for France. The rebellion was over.

Argyll, whose reluctance to shed blood was noticed in London, was replaced
by General William Cadogan (1672–1726), an Irish veteran of Marlborough's
army who had fought at Blenheim, Oudenarde and Malplaquet. Cadogan
sent his men through the Highlands in pursuit of the last rebels, making
a lasting (and unfavourable) impression on the Scots there, but earning
himself an earldom. Daniel Szechi, in *1715: The Great Jacobite Rebellion*,
reports forty executions and more than six hundred prisoners transported
to the Americas, where they were sold as felons into indentured servitude;
some of these indentures were bought by sympathisers.

Most Scots made their peace with the Hanoverian dynasty – obeying
the law, paying taxes and generally getting on with life. One who did not
was Rob Roy McGregor (1671–1734), whose exploits made him a Scottish
folk hero. He had fought in defence of James II against William of Orange
in 1689, but had not been jailed for treason nor deprived of his lands. Rob
(or 'Red') McGregor became a combination of cattleman and rustler; he
also offered protection to his neighbours – for a fee. In an effort to increase
his herd, he borrowed money, but then was unable to repay it. Declared an
outlaw, he fought back with skill and cunning for several years, acquiring a
widespread reputation for resisting local despots and royal tyranny. Finally
captured, he spent five years in captivity before Daniel Defoe's account of
his heroic life induced George I to issue a pardon. McGregor's outlaw life
proved that small numbers of Scots could evade royal troops for a long
time, but also that they lacked the numbers and discipline to defeat the
English and their mercenary troops.

Few campaigns illustrate better than that of 1715 the great difference between trained soldiers and insurrectionists. Mercenaries won almost every time, even when greatly outnumbered.

By 1718 cooler heads began to prevail among the Jacobites. The Amnesty Act persuaded some frustrated and unhappy exiles to return home, and the financial crisis of 1717–18 in France reduced the subsidies that had supported others. James II being long dead, his wife's death in 1718 of cancer was a devastating blow – she had possessed beauty, charm, wit and good sense, and had been devoted to her husband; James the Pretender was on his travels, trying to find a ruler willing to sacrifice British goodwill for giving him refuge. Those Jacobites who refused to acknowledge that the Hanoverian dynasty was firmly in control of the United Kingdom either followed James Stuart around as impoverished hangers-on in his dwindling court or sought an appointment in some foreign army. Those who did acknowledge King George I easily found employment in his army.

James Stuart eventually found sanctuary in Rome, then married the fabulously wealthy granddaughter of King Jan Sobieski of Poland. It was the union of two dynasties without a country.

Scots in Hanoverian service soon became a mainstay of the dynasty and were central to some of the most important legends of the Royal Army – such as the 'thin red line' at Balaclava. The most famous of the Highland regiments, the Black Watch, began as a militia company, but it served in America during the French and Indian War (1754–63) and the American War for Independence (1775–83). Its name was associated with the dark blue, black and green sett that the government issued in 1739 and contrasted so strongly with the red coats of other regular units and, perhaps, because independent units that formed the regiment had once 'watched' the Highlands. Sett refers to the number of threads in a tartan pattern – another reminder of how complicated Scottish culture, history and politics can be.[9]

French Domination of Europe

Louis XIV had not succeeded in all his efforts to expand his borders, but neither had he had failed completely. His annexation of Lorraine had provided him opportunities to send his armies over the Rhine, and his

skilful placing and accepting of brides had allowed him to put a grandson
on the Spanish throne and acquire parts of the Spanish Netherlands.
His army, though blooded by Marlborough and Eugene, had not broken.
His people, though reduced to poverty and starvation, did not follow the
example of their ancestors – there was no rebellion. Even the judges and
nobles were quiet. The times were changing. The passion of past conflicts
was cooling.

Lynn, in *Women, Armies, and Warfare*, cites the example of a British
sergeant in 1710 who learned that his sister was in French service (Lynn
guesses that she was a sutler). Crossing the lines with a bottle of brandy,
she made the occasion into a cheery party; still, when invited to stay with
her brother, she refused – the French food, especially the bread, was much
better, she said. Probably the brandy too.

Under Louis XV French culture and language spread widely among the
enemies of his great-grandfather. In the eighteenth century the French
court was admired – it had the finest palaces and country estates; it set
the styles for clothing, manners and music; its literature, philosophy and
relaxed morals were copied; and now that France was the embodiment
of secular frivolity and sensuality, the king was no longer considered
particularly dangerous to his neighbours' religious opinions or political
foolishness. Gridlock may not be efficient, but it provides few unpleasant
surprises.

In place of a powerful king, France now had strong royal mistresses. One
might well wonder why contemporaries and historians of the nineteenth
century were so impressed by the influence of Madame de Pompadour,
while historians of our own era are not, but she illustrates how much
change France had undergone.[10] Louis XIV had unified France in politics
(emasculating the nobility), in religion (crushing the Jansenists, expelling
the Huguenots, limiting the authority of the pope), in expanding commerce
(establishing state companies) and in restoring national pride. Louis XV
just wanted to get along.

Habsburg Austria, in contrast to Bourbon France, was very Catholic,
very Spanish and very formal. Its triumphs in baroque architecture and
painting were impressive, to be sure, but even in Vienna the French
language was making inroads. After all, there was no one universally
agreed-upon form of spoken German. In contrast, even the exiles from

Versailles spread the use of French. These men were often philosophers rather than political enemies, and everyone felt safe enough to welcome clever speakers – their ideas were amusing, but not likely to be dangerous, especially not their denunciations of organised religion. Everyone could smile at the impassioned responses of the clergy, except the Jesuits, who were losing their hold everywhere outside Austria; almost everyone understood this to be a good thing, since religious passions could so easily turn peaceful citizens into mobs. Educated people came to consider religious enthusiasts semi-deluded mental slaves of arcane practices and superstitions. (Even then they knew how to insult pious believers.) Yes, one should be a Christian – churchmen and pious practices kept the lower classes in line – but taking them too seriously could cost a king his crown.

The eighteenth century was providing opportunities to enjoy the good life. This was especially true for the upper classes, but also for those who produced and sold products, and – if alcohol, tobacco and sugar count for anything – even those involved in the rudest employments. Peace was more common than war, certainly more common than in the past, and wars were not as terrible. 'Limited war' was not without its terrors for the people living in contested areas, but no longer did these wars extend into every corner of every land.

Protestants could pride themselves on their freedom of thought, but Frenchmen who were supposedly Catholic led the way into the Enlightenment, that application of logic and common sense to every aspect of life and belief. The pope, once the bugaboo of Protestant and Orthodox nightmares (occasionally for good reasons), was now an aged recluse, little heeded and little feared. Surrounded by a decaying city – a symbol of his crumbling and moss-covered authority – he was no longer fawned over by visitors, who were now there on a 'grand tour' rather than as pilgrims, visiting churches only to see the art.

If the Habsburgs no longer had much attraction even for Germans, neither did the British court, which after the accession of George I in 1714 was so very German. The king was a Protestant who made dullness into a high art – no festivals, no colour, no imagination outside music. George I was so much like the land of his birth in winter – flat, dark and wet without ever rising to the level of actually raining. His future wife, when informed of the family decision to marry her to him, had shouted that she would not marry that 'pig snout' and fainted when actually introduced. Between arguments and estrangements they had two rather porcine children. Britons often viewed their new king the same way. He responded by preferring Hanover to his newly acquired kingdom, in part because he could understand his subjects there; he never quite mastered English.

English Jacobites hated the Hanoverian dynasty, partly because it was German, partly because it was Protestant, and partly because it was such a dysfunctional family; Scottish Jacobites hated George I because he was not a Stuart. Though the king had distant Stuart ancestors, he never looked nor acted like a Stuart. He had once been a warrior, the commander of mercenary armies. Now George I was the stout foreign gentleman, smoking his long pipe in front of a cozy fire, surrounded by caricatures of courtiers and German mistresses, one with a bottom the size of a British ship of the line, the other thin as a mizzenmast. But even the British navy was something one admired best at a distance. As Winston Churchill said later of naval traditions, what were they but rum, sodomy and the lash?

British political traditions were evolving in equally odd ways. Parties did not yet exist. That is, there were interest groups and alliances of families and ambitious politicians, but Tories were becoming a shapeless collection of country squires who showed up at Parliament to vote against whatever the government proposed – and governments were composed of shifting alliances of so-called Whigs who believed that politics was the practice of deciding who got what, when. Those who called on the winds of reform inevitably sailed onto the rocks of self-interest. It was why so many believed that only an enlightened autocracy could provide both stability and progress. Yet there was something in this rough-and-tumble society, this brutally competitive and corrupt political system, that allowed some people to see past the poverty and unfairness to a future of greater wealth and even to hope for more social equality – at the same moment that opportunities seemed to be vanishing, they also seemed to be opening up. Tories deplored this; Whigs loved it.

Britain offered much that Frenchmen admired – its freedom of thought, its parliamentary system providing checks on royal authority, its literature. But British boorishness contrasted badly when compared with French manners, British drunkenness with French restraint, beer, porridge and turnips compared to wine, truffles and pastry. On the other hand, Britons considered themselves more manly, more honest, more … more … British. Compared to Frenchmen, even English women were more manly.

Conclusion

Western armies were now so efficient that battles were mutual slaughters: the defeated army rarely had to run far because the victors usually could not limp swiftly after them. No ruler could afford this. Armies were too expensive and too fine-tuned to waste in such a manner. To the extent that wars could not be avoided, campaigns were reduced to sieges and fortifying positions that no sensible enemy would assault. In the end, there were ever fewer crises that deserved to become military conflicts. This era became known alternatively as one of 'limited war' and the 'Enlightenment'. The two terms are not synonymous, but neither one can be fully understood without reference to the other – war was not something that intelligent men entered into lightly, and wars were fought for reasons that intelligent men could agree upon, then end the conflict.

CHAPTER FOUR

Gunpowder Empires and Imperialism

The Ottoman Turks created the first 'oriental' gunpowder empire. Their artillery was the decisive weapon in the capture of Constantinople in 1453, but the huge cannons that broke down the walls were too heavy to move about on a battlefield and, therefore, were useful only for sieges. Muskets were another matter. When Ottoman firearms proved effective against the Persians, the Persians adopted them, followed by the Turkish peoples who invaded India under Babur (1483–1530). Thus, one gunpowder regime begat others, and each strove for regional supremacy.

Babur had a claim on Delhi through his ancestor, Timur (Tamberlane, 1336–1405); though the region had been ruled by Muslim sultans since 1206, those rulers had worked with the Hindu majority. That was a practice that true believers like Babur abhorred. In 1526 Babur led his multi-ethnic army on the traditional invasion route over the mountains from Afghanistan to Punjab, where rebels joined him, then he advanced to the Yamuna River, a major tributary of the Ganges. There he overwhelmed local forces in an encounter so hard fought that he angrily executed all prisoners. Upon hearing this, the sultan led his army from Delhi north along the river to Panipat, where the level country allowed him to set up a traditional massive formation of infantry and cavalry behind a hundred war elephants; most of his men were Hindus, a reflection of the policies which had so offended Muslims that some had invited Babur to invade India – promising their support at an opportune moment.

Years before, Babur had hired Ottoman musketeers and artillery experts to train his infantry. How many cannon he had in this expedition, if any, is disputed, but it may not matter much – he certainly had heavy muskets that could fire over the wagon train which held back the Indian cavalry, and the noise frightened the elephants into fleeing back through the infantry.

Still, Babur's success seems to have come less from his weaponry than from his ability to manoeuvre his cavalry units, compensating for their smaller numbers by superior mobility and striking hard. When his horse archers struck the flank of the sultan's closely packed formation, many Indian nobles deserted and the infantry fled in panic.

After occupying the Ganges River valley, Babur founded the Mughal Empire, which soon reached down the river right into Bengal, the wealthy region that is today divided between India and Bangladesh. The Taj Mahal is the best-known Mughal structure, but the red forts in Agra and Delhi probably better represent the spirit of the Mughal state. Later shahs made India into one of the richest and most cultivated regions of the world. Their authority rested on a military machine of immense size and sophistication, their only weakness being the size and diversity of their realm. To govern distant regions, they had to rely on princes,[1] and each prince yearned to be as independent as possible, or even to become shah himself.

Cavalry long remained dominant over infantry in India, but, as Chase points out in *Firearms: A Global History*, the climate was inhospitable to horses. The Mughals learned to compensate for this by relying on smaller numbers of heavy cavalry supported by musket-bearing infantry and artillery. In contrast, the Hindu rulers in the southern highlands could still rely on light cavalry because the climate was more favourable, their horses could go up and down the hills more easily, and European merchants were willing to sell them firearms and mounts. Coexistence was based on Mughal bribes – money was a better incentive for good behaviour than threats of reprisal.

On the whole, most 'oriental empires' did not follow European models, but continued to use traditional arms that were sufficient to deal with local enemies; as a result, native cavalry remained at the centre of their armies. Even two centuries later, when European armies proved themselves equal or even superior to native forces, the rulers were reluctant to adopt Western weapons and tactics. Why abandon proven methods? Why should they antagonise groups that could possibly overthrow them? Lastly, weren't the Europeans still far away and quarrelling among themselves?

It was easy to ignore the fact that in the sixteenth century the Portuguese came to dominate the Indian Ocean trade, driving the Arabs away (the

Chinese had already voluntarily curtailed their once-blooming trade with 'barbarians'). Controlling ports, however, did not give the Portuguese a decisive voice in regional politics, because native rulers were reluctant to cede them a monopoly of commerce; worse, Europeans discovered that native peoples were not dependent on imports. Hence, there was little the Portuguese (and later the Dutch, French and English) could do when local rulers refused to trade.

Eventually, native rulers found it advantageous to trade with Europeans – if their rivals bought Western weapons and they did not, the balance of power might shift unfavourably. Nor could they get around the European near-monopoly of international commerce. From the moment that the Portuguese arrived, their ships controlled whatever seas they chose to concentrate on; while blockade runners could easily slip past the handful of Western vessels patrolling the vast ocean, they could not always find a place where they could exchange their goods.

It was not an arrangement destined to last forever. As Chase noted, the Portuguese weakness was that their position depended on possessing a handful of ports, each vulnerable to attack or embargo by the regional rulers. And so it was for every European trading company – there were so few Europeans and so many natives that the most they could do was to take one side in local disputes, hoping to tip the balance, then ask for commercial privileges – usually a small fort with an attached trading post that typically grew quickly into a small city.

It often happened that when any trading company made an alliance with one Indian potentate, competing companies sought alliances with that prince's enemies. Afterwards, when perceived self-interest changed – native princes being always concerned about former allies becoming their masters – fortifications became more significant. Unless a small garrison could hold out against far superior numbers until help arrived, which might be a long wait, there was little point to having a garrison. But only by hiring local soldiers and encouraging intermarriage with native peoples could the Portuguese provide sufficient troops for guard duty and police duties that required knowing the local languages. This model was copied by the Dutch, English and French who followed them to India.

The Portuguese, as Parker says in *The Military Revolution*, had come east to trade for spices, not to conquer Asia – and the Dutch came to take over the Portuguese enterprise. As an official of the British East India Company noted in 1677, the business was trade, not war. If Asians failed to copy European methods, it was largely because they rarely saw them; moreover, they could defend themselves against the small numbers of foreigners by traditional methods.

The Dutch East India Company became immensely profitable, with a private army sometimes estimated at ten thousand men. Janice Thomson, in *Mercenaries, Pirates, and Sovereigns*, reports that the duke of Württemberg rented out troops to the Dutch East India Company even in 1707, when he needed men himself to hold off Louis XIV's armies. After 1756 the Dutch recruited heavily in the Austrian Empire. They also used Indonesians – between 1715 and 1719 they employed five thousand European and twenty thousand Asian mercenaries.

The Dutch retained their influence in the Spice Islands even after they ceased to be a major player in European politics. That was because when England and France began what some historians call the 'second Hundred Years War' (1689–1815), England needed Holland as an ally; therefore, it would have been unwise to allow its East India Company to root out Dutch merchants, must less deprive them of Indonesia. Instead, the English concentrated on defeating their French competitors. Admiral Ballard, in *Rulers of the Indian Ocean*, praises this restraint as being in the national interest, just as allowing the tiny Portuguese trading posts to survive paid off in goodwill. The trading posts also made excellent hostages for good behaviour.

It would be a mistake to imagine that the Dutch presence was important throughout their possessions – they had but little influence outside their trading stations, and the supposedly subject Indonesians and Malays were proud and warlike peoples, and devout Muslims to boot. Religion was very important to European–Asian relationships, but stereotypes based on modern observations can be as misleading as enlightening. For example, Indonesia – today the most numerous Islamic nation in the world – was not known for fanaticism; rather, Muslims there avoided offending the many Indians and Chinese who lived among them. Business before pleasure, and pleasure before religion. That was the rule of the strict Dutch Calvinists, too.

England

When the first English company was incorporated for trade with India, Queen Elizabeth's realm was far inferior in every respect to the empire of Akbar the Great. The only advantages the English had, other than ships which could sail around Africa, was that they knew India existed (even if they hardly knew anything about it beyond the marvellous tales of merchants and travellers) and understood that they had to learn the languages and what cultural rules applied to traders, while Indians did not care about England, much less its queen, and often saw no commercial advantage in trading with newcomers. What could England provide that they wanted? An additional problem for English merchants was that India had few products that would interest their customers at home. The spice trade was wrapped up by the Dutch, so that even when Englishmen had silver stolen from Spaniards in the New World, what was worth buying? Cotton and silk, of course, and some ceramics: luxury items.

In time English merchants found their own equivalent of spices in Indian tea. That came late, since tea was unknown in Western Europe before its first importation from China in 1609; it was still almost unknown in England in 1662, when Catherine of Braganza of Portugal married Charles II. Niall Ferguson, in *Empire*, says that its first mention in an English newspaper was in September 1658; Macaulay reports that when Monk brought the Scottish army to London to welcome Charles II home, tea was so rare that the soldiers just stared at, or touched it with their tongues. Once tea was introduced at court, however, popular demand quickly followed. Within a few years tea was a major import – and the taxes on its importation became a significant source of revenue. As usage soared, tea supplanted to a degree the consumption of alcoholic beverages.

To transport goods over the vast distances, merchant companies built new and larger vessels called Indiamen. These required a larger navy to protect them from pirates, and then naval bases in the Indian Ocean. As Mahan was to note much later in *The Influence of Sea Power upon History*, trade follows the flag. The ships that bore the flag were warships, using cannon superior to any found in Asia. English traders bribed British politicians into continuing and extending their commercial rights. The risks were great – which explains why only a handful of merchants were involved – but rewards could be spectacular: 20 per cent in a bad year, more when most of the Indiamen made it past blockades, pirates and storms. Significantly, saltpetre, the most essential ingredient for gunpowder, was such a valuable cargo that it became one reason for Dutch–English commercial rivalry.

Also popular at this time was tobacco, the staple of Britain's southern colonies in North America; fish and furs from the northern colonies; and sugar from the Caribbean. Each increased state revenues, which paid for the navy and army that made more trade possible. Only a small number of Britons became rich from this commerce, but everyone sensed that life was getting better. Even those who benefited little understood that Britain was on a rising tide, and that as Britons they could take pride in every success.

Serving in the army or navy was not popular, but aside from those pressed to man the ships, Englishmen understood that they were unlikely to be affected. As long as they were not so careless as to accept a drink from a recruiting officer, they knew that there was always someone else who could be enticed to take the 'king's shilling' in their place – if not native Englishmen, then foreigners; and there were always Scots willing to go anywhere. As time passed, 'anywhere' often came to mean India.

The first English trading post was established on the Carnatic coast in 1611, a part of southeastern India that ran down the coast for six hundred kilometres. Most of the inhabitants were Hindus, but Muslims ruled much of the region by 1692. The dominant ruler was the nawab of Arcot. Inland lay Mysore and the Deccan.

The first English outpost was unsuitable for large-scale trade, but its garrison successfully repelled a Portuguese naval attack in 1612. Later the traders developed a close relationship with the distant Mughal shah, who allowed them to establish new 'factories' along the coast because he was so unhappy with the aggressiveness of Dutch merchants. The Dutch had found strong-arm tactics effective in bringing order into the widely scattered Spice Islands, but Indian rulers preferred the quieter English approach. This was not a policy based on superior morality: England's policy was born of weakness, but it was no less effective for that.

In 1639 the English found a more suitable site at Madras – an island in southeast India on which they constructed Fort Saint George. In return for use of the site, the trading company paid a substantial rent to the prince.

Madras was able to become a centre of trade for merchants and English pirates, partly because it was so far from the capital of the fabulously wealthy Mughal Empire. This early trading post bore little resemblance to the respected 'John Company' of a later time, but it was all that English resources would permit. When Charles II's alliance with Portugal gave English merchants access to Bombay, it was only on the condition that they would support the Portuguese against the Dutch. Disease quickly swept away most Britons who moved there, but the city and its commerce grew so quickly that Bombay became the company's headquarters.

Shortly afterwards the Mughal Empire began to come apart. It had been constructed on the basis of mutual toleration by all religious parties, but when Aurangzeb (1618–1707) seized power from his father, Shah Jahan (the builder of the Taj Mahal), he chose to govern by rigid Islamic principles. This so offended his non-Muslim subjects that he spent his reign putting down revolts; after his death, the peripheral regions broke away. This provided opportunities for Europeans to establish themselves more strongly on the coast.

A new East India Company, reorganised in 1708, made the enterprise more profitable – though it would be easy to exaggerate how much. By 1740 the garrison of Saint George, seven hundred men strong, was double the number of English agents and their families, but less than the three thousand Portuguese and much less than the thirty thousand Indians.

France

France had actually preceded England in Indian trade by half a century, but little came of it until 1664, when Louis XIV's great minister, Colbert, created 'La Compagnie française des Indes orientales', which was supposed to increase the kingdom's taxable wealth (more prosperity = more taxes = more soldiers). A second goal was to weaken the Dutch, who were leading the resistance to French expansion into the Holy Roman Empire. The first stations on the voyage to India were pirate bases in Africa and the Indian Ocean; unfortunately for the royal plans, most of these pirates were Huguenots, Protestants who later became victims of Louis's conversion to an intolerant version of Roman Catholicism.

The French East Indies Company established a mid-voyage station on Madagascar, just as the Dutch and British were stopping in South Africa for fresh food and water, but complete pacification was impossible. At best, Madagascar was a good place to recruit mercenaries and as a base for fleets of pirates.

The major French trading station on the Carnatic coast was at Pondicherry, but there were other trading posts along the coast all the way to distant Bengal. The governor of Pondicherry, Joseph François Dupleix (1697–1763), was ambitious both for himself and his nation. He had come to India in 1715 and by 1742 was governor-general of all French possessions there. In the words of Macaulay: 'The man who first saw that it was possible to found a European empire on the ruins of the Mughal empire was Dupleix. His restless, capacious, and inventive mind had formed this scheme at a time when the ablest servants of the English Company were busied only about invoices and bills of lading.' Most importantly, Dupleix believed that native warriors could be trained by European officers to be the equals of the best soldiers of the West.

There were other French bases in what is today Mauritius and Reunion. Since 1660 there had been Frenchmen in that small island complex lying athwart the trade routes of the Indian Ocean, and over time they expelled their Dutch and English competitors. When coffeehouses became all the rage in Europe in the early 1700s, the French discovered that the local high-quality coffee could be a profitable export. The governor, Bertrand-François Mahé de La Bourdonnais (1699–1753), had come to the East at the age of ten and was even more ambitious than Dupleix. A popular and experienced military commander, he impressed the royal court with his knowledge, his practical advice and his vision of France's future in the East. Appointed governor in 1733, his energy transformed the colony – he introduced a shipyard, sugar cane and indigo production, built roads and hospitals and, according to James Mill in *The History of British India*, dealt with 'the ignorance, the prejudices and the inveterate habits of idleness, of those who opposed him at every step'.

The collapse of Mughal authority in 1739 following the Persian capture of Delhi allowed strong men to carve out territories for themselves: Muslims in the north, Hindu Marathas in the south and minor princes in the Carnatic. The shah, though restored to office by his captor, was unable to bring his forces to bear on these rebels; he recognised the legal existence of nawabs and maharajas, so long as they acknowledged his fictitious authority in distant Delhi.

In 1744, when Bourdonnais heard of the outbreak of the War of Austrian Succession, he sailed to Madras with his small army and quickly persuaded the commander of Saint George to surrender. He fulfilled his promises to the captives that they would be released on parole and could continue their commercial activities, and he additionally promised that he would return the fort to them upon the conclusion of peace. Practical men all agreed that the diplomats in Europe would consider them little more than minor chips on the table, easily thrown into the pile after negotiators had studied their cards.

Dupleix disagreed. When he arrived on the scene, he forced Bourdonnais to yield control of Madras. Admiral Ballard, in *Rulers of the Indian Ocean*, says that while Bourdonnais had little understanding of land warfare, Dupleix had no understanding of naval warfare at all. Forts without fleets achieve nothing, while fleets without forts can bring victory and prosperity. Of course, fleets need bases, especially in waters as dangerous as those on the Indian east coast.

As a sign of his stricter regime, Dupleix paraded the principal Englishmen through watching crowds of Indians to their imprisonment in Pondicherry. One of his generals, Charles Joseph Patissier, the marquis de Bussy-Castelnau (1718–85), was even more successful in the Deccan, inland from Pondicherry. When reinforcements arrived, it appeared that Bussy would roll up the entire English position along the coast. However, the monsoon rains came, bringing all military activities (especially naval ones) to a stand-still.

This ensuing confrontation came much against the wishes of both English and French companies – war interrupts business. However, the naval officers of both nations hoped to enrich themselves by capturing enemy trading vessels, then selling both the cargo and the ships; this caused the conflict to spread onto land, until eventually these 'Carnatic wars' involved every state in the region. It would be incorrect to attribute too much importance to European influence on Indian politics yet, because India was a huge region – populous, wealthy and self-assured – with a wide variety of religious convictions ('persuasions' did not exist in India) and ethnic origins. All saw Europeans as convenient commercial partners, but not as a military danger. Indeed, many considered Europeans incapable of possessing significant martial characteristics.

That mistake came partly from the kind of merchants they encountered, partly because the managers of the trading companies had been told to avoid distractions (especially the expensive distraction of local conflicts), and partly due to the natives' self-satisfied belief in their all-around superiority.

There was one disturbing moment. In 1746, after Dupleix rejected the demand of the nawab of Arcot to surrender Madras to him – as had been agreed earlier – the prince sent his son with an army to besiege Saint George. When the French ran out of water, they sallied out to fight. The five hundred Frenchmen, skilfully employing field pieces, routed the besiegers. The nawab then took the field personally with ten thousand men, but he did no better – 230 French supported by seven hundred native troops defeated him too. It was now apparent that even a small European army supported by native warriors could defeat much larger native forces using traditional weapons and tactics: the French artillery was not only more deadly, but could fire much faster. At this point many Europeans began to ask if even larger bodies of native troops could be trained to use European weapons and methods, and to what extent European officers and non-commissioned officers could instil order and discipline in troops accustomed to fighting in disorderly masses. Dupleix saw the potential of dominating the subcontinent with a European-trained army.

Peace came to Europe in 1748, but the war in coastal India continued, fought by proxy, the French and British each supporting claimants for office who became increasingly dependent on their aid.

Persia

All the great states of Central Asia owed much to the memory of thirteenth-century Mongol hegemony, when universal peace had been imposed by brutal force, but also to the belief that all followers of Islam should be in one state, with all subjects rendering obedience to one powerful leader. The gunpowder revolution that began about 1450 was centred on powerful rulers attempting to make those ideals into reality, as well as those attempting to resist.

Shah Abbas the Great (1571–1629) was able to re-establish Persia as a great state by rebuilding his army on the basis of firearms. Hiring an English advisor, he divided his army into three bodies – the slave infantry, the musketeers and the artillery. He paid them all from the state treasury, the money coming from tolls on trade and taxes on industry and commerce. It took the shah fourteen years to pacify Persia, but eventually he was welcomed by tribal leaders and long-oppressed Shiites. Abbas began his attack on the Ottomans in 1602, a moment when the Turkish sultan was distracted by war with Austria, an uprising in Egypt and by internal riots. With weapons from Spain and other European countries, he crushed the Ottoman army in September 1605, then he pushed on into Anatolia, ravaging the countryside while avoiding pitched battle.

He repelled the Ottoman counter-strike in 1610, then signed a truce in 1612; after five years of peace, inconclusive fighting resumed, followed by another truce. Abbas's next great opportunity came in 1622, when civil war broke out in Turkey – the insane Mustafa I (1591–1639) murdering Osman II (1603–22), followed by supporters of the eleven-year-old Murad IV (1612–40) challenging his authority. While the Turks fought over the succession, Abbas swept into Iraq, capturing Baghdad and other cities, slaughtering Sunnis (who were considered loyal to the Ottomans); he tried to limit tribal fanaticism by recruiting Georgian and Armenian converts – an obvious imitation of the sultan's elite corps of janissaries – but without much success.

The Persian threat to Constantinople had the effect of quieting political infighting (external threats often have that effect). When Murad restored internal order, he still had too many distractions to drive the Persians back, but he was able to limit future Shiite gains; after Abbas's death, Murad recaptured Tabriz in 1634 and Baghdad in 1638 (executing the entire Persian garrison, perhaps as many as thirty thousand men). The peace treaty of 1639 guaranteed Shiites religious freedom and Persia full independence – concessions that Murad could have made long before. When the sultan died shortly afterwards (from alcoholism), the public was delighted. It seemed as though peace was guaranteed, as was the case.

When the next war broke out eighty years later, that was not because either Persia or Turkey wanted it, but because Afghans of the Ghilzai clan were eager to expel the Persians from Pashtun territories. The Ghilzai, who were the core of the modern Taliban, were centred at Kandahar; their ruler, Mir Mahmud Hotaki (c.1697–1725), saw three directions of possible expansion – north into Turkish and Uzbek regions, which were currently unstable, east across the mountains into the Indus River valley (now Pakistan), and south into the Safavid empire of Persia. The latter, being weak but rich, was the obvious first target. In 1721 Mahmud crushed the Persian army in a great battle at Gulnabad, then, when the shah of Persia peacefully abdicated, named himself as successor. It did not take Mahmud long to murder the former shah and all his relatives, then to massacre thousands of scholars at Isfahan. Afterwards he advanced on Shiite areas, long associated with Persia but held by the Ottoman sultan. The ensuing war was fought in what is today Iraq, but without either side achieving victory.

If Mahmud had not been murdered, with a civil war following, the history of Afghanistan and Persia, and perhaps Iraq too, might have been very different. But a talented Turcoman warlord, Nader Shah (1688–1747), was able to rally the dispirited Persians and throw out the steppe nomads. Nader had begun as a leader of outlaws, subsequently ruling through figureheads until the sheer incompetence of the ruling family required him to take over personally. As he advanced into Afghanistan and was about to crush the Pashtuns, the Ottoman sultan intervened. However, Turkish efforts to keep Persia weak did not work as planned – Nader first defeated the Afghans in 1729, then the Ottomans in 1730. The Ottoman response to this was ferocious – Turks were not known for quitting. Fighting raged up and down the frontier (even involving the Russians in Georgia, at that time a Persian tributary), and the sultan's failure to crush the upstart led to his overthrow in 1730. Nader's siege of Baghdad failed in 1733, but with Russian assistance he drove the Ottomans out of what are today the eastern provinces of Iraq.

Nader's reorganisation of his multi-cultural army made him less dependent on his Persian subjects, who were oppressed taxpayers and religious zealots – both prone to revolt. He tried to evade this danger by having an overwhelming, ever-successful army of steppe horsemen and by paying this army with the plunder of conquered countries.

His first task was to build a new army, often using recruits drawn from regions likely to revolt as soon as he rode off over the horizon, thereby weakening them. He required subject khans to send him men, whom he trained as both disciplined infantry and dashing cavalry. He relied on a musket so heavy that it had to be transported by camel – it fired a one-pound ball that could penetrate any armour – and on mobile cannon. He did not have many siege guns, but he was relentless, rarely giving up until an enemy was routed or a city or castle surrendered. Nader's reputation for mercy served him well, as did his practice of offering moderate terms.

Nader had grown up with the bow and spear, but early in life had seen their limitations. His emphasis on firearms, together with his own military genius, allowed him to crush his enemies, then enlist their surviving warriors into his army. Once potential rebels were far away, enriching themselves in newly conquered lands, he thought he could make his chaotic but compliant empire into a great military power. Indeed his army became huge – a massive tax burden – more numerous than the Austrian and Prussian armies together, and, to judge by his successes against the Ottomans and the Ottoman victories over Austrians, it was as effective a war machine as either.

Having made peace with the Turkish sultan, Nader turned on the Afghans again, crushing them in 1737. He then invaded India, where the incomparably wealthy Mughal shah ruled from a jewel-studded peacock throne over multitudes of industrious and warlike peoples. The battle of Karnal in February 1739 was an old-fashioned contest of traditional armies – Nader having 55,000 warriors and employing camels, his opponent 150,000 (or a million) men and using elephants. The difference was partly in firepower, partly in unity of command and purpose, but mainly in generalship. Nader's victory was a hard blow to the Mughal Empire and its proud traditions. Though Nader allowed the shah to retain his title and his fortress in Delhi, he took away both his reputation and the famous peacock throne (later destroyed, but henceforth identified with Persia). Nader's victory proved that the Mughal shah lacked the ability to defend his state against a distant foreign barbarian; soon rebellions proved that he could not defend it against sophisticated domestic rivals.

As Axworthy explains in *The Sword of Persia*, Nader's army was invincible because of his emphasis on discipline and firepower, but such characteristics came at a cost that ruined his taxpayers. These developments, paralleling what had occurred across Europe in the past century and a half, came about so swiftly that Persian society was not able to adjust appropriately. Basic reforms were needed, especially in encouraging economic development and in tying those developments to military needs, but Nader had no interest in such matters. All he wanted was more money.

Nader's problems were multiple and pressing. The Ottomans were on one side, the many Afghan peoples on the other, with restive Persians at his back. For years he successfully fended them all off – but at a heavy cost. As his army expanded across the Gulf into Oman, it defeated enemies in the Caucasus region and crushed rebels who believed that he had perished in India. Nevertheless, he grew paranoid, seeing conspiracies everywhere. His health declined, depriving him of vigour and sleep. He could have given more authority over to his sons, but he had seen that rulers who failed to hold the reins of power firmly lost control of the unruly beasts of empire. Bitter experience and impossible demands for taxes turned his once popular government into a reign of terror – he blinded his most talented son for daring to think independently, then slew long-time companions who had led armies to brilliant victories. Eventually, he spent more time in his harem and less discussing pressing problems, practices that resulted in erratic changes of policy and brutal retaliations. His last war against the Ottomans, 1743–6, ended with a combination of unsuccessful sieges and battlefield victories, but only a slight expansion of territory. Persia disintegrated after his assassination in 1747 – the army fell apart, the individual units going home to resume ancient feuds. The 'Napoleon of Persia' had not been able to bring together the Shia and Sunni, much less the Afghan, Persian, Pashtun, Kurd, Turcoman and other peoples of his empire. The Persian core recovered eventually from the wars of succession that followed, but Persia was not to be a great power again.

As the Persian and the Mughal empires declined, martial sects on their periphery were adopting European weapons – the Marathas in India being the most important, but also Sikhs, Caucasus peoples, even Malays. Groups previously despised were becoming self-confident.

The Maratha Confederacy, Hindu lords representing ninety-six martial clans, all fiercely resentful of Muslim monotheism, lay inland from the Carnatic coast in South India. After Nader's assassination, the Marathas occupied much of the shattered Mughal state. Their ambitions, however, were challenged by the Pashtuns of Afghanistan, who rode through the Khyber Pass into India.

Afghanistan

To the north of Persia a new state arose, ruled by Ahmed Shah Abdali (1723–73), the commander of Nader's heavy cavalry. He led his fellow tribesmen, the Pashtun, into both Persia and India, sacking Delhi in 1756 and defeating the army of the newly powerful warrior sect of Sikhs. His cavalry wore heavy armour and carried muskets – not exactly the light horsemen one might expect from north of the Hindu Kush, but reminiscent of the Parthians who had stuck terror into Roman legions.

When this Islamic advance reached the Maratha Confederation, it provoked a counteroffensive into the Punjab; in response Ahmed Shah declared a jihad against the Hindu unbelievers. The decisive encounter came in January 1761 at Panipat, near Delhi, when one hundred thousand warriors conducted a mutual massacre. The Maratha artillery had been trained by the French – 150 cannon – and dug in behind extensive earthworks, but eventually they ran short of supplies. In preparation for a desperate sally to break through Ahmed's siege lines, the Maratha soldiers rouged their faces with saffron – a sign that they would either prevail or die – then wheeled out the cannon behind a line of French-trained musketeers with bayonets. The light cavalry was held in reserve until the Afghans had been worn down.

In the opening stages, the battle played out as planned – despite initial aiming errors, the European-style musketeers and artillery shot the charging Afghan cavalry to pieces before advancing against infantry armed with outdated matchlocks, and mowed them down. Then a premature cavalry charge negated that advantage – the commanders of the horsemen either could not bear missing the glory or were persuaded that the Afghans were ready to break. However, their half-starved mounts were not equal to the task. Worse, the infantry had now advanced beyond the covering fire of the artillery and the command structure broke down, so that reserves were not quickly brought up.

When Ahmed deployed his own mounted musketeers and the camel corps, with its two thousand mounted light cannons (which could fire over the heads of Muslim horsemen directly into the Maratha cavalry), his Afghan cavalry swept down on the Hindu lines, breaking them, then wiping out the Maratha household troops and capturing tens of thousands of poorly trained troops which had been waiting in the rear.

Ahmed ordered the beheading of ten thousand prisoners, then led tens of thousands of noble captives off to Afghanistan as slaves. The slaughter among his own troops, however, had been so substantial that his state declined as much as the Maratha Confederacy. In the place of the Islamic and Hindu powers came a revived Sikh Confederacy in the Punjab that reached all the way to the Khyber Pass.

Black comments in *Warfare in the Eighteenth Century* that the battle of Panipat illustrates why the Indians were not so worried about the British military challenge – they had more serious problems right on their border.

Madras

The Maratha Confederacy had been unable to expand into northern India, but it extended its influence towards the coasts. Macaulay described this with his usual combination of narrative skill and strong opinions: 'Every region not subject to their rule was wasted by their incursion. Wherever their kettle-drums were heard, the peasant threw his bag of rice on his shoulder, hid his small savings in his girdle, and fled with his wife and children to the mountains or the jungles, to the milder neighbourhood of the hyena and the tiger.' William McNeill, no mean writer himself, in *The Rise of the West* attributed the Mughal collapse to both disunity among the princes and their inability to win the support of their Hindu subjects; the authority of 'weak and debauched' emperors, he said, was largely imaginary. More recently, Ferguson argued cogently in *Empire* that this situation, which Europeans considered 'anarchy', was exactly what Europe had been going through. Indian states, like European ones, were modernising their tax systems to pay for large standing armies. It would have been only a matter of time until order was restored, but meanwhile the European posts had to protect themselves – equipping and training troops from the warrior castes of India.

It was in this period that French influence reached its peak. Dupleix contributed weapons, instruction and officers to the Maratha Confederacy; the British, naturally, did the same for its enemies, though less effectively. This was because, as Black suggests in *Warfare in the Eighteenth Century*, the costs of new weapons – muskets and cannon – had become a disruptive burden. The East India Company had been founded to make money through trade, not by raising armies – or equipping them.

It was at this moment that fate called forth Robert Clive. While there is no active agent called 'fate', those who dislike the 'great man' theory of history, or are reluctant to admit to any Indian shortcomings whatever, might admit that Britain experienced some damn good luck right then.

Perhaps no soldier of fortune should be more famous than Robert Clive. Born in northern England in 1725 to parents with a solid position in local society and politics, but not wealthy or prominent, he was seemingly unsuited either for study, work or the life of a minor official or merchant. Clive was unable to concentrate, to work quietly, to take orders or even to focus his aggressiveness and desire for action. He was bright enough, everyone agreed, but he was nothing but trouble. Even his indulgent parents were happy to see him sail for India. The East was no place for useful or promising children – disease, dissipation and drink were real dangers – but perfect for those who could not fit in at home. For this reason the British government sent Scots and Irish to India and other tropical climes. Kevin Kenny, in *Ireland and the British Empire*, notes that at the battle of Wandewash (1760) the French commander was Thomas Arthur, the count of Lally, born in Galway, and the British commander was Eyre Coote, born in Limerick. Irish soldiers served in both armies. Service in the colonies was, Kenny says, a form of banishment.

Clive's passage took almost a year. Stranded nine months in Brazil, he learned some Portuguese, a skill that became valuable later, because he lacked the patience to learn any of the many Indian languages. Being still a growing boy, none of his clothes fitted when he finally arrived in Madras.

He was immediately bored. Clive disliked the climate, hated the work and was earning too little to cover the cost of his transportation and the long lay-over in Brazil; moreover, he had made no friends. Twice he attempted suicide, but the properly loaded pistol misfired each time, persuading him that fate or God must be preserving him for some great work. Fate again. Fortunately for him, the governor gave him the run of his library.

It was at this point that war came. When Dupleix arrested the leaders of the English mercantile company, Clive slipped away in the disguise of a Muslim, reached an English fort in Bengal and enlisted in the forces of Stringer Lawrence (1697–1775), an experienced soldier who had seen combat in Gibraltar, the Low Countries and Culloden, and was universally admired for courage, ability and honesty.

Clive, in contrast to Lawrence, was just twenty-one, a minor officer with no military experience or training. However, Lawrence realised that Clive was a natural leader of men; with a generosity not widely known even among the greatest of generals, Lawrence gave Clive men and responsibility.

Nature assisted. As Admiral Ballard reminds us in *Rulers of the Indian Ocean*, the French were always to the leeward, so the southwest monsoon allowed British merchantmen to run before the wind past the blockading fleet. Therefore, the British could wait in safety, while the French had to keep watch on the high seas. Inevitably, this strategy played out to the French disadvantage – Bourdonnais was caught by a tremendous storm common to the Bay of Bengal and had to limp back to Mauritius with his surviving ships. Abandoning plans to strike at British bases too widely dispersed to be defended effectively meant missing his only opportunity to win the war. The next year a large British fleet under instructions to take the French coastal bases suffered the same fate.

Peace was concluded in 1748, with Madras restored to the English; but Clive made only a perfunctory effort to resume his civilian career. When Lawrence requested him to return to military service, he instantly agreed. Political turmoil in the region had become worse, allowing the French to make alliances with local potentates. Lawrence decided to counter this, believing that any prince threatened by French allies would welcome English support.

Still, on the whole the situation was unfavourable to the English. Dupleix was besieging Trichinopoly, the last, weak stronghold of the weakest candidate to rule the coast. He had amassed a fantastic personal fortune, dressed extravagantly in order to overwhelm native eyes used to elaborate jewel-bedecked, colourful costumes, and he commanded thousands of French and native troops. With such showmanship, he won over important native princes. As Marshman comments in *The History of India*, 'An Asiatic prince never considers himself bound by any principle of honour, or even consistency; his own supposed advantage is the only rule of his conduct, and he changes sides without the smallest scruple. Dupleix persuaded the Nabob that the English were the weaker party, and the Nabob did not hesitate for a moment to abandon them.'[2]

Clive, in contrast, had only two hundred English and three hundred sepoys, a term originating from the Persian word for soldier – it would soon mean Indian soldiers in the employ of a European power. Sepoys were not simply Indians given Western weapons – in *Battle*, Lynn stresses the Asian origins of their system of values (caste, religion, honour) that made them so formidable. It was no accident that Clive and his successors never allowed any missionary to approach them, that they paid them promptly and honoured their services. What the British brought were drill and discipline, better weapons and more effective combined arms.

There was really no choice. As Chase points out in *Firearms: A Global History*, it was not practical to transport a European army to India. Moreover, there was the matter of disease – which incapacitated many of the Britons who did not die outright. Nevertheless, British officers were able to train Indian troops more effectively than anyone had imagined.

While some sepoys were Muslims, most were Brahmans, who found in the regiments a new form of community, complete with wives and families following them on campaigns. Clive and his successors had to avoid requiring them to eat at a European-style mess, since no high-caste Hindu could eat food prepared by a lower-caste cook; in time 'John Company' required all British officers to master Hindi before assuming their duties.

That was in the future, of course. When Clive faced the French at Trichinopoly, only two of his officers had ever seen action, and only four had any military training. But Clive, whose personality had prevailed on the company's officers to entrust the relief of the fort to him, persuaded his men to attack the nawab's capital at Arcot. Rushing to the gates in the midst of a violent thunderstorm, he convinced the garrison that he had a much larger force; generously, he allowed them to evacuate without being slaughtered.

The next day the garrison discovered how small his force was. Gathering reinforcements to the number of three thousand men, the Indians established a camp nearby and then went to sleep, certain from sounds of carpentry that the Englishmen were labouring to improve the city's defences. Clive had indeed been driving his men hard, but after dark he led them out, attacked the besiegers, scattered them to the winds and returned to the city without having lost a single man.

In response, Dupleix sent an army of ten thousand men, among whom were 150 French soldiers. This time the siege was properly conducted – a breach was blown in the walls, then efforts made to widen it. Meanwhile, Clive's numbers dwindled, his supplies began running out, and hope of relief almost vanished, but he insisted on persevering, requiring his officers to take no more rations that they supplied their troops. When Clive's sepoys saw the English starving, they offered to live off the rice water, giving the rice to the Europeans, who needed it more. Fifty days passed.

Then fate (again) called forth a *deus ex machina* – the god in this case being a Maratha faction which had been mistrustful of the French, but had not seen any way of opposing them until Clive appeared. First, of course, they had to rescue him. When the besiegers heard of the approach of this Hindu army, they made one last effort to storm the fort, using elephants with iron plates on their heads to batter down the gates, rafts to carry men over the wet moat, and masses of men to assault the wall that was only protected by a dry moat. Three desperate efforts in the course of an hour failed. The besiegers then retreated, leaving four hundred of their number behind, but having slain only five or six of Clive's men.

Now, miraculously (as always) the men commanding Saint George found two hundred English soldiers and seven hundred sepoys to relieve Arcot. When they arrived, Clive hurried in pursuit of the retreating besiegers, brought them to combat and routed them. When six hundred sepoys from the French army came over to him, Clive had sufficient manpower to win several more victories.

Next, again miraculously reinforced, Clive prepared to attack Trichin- opoly. At this point, however, cooler minds prevailed – command was given to Lawrence. It is a credit to both men that there was no crisis. Lawrence had always treated Clive well, and he did so now as well. Like a team in harness, they marched on Dupleix.

The French commander had only one weakness, he himself admitted – he did not like the sound of gunfire; he needed silence and tranquillity, not noise. He had not been trained as a soldier, and he knew better than to pretend otherwise. His practice had been to entrust military affairs to experts. Unfortunately, at this moment there were none left. Moreover, his French troops were, in Macaulay's words, 'the sweepings of the galleys'.

Clive's new men were hardly better, 'the worst and lowest wretches that the Company's crimps could pick up in the flashhouses of London'. In their first engagement, they all ran away at the first shot. But Clive, though desperately ill (as the subcontinent's climate eventually made almost every Englishman), whipped them into an army and brought the war to a victorious conclusion.

The outcome was essentially foregone – British resources were simply overwhelming; Dupleix lacked money, men and naval support. However, chance plays too great a role in human affairs for us to imagine that overwhelming strength always prevails.

Clive married and returned home in triumph. Dupleix, in contrast, had his last great offensive – a gigantic army of two thousand Frenchmen, hundreds of thousands of Indians, hundreds of cannon and over a thousand elephants – disrupted by a mutiny among his officers, who wanted a larger share of the booty. When they quit the army, their units dissolved and the rest of the army went home. Dupleix was summoned back to France in 1754, having spent his entire fortune in his country's interest. His frustration in seeing the great enterprise abandoned by the king was made worse when Louis XV's ministers refused him any kind of recognition or financial support. He died in lonely poverty.

Bourdonnais did no better. After quarrelling with Dupleix, he was captured by the British at sea, so that the war was over before he reached the royal court to explain his strategy for victory. The king ordered him secretly imprisoned in the Bastille, where he was held for two years. He was acquitted of all charges in 1751, but by then his health was ruined and his fortune lost; he died two years later in poverty. Only Bussy came away with honour. He maintained himself in the Deccan until 1758, when Lally assigned him to the far less significant post at Pondicherry – thereby resolving their dispute over strategy – and took over command in the Deccan himself. Bussy was captured by the British, but, because of his generous behaviour in the past, was allowed to sail to France. He returned to India in 1782, but achieved little.

Louis XV came out of the war better than he had reason to expect – the peace treaties allowed him to retain unfortified trading posts that, in fact, continued to belong to France until their incorporation into India in 1954. His officers had done well, but the king had failed to put sufficient resources into either India or Canada to assure them victory. As Mahan noted, when the French navy was driven from the seas, it became impossible for French merchantmen to ply the seas. By 1759 French goods became so scarce that the merchants had no choice but to raise their prices. This drove Indian purchasers (both in America and Asia) to British competitors.

Clive had done better, but his fortune lasted only two years. He spent lavishly (establishing an unfortunate precedent for everyone else returning home flush with Indian loot), ran for Parliament, but lost his seat to superior political manoeuvring, and in 1755 returned to India as a lieutenant colonel in the British army. This time he had the full support of the British government, especially that of William Pitt (1708–78), the secretary of state after 1756, whose grandfather ('Diamond' Pitt, 1653–1726) had acquired a fortune as governor of Madras.

Bengal

Clive's assignment was to deal with the 'problem child' then ruling the incredibly rich state at the mouths of the Ganges River – a land producing rice, sugar, fish and fine cloth, but few soldiers. When Mîrzâ Mohammad Sirâjud Dawla (1733–57) succeeded his grandfather as nawab, there was dissention in the royal family, and in his bureaucracy after he replaced too many officials. The prince was resentful of British influence and appalled by the foreigners favouring Hindu merchants, their refusal to pay taxes, their mixing in court intrigues, and most of all for bringing their quarrels into his lands. But he was too impatient to plan carefully, so that he entered into war with Britain only half prepared. Macaulay wrote that:

> Oriental despots are perhaps the worst class of human being; and this unhappy boy was one of the worst specimens of his class. His understanding was naturally feeble, and his temper naturally unamiable. His education had been such as would have enervated even a vigorous intellect, and perverted even a generous disposition. He was unreasonable, because nobody ever dared to reason with him, and selfish, because he had never been made to feel himself dependent on the good-will of others. Early debauchery had unnerved his body and his mind. He indulged immoderately in the use of ardent spirits, which inflamed his weak brain almost to madness.

Macaulay, whose provocative sallies lent spice to his narratives, added that 'Whatever the Bengalee does, he does languidly. His favourite pursuits are sedentary. He shrinks from bodily exertion; and, though voluble in dispute, and singularly pertinacious in the war of chicane, he seldom engages in a personal conflict, and scarcely ever enlists as a soldier.' Macaulay, who knew

India well, shared the common prejudice of the times that native peoples were to be prized according to how much they resembled Britons – warlike, self-confident, moral and reserved.

More to the point, Bengal was not a strong and stable state, but a new political unit. The nawab had only been in power for months, and he was not a person to inspire love or confidence; even his own family mistrusted him. Moreover, with Ahmed Shah sacking Delhi in 1756, he should have known that he could not expect assistance from the Mughal ruler; in fact, he had just been required to send some of his best troops to assist the shah. A circumspect avoidance of war was called for, but when the British mounted cannon on their fortifications in expectation of a new war with France (the Seven Years War, 1756–63), the young ruler was so offended that he prematurely led his army against Fort William at Calcutta.

The British governor fled, followed quickly by the military commander. Not surprisingly, the fort fell quickly. Dawla had the prisoners stuffed into the basement prison, probably neither knowing nor caring that 146 people would not fit into the chamber, which became infamous as the 'Black Hole of Calcutta'. To pleas for mercy the jailers responded with laughter, and that the nawab had gone to sleep and would not be wakened. In the morning twenty-three staggered out – the rest had suffocated. A few survivors were released, though several were tortured, and the one surviving woman was escorted to the prince's harem.

In Madras the British decided upon war, with Clive to lead the army. Nine hundred British troops and fifteen hundred sepoys were all he had to fight one of the most powerful rulers in India, a prince who had equipped his troops with European weapons and hired many European artillerymen (artillery long remained a foreign specialty – first Turks, then Europeans – even after Indian foundries were producing excellent cannon). The campaign began well, but then the British governor accepted the nawab's generous terms of peace (and recompense for all losses) – war had broken out in Europe, and if a French fleet appeared, the governor would need all of Clive's men back in Madras.

Clive understood that the nawab could not be trusted. First, there was Dawla's personality, his instinctive reliance on lies and betrayals; second, there was evidence that he was negotiating with the French. Consequently, Clive did not break off the campaign, but struck at the prince's principal fortress, taking five hundred European troops prisoner. He then orchestrated a conspiracy to topple the tyrant, to replace him with a disillusioned Arab mercenary, Mir Jafar.

Syed Mir Muhammed Jafar Ali Khan (1691–1765) had been an earlier nawab's military commander. Not satisfied with marriage to the ruler's half-sister, he conspired to occupy his office, too. He was removed from command, but not murdered. Dawla, desperately in need of an experienced commander, called him back into service. He was thus available for Clive's purposes.

Stealing from a thief not being easy, Clive stooped to intrigue and trickery so low that even the worst intriguers and tricksters of his own nation were appalled – a difficult task in those days when corruption and government were almost synonymous. While Clive believed that he had persuaded Mir Jafar and a bevy of Bengalese merchants and officials to betray their master, his officers and civilian officials were sceptical – the Bengalese rulers may not have survived by courage, but they had cunning aplenty. Confident that the prince's army would not fight, in June 1757 Clive marched north from Calcutta to Plassey, where the Bengalis were waiting.

Clive had three thousand men, two-thirds being sepoys trained by English officers. The nawab had forty thousand infantry and fifteen thousand cavalry, many drawn from distant warlike peoples; he had fifty cannon drawn by white oxen and pushed by elephants. The most difficult part of Clive's campaign may have been in crossing the Hooghly (Bhāgirathi) River. No river crossing in the face of an enemy is easy, but Clive encountered no significant opposition – Dawla had not entrusted Mir Jafar with overall command, nor any of the competent Frenchmen present, but gave the orders himself. Mostly, it appears, he did not know what orders to give and therefore gave few.

For Clive's part, it was not clear whether Mir Jafar would honour his part of the bargain, to bring his part of the army over to him. For good reasons Dawla and Mir Jafar mistrusted each other. Moreover, their unpaid troops were mutinous and lacking in confidence, and only a few French troops were present. Clive, hoping for the best and knowing that retreat would be such a fatal blow to his prestige that his outnumbered men might not be willing to fight later, plunged ahead – literally plunging into the uncharted waters of a great river, then leading his forces into a mango grove which the prince's excellent cavalrymen hesitated to enter. The next morning, despite having heard nothing from Mir Jafar, he moved out of the marsh sufficiently to deploy his artillery and align his men. He drove off an uninspired cavalry charge, after which a downpour interrupted the combat.

The British force took shelter under the trees and covered their weapons, but the French and Indians obediently remained in line – artillery, elephants, cavalry and infantry – and their weapons became soaked. Mir Jafar remained in place, too, ready to join either side, perhaps, as soon as it became clear who was winning. When the storm passed, the British powder was still dry, that of their foes wet. When Clive ordered the advance, he was met by a general counterattack along the line – except for Mir Jafar, who waited to see what happened. As British musketry cut the opposing ranks to pieces, the Indian army began to crumble. Mir Jafar remained waiting.

When the last cavalry charge was repulsed, Clive's men advanced on the prince's camp, slaying the French gunners who stayed by their weapons to the last. Clive's casualties were twenty Britons, sixteen sepoys. The prince fled on a camel, surrounded by servants, while Mir Jafar's forces remained in place, unengaged, though Clive's flank was now exposed. Afterwards, Mir Jafar withdrew and was rewarded with the prince's office. Dawla was soon executed by one of his principal lieutenants, probably on orders from Mir Jafar's son. He was mourned by none except modern nationalists who believe Dawla's resistance to Britain excused his incompetent political and military leadership. In contrast, Mir Jafar's name came to mean traitor.

Clive did well. He presented the company with 800,000 pounds sterling. When he himself toured the royal treasury, he 'walked between heaps of gold and silver, crowned with rubies and diamonds, and was at liberty to help himself'. Macaulay's lyricism imagines the masses of coins, some dating from the earliest contacts with Europeans, or even earlier, from Venetian trade. Clive took between 200,000 and 300,000 pounds. To his credit, he later established rules that made it impossible for anyone to duplicate his feat, and by guaranteeing company officials good wages, he eliminated the prime cause of corruption. Clive was still only thirty-four.

Southern India

In 1759 there was still a strong French position anchored on the strong fortifications of Pondicherry and good alliances with the native princes inland, but all were now in danger. If Louis XV had sent an army and a fleet to India earlier, the situation might have been saved. As it was, only the genius of Lally (1702–66), one of the finest soldiers in the French army, offered any hope of salvation. He was the son of Gerard Lally, an Irish exile, and his noble French wife. In the War of the Austrian Succession, he had fought with distinction at the head of the Irish brigade in Germany, in Scotland as an aide of Charles Stuart, and the Low Countries; everyone agreed that he had earned the title marshal of France.

The results were disappointing. Everything went wrong – Lally offended his officers, failed to inspire his soldiers and treated the natives as slaves. Lacking money, he attempted to recover a debt from a nearby native ruler. This brought him into conflict with the British in 1759.

Lally had an imposing number of European soldiers for the times – 1,300 French soldiers, 150 French cavalry and 1,800 sepoys – an army able to challenge that commanded by Colonel Eyre Coote (1726–83), who had begun his career in a well-travelled Irish regiment of the British army and fought at the battle of Culloden. Coote was colonel of the first regiment to be sent to India and had fought at Plassey; now he commanded one regiment of regulars and another of Highlanders, together with sailors to handle the artillery – a force he estimated at 1,700 Europeans and 3,000 sepoys.

At the battle of Wandiwash (Vandavasi) Lally did what he could to counter Coote's superior firepower, but his soldiers were reluctant to close with their enemy. His men, it appears, had the better judgement, since eight hundred were killed or wounded in the engagement. Even at the moment when Lally had sensed victory, after the British lines had been shaken by his artillery, his cavalry commanders refused to charge, calling the order suicidal. When Lally at last found an officer willing to lead his men against the centre of the British line, the formation was cut to pieces by cannon and volley fire. Lally was still fighting at that contested point when the explosion of a French caisson eliminated much of his artillery, leaving his left flank vulnerable to a British bayonet charge. Lally's surviving men abandoned their weapons and fled, reaching the coast at Pondicherry four days later. Central India had been lost. Afterwards the French sepoys came over to the British, followed by enough European soldiers to create a special body of 'French volunteers'.

Lally fell momentarily into depression, then rallied his forces to defend Pondicherry. At one moment, with French reinforcements promised and the blockading British fleet almost destroyed by a storm, it looked as if he might sustain a French presence in southern India until the end of the war. To almost universal surprise, the British commander restored his surviving ships quickly enough to resume the blockade. Starvation did the rest. Without supplies or hope of obtaining them, Lally surrendered Pondicherry in 1761 and was taken to Britain. Hearing that he was accused of treason, he insisted on returning to France. Warnings by his friends were all too well-founded – Lally was arrested and held two years in prison before his trial, then found guilty and beheaded. Louis XV needed a scapegoat and Lally fitted the role.

Bengal Again

As if there were not complications enough, that same year the Dutch in the East Indies (modern Indonesia) saw in the chaos in Bengal an opportunity they could exploit. Invited secretly by Mir Jafar to intervene, they arrived suddenly on the coast of Bengal with seven ships and fifteen hundred men, half of them Europeans. Their goal was to seize the sources of saltpetre, the most essential ingredient of gunpowder. Clive acted promptly, killing or capturing almost the entire force. From that moment on, it was clear who governed in Bengal – Clive, not Mir Jafar.

Mir Jafar's son, Meerun, believed that the way to restore the normal order was to catch the foreigners unaware and massacre them. However, before his plot was ready, the son of the Mughal shah invaded, forcing him to ask for British aid. In early 1760 the Bengali army met the invaders at Patna – a six-hour battle that ended in the total rout of the Mughal forces. Hours later Mir Jafar's son was struck by lightning, after which Mir Jafar went insane. When the British appointed the prince's son-in-law, Mir Qasim (Kasim), as his successor, they were repaid lavishly in money, jewels and new monopolies. But Mir Qasim was not willing to remain a European tool. Having seen the value of the Western way of war, he employed an Armenian merchant to raise 15,000 cavalry and 25,000 infantry trained in European methods, with his own impressive arsenal and cannon-foundry; he also acquired French troops and made alliances with neighbouring princes. He reconciled with the Mughal emperor, Shah Alam II (1728–1806), whose title was more impressive than his armies – though Alam was still the shah, and that was nothing to deride. Then, in 1763 Mir Qasim prematurely declared war on the British, who were able to declare him deposed, bringing back Mir Jafar as a figurehead for their rule. When Mir Jafar died two years later, nobody noticed or lamented.

The British-led army defeated Mir Qasim at Buxar in October 1764 in one of the most one-sided battles in Indian history. His revenge was to murder all European prisoners, using a Swiss mercenary from the French army, Walter Raymond, as his instrument. Mir Qasim ended his life in obscure poverty, while the defeated shah became a British puppet.

This was a cruel episode even by Indian standards. When Major Hector Munro (1726–1809) had faced a rebellion by sepoys just before the battle, he refused their demand for more pay, then surrounded them, seized the ring-leaders and tied them, Mughal fashion, to the mouths of cannon. With due ceremony, by blowing them into pieces, he restored discipline in his army. Munro was a Scot of aristocratic origin who spent much of his life in India, returning home considerably enriched. The historian Marshman wrote disdainfully of these sepoys, 'There is no instinct of obedience in native armies in India, as those in Europe, and their natural condition under every dynasty, native or foreign, Hindoo or Mahomedan, and in every province, has from time immemorial been that of insubordination. The British army of sepoys was no exception to the general rule.' These were actions and opinions typical of the era. Modern scholars who appreciate the institutions and attitudes that Britons brought to India may wish that they had not done so at the point of a bayonet, but do not often say how this might have been done.

The Results

The Seven Years War had been a worldwide conflict. In America it is known as the French and Indian War; in Asia it could be called that as well. Britain won in both theatres, and in Europe too. And the results were momentous. Ferguson reminds us that, had the French won this war, just the population of India learning French would have made it the world language today, not English. The difference was that England could raise money on credit, and the French could not. India was more than the 'jewel in the crown': it was, he says, a whole diamond mine.

Clive was not ungenerous. Left sixty thousand pounds in Mir Jafar's will, he donated the money to a fund for invalid officers and soldiers. Subsequently, though he declined large gifts from a variety of native rulers, he was hounded by his generation's version of the gutter press, snubbed by the traditional aristocracy and investigated by Parliament. At first Clive was honoured for having achieved much with small resources, but in the long run no one was proud of his deceptions. He might have been 'astonished at his own moderation', but no one else was. As Macaulay wrote in 1840,

> English valor and English intelligence have done less to extend and to preserve our Oriental Empire than English veracity. All that we could have gained by imitating the doublings, the evasions, the fictions, the perjuries which have been employed against us, is nothing when compared with what we have gained by being the one power in India on whose word reliance can be placed. No oath which superstition can devise, no hostage, however precious, inspires a hundredth part of the confidence, which is produced by the 'yea, yea,' and 'nay, nay,' of a British envoy.[3]

The importance of securing the loyalty of the sepoys cannot be over-stated. As Macaulay assured his readers, the sepoy 'knows that, if he lives a hundred years, his rice and salt are as secure as the salary of the governor-general; and he knows that there is not another State in India which would not, in spite of the most solemn vows, leave him to die of hunger in a ditch as soon as he had ceased to be useful.' There is surely a lesson for every government and each of us in that, even for those who believe that the prideful historian overstated the facts. Lynn, one of our most insightful historians of that era, notes in *Battle* that Indian rulers should have been more effective in combining European and Indian military traditions, but they were not. They raised larger armies than the East Indian Company and equipped them better, but Indian rulers came and went, disrupting the development of regimental loyalty which made the company's sepoys so formidable. The company's policies were essentially unchanged year after year, protected by distance from the meddling of Parliament, religious zealots and unimaginative military commanders.

Lynn further remarks on the importance of culture. When sepoys took an employer's salt, it was a symbol of commitment so important that it was put into the sepoy's oath. The sepoy's belief in reincarnation was also significant – a soldier could not kill, nor could he be slain, but would be reborn; death in battle was a sign of right conduct.

The number of sepoys was still not large. As Parker estimates in *The Military Revolution*, they had grown from two battalions in 1758 to ten (nine thousand men) in 1765. This is a small force for protecting British trading posts from the warriors available to Indian rulers. But their successes demonstrated that military values rooted in cultural traits make armies effective, not weapons or courage. Officers – given sufficient time and support – can develop these values in soldiers. If the cultural traits run contrary to the essential military values, even foreign officers find the task daunting. Since learning is a two-way street, success is rarely achieved by mindlessly imposing foreign values on any culture, much less on a culture with proud military traditions of its own.

India took full revenge on Clive – he died in 1774, not quite aged fifty, from the ravages of numerous tropical diseases. His admirers regretted that he was not able to employ his talents against colonial rebels in North America.

What did all this mean for the East India Company, which had fought the wars first to keep its foot in the India market, then to kick the French out? In 1772 it was almost bankrupt. To save it, the British government lowered taxes on tea sales in America, hoping to accomplish two goals at one and the same time – to save the company, which was suffering from an American boycott, and to establish the government's right to tax colonists without asking their consent.

And what did this mean for the British view of their first empire? Modern scholarship is divided on this issue. The dominant view seems to be negative, citing the trial of Warren Hastings, the governor of Bengal, as proof that colonialism was one long era of economic exploitation and human rights abuses.[4] The opposite view was that the Hastings trial was proof that Britain was determined to curb such abuses; in that sense it was part and parcel of an evolving awareness of the ambiguity of power that powered demands for political and social reform and led to the foundation of the first abolitionist society. The beginning of the Industrial Revolution, followed by the French Revolution, changed British views of their future role in the world; in many ways, of course, this new view reflected past ones.

One question worth pondering is why is it that we reserve our praise for cultures which excel in war rather than for peaceable and productive peoples such as those in Bengal? Perhaps it is political attitudes that determine which answer the individual reader chooses.[5]

The Great Game

The future of British India was still not certain. Commercial and political success might yet prove fleeting. The third battle of Panipat had left central India in turmoil, but not in collapse, and great Muslim and Hindu armies still contested for supremacy; their strength was such that none paid much attention to the foreigners far to the east. In 1775, when the Maratha Confederacy went to war over rival candidates for the office of prime minister, this encouraged the new French king, Louis XVI (1754–93), to take one last great gamble. Possible control of Asia was worth placing one more bet on the green felt – an analogy that French society would have understood well.

The effort failed, after which France ceded this theatre of war to Great Britain, and Britons came to rely on their sepoy regiments to hold what they had acquired. But the situation was sufficiently fluid that Russian generals imagined they could reach India and prevail there. After all, every successful invasion of India had come from the north.

'The Great Game' – the contest for control of Central Asia – could have been won by either Great Britain or Russia, but for a time it appeared that the winner would be China. There were obstacles, each realised, but surely modern weapons could overcome them. There were comparatively few people in the vast, dry, flat lands, but they were only mounted tribal warriors. As for the rugged mountains, there were always allies to be found there who would happily fight ancient enemies. Distance was a problem, but even that could be overcome.

The Russian dreams were not new ones. Peter the Great's southward move into the Caucasus region in 1722–3 had been initially successful, thanks to the fleet that accompanied the infantry along the coast of the

Caspian Sea. He hoped to bring pressure to bear on the Ottoman Empire and to take advantage of the collapse of Persia, but neither happened. His generals could not pacify the rugged interior, and, according to Black, in *Warfare in the Eighteenth Century*, 130,000 Russian soldiers died of disease before the army withdrew in 1732.

The vacuum of power east of the Caspian was equally illusory. When Peter sent columns towards Afghanistan in the hope of opening a route to India, they reached Khiva in 1717, but soon found themselves surrounded by a large force of irregulars. After two days of siege, the army accepted an offer to leave peacefully, but was attacked on the march and annihilated. A second expedition, in 1719, to occupy gold fields, was similarly destroyed. (This was a fate that the British should have expected when accepting a similar offer in Afghanistan in 1838. Of the army of 4,500 in Kabul four years later, supported by perhaps 10,000 civilians, only forty escaped and only one was a Briton.)

Subsequent advances were more cautious. Forts were constructed on the frontiers, then at strategic locations (i.e. where water was available) and cities occupied. Most importantly, alliances with weaker tribes made warfare against stronger ones possible. There were always weaker tribes available.

The swift advance in military skills and technology was building a degree of self-confidence and ambition in Europeans matched only by previously unknown Asian and African feelings of inferiority. Asian efforts to duplicate European military methods were limited to adopting only the weaponry – gunpowder regimes. Changing ancient traditions, to learn the secrets that lay behind the weapons, was not yet acceptable.

In the 1850s Marx denounced 'oriental despotism', accusing it of resting on foundations of class and caste, ignorance, superstition and oppression that had to be swept away; in so doing, he praised British colonialism for unwittingly bringing about the only social revolution the region had ever known. (That is, military regimes came and went, but at the level of the farmer and artisan, nothing ever changed.) Opponents of imperialism, sentimental about the simple joys of village life and outraged by Western arrogance, disagreed. This began a conversation which has lasted into the twenty-first century, most recently with Ferguson's book subtitled *The West and the Rest*, arguing that competition, science, property rights, medicine, a consumer society and the work ethic combined to make all the difference. Today these are no longer exclusively Western virtues, but traditional elites and enlightened despots still pick and choose among practices which work best when they are mutually supportive.

The debate is far from over, but it is also hoped that this book will help explain how a comparative handful of Europeans were able to conquer wealthy and sophisticated peoples half the world away.

CHAPTER FIVE

Overlooked Wars

The great wars of 1700–17 left European rulers and their subjects exhausted. While minor conflicts abounded (including one in Italy that found Great Britain and France, recently deadly enemies, fighting together against Austria, Britain's long-time ally), most rulers were strongly opposed to another great international war; more importantly, perhaps, their bankers feared that a new war (and the associated borrowing) would endanger their ever recouping their earlier investments. Every monarch on the continent (in Britain only slightly less so) was staggering under the weight of debt and the accumulated anxieties of repeated crises; in Britain there was criticism that Hanover's concerns seemed more important than British interests.

There was an eagerness to enjoy life again – to build palaces and churches, pose for portraits, buy large paintings of mythological scenes with nude women, dance at great balls, race horses and entertain the public with parades and ceremonies. There was also a change in habits of thought, moving towards those we associate with the Enlightenment; the most important of these was to ignore conflicts over religion and concentrate on improving life here and now. This meant investing in public works projects that promised to increase public happiness (i.e. commerce), and augment government revenues. This latter point was very important, because more revenues could make possible all the projects that seemed useful and desirable or even merely necessary. Also, more revenues could be used to improve and enlarge the armies, all of which would otherwise be neglected in an era of peace.

Some may have sensed that preparing armies for a future war *almost ensured* another one, yet not preparing the armies *certainly assured* another war. There was always someone out there ready to take advantage of a weak neighbour – as Poland–Lithuania's unhappy fate would amply demonstrate.

Austrian Efforts to Create a Modern Army

Emperor Charles VI was not a brilliant man – his five years in Spain, 1706–11, proved that – but he was stubborn. When he returned to Vienna to become Holy Roman emperor, he never gave up the dress and customs of the Spanish court; nor did he cease to dream about becoming king of Spain. Nevertheless, he was realistic. He was also good at choosing among policies and picking the men to implement them – good enough that, for two decades, it appeared that he had made his Austrian lands more powerful than the much richer and more populous kingdom of France. He had emerged from the War of the Spanish Succession with most of the contested lands in Italy and the Rhineland, with vast acquisitions in the Balkans, and great influence in Poland. He failed in his efforts to regain the crown of Spain partly because his allies, Britain and Holland, did not want to see that much power collected in one ruler's hands; they joined with France to thwart him.

Although it was not apparent at the time, Charles's position rested on weak foundations. Italy could be held only by an army of occupation, and more garrisons were tied down on the French frontier. The Balkans had been devastated by war and the associated epidemics and famines; efforts to resettle the vacant lands were only partially successful. Belgrade was intended to be a German city, but many Serbs moved there, while the rich bottomlands of the Banat slightly to the north that were intended to be multinational became largely German. Belgrade prospered from the construction of Roman Catholic churches and monasteries, but it was the Banat's food production that promised a happier future.

Finance was the crucial factor for military preparedness. Charles received some money from the pope and German states, but in the end he had to rely on his own lands. Karl Roider, in *The Reluctant Ally: Austria's Policy in the Austro-Turkish War*, describes the two great financial institutions of his realm – the Hofkammer (privy council) and Hofkriegsrat (war council). The former was responsible for raising money, the latter for distributing it. For military affairs, therefore, the Hofkriegsrat was far the more important, and during the interwar years it was dominated by the legendary field marshal, Prince Eugene of Savoy.

Eugene – the 'little Capuchin' – was technically an abbot, but other than not marrying or making a spectacle of his sex life (unlike many contemporary churchmen who relished their notoriety), one would hardly have known it. His efforts to reform the army centred on a handful of basic changes:

1. Taking control of the regiments from their commanders, who were accustomed to raising, training and equipping the units themselves. This was only partially successful, because the practice of selling officer's commissions was too deeply ingrained and because too many noble families profited from holding nominal command of regiments.

2. Making the units more uniform, with three thousand men in each regiment, three battalions per regiment, and all men wearing grey overcoats and mitred hats (except for the grenadiers, who wore tall bearskin headgear). The state provided mounts to the cavalrymen, a practice that presumably reduced the percentage of undisciplined nobles among the horsemen.

3. Reducing competition between recruiters so that they could concentrate on men between the ages of twenty-five and thirty and to avoid those unlikely to become good soldiers (students, artisans and nobles); also not to enlist Italians, Poles, Croatians and Hungarians (and, of course, no Frenchmen like himself). The approach was thoroughly mercenary – to offer bonuses for enlistment, then provide regular pay. Efforts to identify and punish those who would collect the bounty, then desert, were only partially effective.

The obstacles were too weighty even for Eugene to move. First of all, most of Austria's income was already spoken for – court expenses, other military commitments and a crushing debt. It was a burden that Austria could manage in peacetime, but not for another long war. Second, there were political rivals who overlooked no opportunity to undermine his position. Third, the estates and the princes of the Holy Roman Empire wheedled reductions in their monetary contributions. Fourth, as Eugene grew older, he came to enjoy his low-stakes card games, his conversations with interesting men and pretty women, and a pleasant glass of wine in the evening – he lost interest in the frustrating details of administration.

The army slowly declined in efficiency. Veterans were released, to be replaced by younger and cheaper men. Training was neglected –

ammunition was expensive, war games even more so, and the soldiers were needed for agricultural labour, construction and public works.

Turkey Awakens from Sleep to a Nightmare

After the Ottoman army defeated the forces of Peter the Great, Ahmed III (1673–1736) had no desire to fight another European war; his interest was in a comfortable life, surrounded by compliant ministers and women, flowers and literature. He enjoyed the company of Europeans and two of his wives were French; several of his governors were Greeks (Phanariotes), and he soothed the discontent of religious and ethnic minorities by giving limited authority to their spokesmen. He was not a pacifist, but he saw wars as expensive distractions. In the 1720s his conflict with Persia had wound down to pacification efforts; although his troops had occupied Baghdad and Azerbaijan, it was not clear that he could avoid raising taxes. Nobody could say whether the climate would not defeat Ottoman armies as it had earlier foreign occupiers, or if the logic of geography would not inevitably pull the sultan into an invasion of Persia, or if peace would allow the Shiite heresy to spread into Sunni Turkey. The conflict had been managed by his grand vizier, Damad Ibrahim (1666–1730), who was so extraordinarily competent that Ahmed rewarded him with one of his many daughters, and the vizier's sons with two more. Both men were patrons of the arts who had presided over what subsequent generations would call the Tulip Era, a time of cultural revival and splendour. However, beginning in 1729 the Persian war went sour.

Damad Ibrahim, who had overseen the victory over Peter the Great in 1711, did not hurry to the endangered frontier himself. This was perhaps a mistake, because it turned out that the army was not ready for war. The sultan and grand vizier had spent grand sums on garden parties and entertainment, on artists and architects, but relatively little on armaments. Now they had a new and expensive crisis. Where could they get the money?

Damad Ibrahim met the budgetary crisis by spending money on the army that would normally have been used to support the refugees crowding into Constantinople. Since he could not ignore the plight of the newcomers, he allowed them to practise their trades right in the capital: this outraged the established guilds, which complained about unfair competition. When he delayed paying the quarterly salaries of the janissaries and other troops, those men then had to seek civilian employment too. His attempt to reduce the silver content in the coins met the fate of all inflationary efforts, in that the valuable old coins flowed out of the country or were melted down, leaving only debased ones for the tax farmers; soon counterfeiting became a major problem. To offset the inflation, he increased taxes. Meanwhile, the sultan contracted French architects to build new palaces and summer homes. This was the outward symbol of a Westernising trend that was viewed suspiciously by his subjects.

There were the inevitable conspiracies at the court and repeated uprisings in Egypt and other territories. Eventually, critics of the grand vizier's policies concluded that change could come only after his removal. The critical moment arrived in August 1730 after the sultan and grand vizier marched out of Constantinople in a great display of martial splendour, announcing that they were on their way to the Persian front. When it became known that they had stopped in Scutari, on the opposite shore of the Bosporus, and had no intention of going further, a riot broke out in Constantinople.

The instigator was an obscure Albanian second-hand clothes dealer, Patrona Halil, a former janissary with a history of joining protests, who by now had been reduced to working in a bathhouse. At the onset he had no more than twelve followers, but his denunciation of the sultan's surrender of territories to unbelievers (Christians) and heretics (Persian Shiites) quickly enlarged that number. The sultan and his officials hurried back, but too late. Unemployed janissaries had joined the rioters, then opened the prisons and released slaves from several galleys. The sultan, who had never been known for his strong nerves, first delivered Damad Ibrahim to the mob – mercifully strangling him beforehand – then accepted his own removal. Ahmed III lived six more years as a prisoner in the Topkapi palace, though nothing is known about the details of his confinement. His appearance in Voltaire's *Candide* among other exiled rulers at the carnival in Venice was pure fiction, but the philosopher's advice to leave high politics to others and to concentrate on cultivating one's own garden has the power of truthfulness.

Voltaire's readers were shocked that Candide and his friends found happiness as simple gardeners in Turkey. It was not easy to argue that life in the country was preferable to the gambling dens of Paris, but it still seemed obvious that manual labour eliminated society's three great evils – idleness, vice and poverty. As Voltaire's witty sallies were widely quoted among Enlightenment intellectuals, the Catholic Church put *Candide* on its Index of Forbidden Books.

Meanwhile, in the real Constantinople of 1730 power was held by Patrona Halil, who retained his working-class rags to disassociate himself from the luxury-loving habits of his predecessor.

The new sultan, Mahmud I (the hunchback, 1696–1754), distributed money liberally and allowed Patrona Halil to double the number of janissaries – a sign that the illiterate upstart and his equally illiterate associates were preparing for war. After two months the sultan obtained the help of the Tatar khan, then lured Patrona Halil to the palace, murdered him, and ordered the rebel leaders rounded up and killed. In the next four years there were four grand viziers and even greater turnover in the lesser offices – Albanians were removed from their commands, coffeehouses and baths were closed, and the number of executions was estimated by the Venetian ambassador to top ten thousand. Even so – or because of these measures – conspiracies continued to appear. Counter-measures included forbidding contact with foreigners, increasing taxes and liberal gifts of coins that were ever more worthless.

Nothing seemed to be going well – not only was the Persian war going badly, with 'Russian deserters' serving as engineers and artillerymen for the Persians, but one epidemic after another swept the capital and provinces. In 1733 the Venetian ambassador reported that three hundred members of the grand vizier's court had perished.

Fortunately for the sultan, Nader Shah turned his attention first to Afghanistan, then India. That upstart, who had taken over the disintegrating Persian Empire in 1720 and made it the dominant military power of the region by 1730, saw conquests elsewhere easier and more profitable than fighting the sultan over impoverished mountains and deserts; and he had already taken rich lands between the Tigris and Euphrates rivers that no power based on the Mediterranean had ever been able to hold for long.

As the new sultan's situation improved, he resumed the Westernising programme that had been cut short by the revolution. He hired Claude Alexandre, comte de Bonneval (1675–1747), a French officer who had served capably in the War of the Spanish Succession, first for the French against

Austria and England, then for the Austrians against the French, and then for the Austrians against Turkey. Though badly wounded at the battle of Petrovaradin, he recovered quickly enough to take part in the capture of Belgrade. Court-martialled for insulting his commander in the Austrian Netherlands, he lost his command, his honours and his pension. As soon as he could, he went to Venice, then sailed to Constantinople to offer his services to the sultan. He organised a school to teach artillery tactics. Not surprisingly, many Ottoman officers were jealous of this French mercenary's swift rise to prominence.

French Recovery

Peace was in France's interest. There was simply nothing worth fighting over. Meanwhile, French prestige grew apace, based on leadership in the arts, architecture, literature and the emerging fields of science and philosophy. Early in his reign Louis XV was a handsome man, an engaging ruler and totally without ambition.

His government was managed by Cardinal André-Hercule de Fleury (1653–1743), his tutor, and since 1726 first minister. This was perfectly in line with French tradition, but so were complicated political intrigues that could not be afforded without a reform of the monetary system. Fleury's predecessor had been persuaded by John Law (1671–1729), a prominent Scottish economist, that trade – not the mere possession of bullion – was the best measure of a nation's economic health. Law had been a successful speculator, but it was his arguments against private monopolies and tax farming that brought him to the regent's attention in 1716. Law established private banks and began printing paper money. The theory was that this was a good means of stimulating trade and industry without putting government credit at risk. The paper bills were to be backed by gold, but – as so often happens – the temptation to print more money was irresistible; these bills were backed only by the government's promise to redeem them. Given the poor royal record on repaying loans, this promise gave experienced lenders pause.

As the increase in the money supply and easy credit led to inflation, speculators offered to safeguard people's money by investing it in new enterprises similar to British and Dutch companies that had earned great profits. The most important of these enterprises was the Mississippi Company, a joint stock company that absorbed the East India Company and whose stock rose and rose – until 1720, when the bubble burst. The financial panic led to a downturn in the economy that was reversed only after Fleury returned the currency to hard cash and began to pay the interest on royal debts. When confidence returned, Fleury began an ambitious programme of building roads and canals based on requiring peasants to work on the projects for low wages. His careful management of the budget left the army and navy with insufficient funds to remain effective, though that did not matter much, Fleury reasoned, because he intended to avoid war. That would have been easier if he had been as restrained in his relationships with Germans as he was with Great Britain. However, he could not refrain from trying to build up a pro-French party in the Holy Roman Empire, then interfering in Polish affairs when the opportunity arose.

Louis XV had the looks of a king and the brains, but not the temperament. He was sufficiently intelligent to understand all the problems, but not wise enough to choose confidently among alternative policies. Timid in such matters, he relied on his advisors; shy, he preferred the quiet of family life and the company of attractive women – most famously Madame de Pompadour (1721–64). The soft-porn portraits by François Boucher (1703–70) tell us much about the king and his court, and about the women who became known as courtesans. The most famous painting, other than that of the aristocratic and refined Pompadour, was the nude fourteen-year-old Marie-Louise O'Murphy de Boisfaily (1737–1814), the daughter of an Irish officer who had become a shoemaker in Rouen.

Attractive was not a word easily applied to the woman Louis XV had wed – Maria Karolina Zofia Felicja Leszczyńska (1703–68), the daughter of the exiled king of Poland. She was chosen because Fleury was concerned about Louis's health and did not want to wait until a suitable royal princess came of age – after the succession crises at the end of Louis XIV's life, he wanted the young king to produce an heir quickly. Maria was healthy, pro-French and available. She provided France with a large number of potential dauphins and princesses, and she did not complain about her husband's mistresses. In time Louis developed a cold and imperious public character that hid his inner doubts about his abilities. This may have saved his own mental health, but it cost him the hearts of his subjects.

1. All soldiers, but especially mercenaries, had used threats, torture, mutilation and execution to locate hidden money, to take revenge for resistance, or simply to intimidate the population. The punishments depicted here were some used by judicial authorities.

2. The new state armies proved their worth in 1683 when Catholics and Protestants put aside their religious difference to march to the relief of Vienna, then close to falling to Turkish besiegers. Previously Ottoman armies had been almost unbeatable; afterwards Christian forces were superior. In the foreground left is King Jan Sobieski of Poland, with the German and Polish forces pouring over the Kahlenberg (Bald Mountain), hurrying to the relief of the beleaguered city.

3. Strasbourg (Strassburg) was the most important city on the Rhine. It also lay near the traditional 'Spanish Road' along which Habsburg troops marched to the defence of the Netherlands. Louis XIV considered its possession essential to his plans for expansion into the Holy Roman Empire.

4. The Rhine at Kelheim, where German fortifications frustrated French marshals until Louis XIV forged an alliance with the duke of Bavaria.

5. George I on the royal barge on the Thames in 1717, accompanied by George Frideric Handel and listening to the composer's *Water Music*.

6. Horses hauled boats in Russia from the Don River to the Volga River.

7. The steppe near the Dnieper River.

8. Between 1709 and 1715 Antione Watteau painted this sorry spectacle of a French officer leading eight undisciplined recruits to join their regiment.

9. Apotheosis of Prince Eugene of Savoy (that is, his being declared a deity, an appropriate honour for Austria's greatest general). Marble statue by Balthasar Permoser in the Österreichische Galerie, Vienna. Appropriately for such a modest man, he shrinks back from the honour. Almost every visitor to Vienna will visit his palace, now the Belvedere museum and gardens.

10. Raphael Donner (1693–1741) produced this version of St Martin and the Beggar for Prince-Bishop Emre Esterhazy, in 1728. Made of lead, larger than life, it decorated the high altar of the cathedral at Bratislava (then called Pressburg). What struck contemporaries was the artist portraying the knight as a hussar.

FRIDERICUS
Dei Gratiæ Rex Borussiæ,
Marchio Brandenburgensis Sacri Romani Imperii
Archi-Camerarius et Elector etc
Natus d 24 Ian 1712 succedit
d 31 Maÿ 1740

11. The young Frederick the Great (*above*), based on a portrait by Christian Wolfgang. Much more familiar is the 'Old Fritz' who had mastered the art of war and earned the love of his officers and men. This bronze statue (*right*) was kept in his favorite palace, Sans Souci, outside Berlin at Potsdam.

12. Leopold von Daun had reformed the Austrian army after the defeats in the War of the Polish Succession and the Turkish war. He persuaded his soldiers that they could stand up to the French and Prussians, but he was a cautious commander, never asking more of his men than he believed they could achieve. Standing on the defensive generally worked well, but not against Frederick the Great. Only after his death, when others had an opportunity to face the Prussian king, was Daun's greatness recognised.

13. The strange geologic formations overlooking the Elbe River were a formidable barrier to the movement of armies in the eighteenth century. In more modern times these mountains, which separated the Czech lands from Germany, were an essential component of the Czechoslovak defensive system. When the 1938 Munich conference insisted that they be surrendered to Hitler, the Czechs could no longer defend themselves.

14. Landscape in the Kyffhäuser by Johann Alexander Thiele. The fortress was on the highest point of the hills along the border of Sachsen-Anhalt and Thuringia.

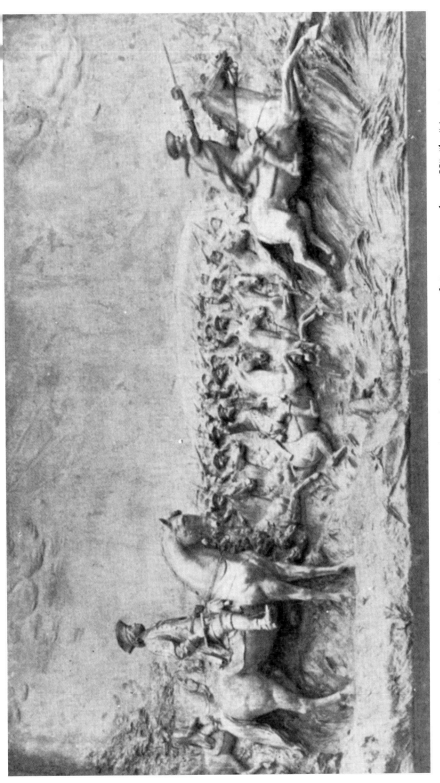

15. The charge of the Walloon dragoons at the 1757 battle of Kolín is from the monument of victory erected near Křečhoř in 1898.

16. Fragonard (1732–1806) was among the most popular Rococo painters. *The Swing* illustrates the carefree life at the court of Louis XV.

17. The opposing commanders in India saw themselves in thoroughly European terms. Nothing in any of these pictures would suggest that they had ever served in Asia.

To the extent that a picture can tell a story, Clive (*left*) radiates authority, just as Dupleix (*below, right*) suggests self-confident nobility, while Bourdonnais looks like a commoner. No matter how good Bourdonnais's judgment was on the deck of a man-of-war, when it came to selecting this artist, he was totally at sea.

18. Richard Montgomery reviews the troops at Crown Point prior to moving up the Hudson River towards Canada. Born in Ireland, he had served in the British army in America during the French and Indian War, after which he settled there. In 1775 he chose to side with his adopted country. American hopes were high that French Canadians would make a similar choice to break with Great Britain.

19. Washington and de Steuben greet Lafayette at Valley Forge. These two officers helped the Continental Army emerge from suffering through the Pennsylvania winter as an improved fighting force. Washington was one of the finest horsemen in America.

20. Washington and Rochambeau at Yorktown in October 1781. Cornwallis chose to be ill rather than surrender his sword personally, and his British and Hessian troops showed equal disgust when they marched out between the aligned French and American forces. The moment was, according to legend, symbolised by the British army band playing the popular tune, 'The World Turned Upside Down'.

The regent had hoped that putting the aged Marshal Villeroy in charge of the youthful king's education would prepare him to lead armies and command a great state, or at least to polish the skills of a courtier, but the marshal had no more success in this than he had had against Marlborough.

In 1728 Fleury decided to renew the once-strong ties to the Ottoman Empire. Sending Louis Sauveur Villeneuve (c.1680–1745) to the Sublime Porte as ambassador, he assured him a hearing by having him arrive on board the flagship of an impressive fleet of warships. To his surprise, the grand vizier, Damad Ibrahim, only enquired about the availability of plants from the gardens at Versailles, then dismissed him. The next interview was eight months later.

The situation hardly changed after the revolution of 1730. Mahmud I left politics in the hands of swiftly changing grand viziers, retiring to his palace to enjoy his wives and write poetry, ignoring the political turmoil. Grand viziers were ready to imagine great victories, but not to take steps towards achieving them: none were ready to make war until the army was stronger and the political situation more favourable. Lord Kinross notes in *The Ottoman Centuries* that Villeneuve did what he could to assist the Turks to be ready when the time came, but it was clear that the Turks wanted France to declare war on Austria before committing themselves to a potentially disastrous conflict. Louis XV's ministers had no intention of doing that.

Russian Recovery

The fateful year of 1730 had as much effect north of the Black Sea as on the two great states to its south. In that year Anna Ivanovna (1693–1740), the niece of Peter the Great, became tsarina (empress) of Russia. Twenty years earlier she had married the heir of the duchy of Courland, Friedrich Wilhelm Kettler (1692–1711), in order to tie that small but strategic territory to Russia. Kettler died two months later, perhaps from overeating. Peter allowed Anna to retain the title of duchess, but put his son by his first wife – Alexei (1690–1718) – in charge of the government. Alexei was supposed to learn from this window on the West how France, Britain, Denmark and Sweden had made themselves so powerful, but he was a poor pupil who disliked his father and most of his policies. To secure her position in the intrigue-filled court, Anna took as her lover first the Kettler family's chief advisor, then Ernst Johan von Biron (1690–1772). In keeping with the Byzantine complexity of the court (which was excellent training for later managing the court in Moscow), Biron had been introduced to Anna by his sister, who had also been the advisor's mistress. (He was totally unrelated, as best we know, to the French officer bearing the same family name.)

Ernst Johann von Biron was the grandson of a groom in the ducal stables of Jacob Kettler (1610–82). Kettler had shown what a man of talent could do with even a small state surrounded by powerful neighbours who were constantly at war with one another – under his guidance trade had brought prosperity, and he had founded colonies in Africa and the West Indies to provide sugar and other commodities that sold well in the region. He encouraged his subjects to improve themselves and their lot – opening the way upwards even for a lowly born person such as Biron, whose ambitions were unfocused but unbounded. After being expelled from the university in Königsberg in 1714, Biron had gone to Russia to seek his fortune, but the outbreak of peace caused him to return to Courland. In 1716 Alexei fled to Austria, then allowed himself to be enticed back to Russia, where he was tortured to reveal the names of his fellow conspirators – who were then executed gruesomely, some broken on the wheel or impaled; Alexei himself died from the mistreatment.

This left Anna as sole ruler of Courland, where over the years she came to admire all things German, and began to introduce reforms advocated by German and French intellectuals. When Anna became tsarina in 1730, she brought Biron with her to St Petersburg.

As a result of their Western orientation, Anna and Biron were almost instantly disliked by Russian nobles and churchmen. According to Roider in *The Reluctant Ally*, Biron's only positive skill – other than being very charming to a very plump tsarina – was his knowledge of horses. Given his background, this was not surprising.

Biron's elevation to prominence was one of the swiftest in an era when it was not unusual for personality, education and manners to lift a person over the heads of men whose feet were mired in genealogy; that fact, combined with Biron's obnoxious arrogance, made him thoroughly hated. To guarantee himself friends in high positions, Biron promoted family members and Baltic nobles to offices in the Russian army and bureaucracy.

Another prominent German promoted by the tsarina was a general whom Roider calls the archetype of eighteenth-century adventurers. Burchard Christopher Münnich (Minnikh, 1683–1767) was a dashing figure of ideal physical proportions and mental swiftness. Born in Oldenburg in northern Germany, he enlisted in the French army, then served in the armies of Hesse and Saxony before going to Russia. As president of the Council of War in 1732 he established the school of cadets and reorganised the army. Bruce Menning, in his essay in Kagan and Higham's *The Military History of Tsarist Russia*, credited him with making a bankrupt system into an effective army on the Prussian model.

Another was the foreign minister, Heinrich Johann Ostermann (1686–1747), who had been selected by Peter the Great and hence was prominent among Anna's closest advisors. His policy was based on friendship with Austria, which would allow co-ordination of policies against Turkey. Like the other Germans in Russian service, he watched with interest the sultan's difficulties in his wars with Persia. Ottoman weakness always meant Russian opportunity; at that time Turkey seemed very weak indeed.

The sultan and his officials faced a strategic geographic problem. There were only two routes from Turkey to Persia – one through Syria, the other through the Caucasus region into Azerbaijan. The former required crossing mountains and desert; the latter followed the shore of the Caspian Sea directly into the Persian heartland. Awkwardly, the best route to the Caspian Sea led through Chechnya and Dagestan, vital territories already subject to Russia. This made it all the more important for the sultan to protect the Crimean Tatars, who had traditionally made the steppe along the Black Sea safe for Turkish armies. Anna's generals argued that blocking this invasion route would weaken the Ottoman sultan.

This could best be done by crushing the Tatars and occupying the Crimea. But what then? That was the question everyone was asking, especially the Austrians, who feared that the tsarina's armies would push down the western coast of the Black Sea towards, or perhaps to, Constantinople. Everyone also believed that the Russians did not dare move alone. Only if the Austrians tied down much of the Ottoman army could the Russians strike. And that seemed impossible . . . except to Fleury.

Fleury's plan, incredibly complex as only vague dreams can be, required Austria to become involved in a Turkish war so that the emperor could not take a firm stand against his reordering the balance of power in Central Europe in France's favour. Vaguely in the background was a concern that Charles VI would recover the Spanish throne – then in the hands of the erratic Philip V and his domineering wife. Fleury found suspicious the Habsburg use of Spanish court etiquette, but a better explanation was Charles VI's personal taste. Still, the French minister was not alone in fearing that some day France would once again be surrounded by hostile Habsburg states – therefore, he wanted a weak Austria. The question was, how could he achieve this without the neutral or semi-neutral German states coming to the emperor's defence? The answer seemed to be to make Poland into a firm ally.

This alliance would also make the embarrassing royal marriage to the daughter of a deposed monarch more respectable. The match had, after all, been hurried by concerns about the young king's health. It would just look better if the queen's father was a real king again, not a failed monarch living in exile.

The War of the Polish Succession – the First Overlooked War

Fleury's opportunity came in 1733, earlier than he had wanted, since Austria was still at peace. When Augustus II, the king of Poland, passed away, most observers believed that the election of his son would be a mere formality. The presumptive heir was one of the weightiest men in Germany – Augustus III (1696–1763), the elector of Saxony, a fleshy man with no appetite for exercise or politics. In almost no way did he resemble his numerous half-brothers. Instead, he took after his fat and oversexed royal father. (In *A Tale of Agony* Pawel Jasienica called him a mindless mass of blubber and said that 'the roster of kings never saw such a moron.') The only objection was that raised by his nobles and clerics, who considered Augustus a puppet of his Habsburg wife and her father, Charles VI. French propaganda had prepared Polish public opinion to reject the Saxon connection, and now French assistance (i.e. bribes) provided a standard-bearer – their former king, Stanislas Leszczyński. After his defeat in the Great Northern War, when Stanislas had been a Swedish puppet, and his abdication, he had withdrawn to France. Because he had been loyal to French interests, Louis XV's regents gave him a small territory at Zweibrücken on the Rhine, then the unoccupied palace at Chambord; after 1725, when he became the father-in-law of the king, he was given Lorraine. This latter act involved the removal of Leopold Joseph (1679–1729), one of the best Austrian generals and the father-in-law of the presumptive heir to the Habsburg lands, Maria Theresa (1717–80). Louis XV wanted Lorraine in safe hands, even if Stanislas never had any past connection with that territory.

Stanislas's appearance in Poland came as a surprise to everyone – he had travelled there in disguise. Had he been identified en route, he would have been hauled out of his coach and immediately imprisoned. Winning unanimous approval of the nobility and clergy (as was required of any Polish election), he was proclaimed king. Immediately, the Russians, Austrians and Saxons declared the election invalid – the emperor especially could not allow a pro-French ruler in Poland. A Russian army invaded, while the Habsburg armies gathered on the Rhine to meet the expected French invasion. Polish resistance was easily crushed. As Pawel Jasienica remarked, Polish and Lithuanian methods of warfare were terribly outdated, whereas Russia had a modern army and a tsarina willing to do whatever was necessary to get her way.

It was a strange war in many ways. Soldiers, often unpaid and unenthusiastic, deserted in droves; those who remained in arms fought reluctantly. What else could one expect of armies hurriedly raised from the dregs of society? Officers were often coolly professional, risking their lives to inspire whatever loyalty they could from their men, calmly assessing the movement of forces, the cost of battle, the likelihood of defeating the enemy (but never entertaining the idea of destroying him). The theatrical aspects of war were in full bloom – never better on display than in the conduct of a siege, which usually ended with the defenders marching off with weapons and personal effects, to be met in only a few days on another battlefield. Uniforms, ceremonies, banquets and parades disguised the fact that most manoeuvres were more about finding fodder than taking strategic points – horses had to be fed – and since troops were not trusted to return promptly to camp after ravaging the countryside, officers went from village to village with lists of supplies to be provided. Not surprisingly, farmers and townspeople chose to comply – nobody wanted a visit from the cavalry. Diplomacy moved slowly, but missed nothing – no cavalry forager was more exacting than the bureaucrats in the foreign affairs office. The exchange of letters and notes proved that the theatre of war had its counterpart in royal courts.

Although France could not impose its will in Poland, Louis XV's field marshals had considerable success along the Rhine. It took Prince Eugene months to recruit new soldiers, more months to train them, and, in the end, their numbers were insufficient. All he could do was slow the French advance, wearing down both the French army and Fleury's finances. When it came to relieving a great fortress on the Rhine, Eugene concluded that the troops contributed by the German princes were of such inferior quality as to make an attack far too risky. Since Eugene was known for taking risks, this was a strong condemnation indeed. His enemies insinuated that the prince was merely too old for such an important command.

The Habsburg situation was even worse in Italy. Spain and Savoy (Sardinia) entered the war, temporarily occupying Milan; although Austrian armies managed to recover northern Italy, they lost Naples to Charles III (1716–88) of Bourbon, one of the least handsome and worst-dressed members of the Spanish royal house – a family not known for good looks or brains under the best of circumstances. Fortunately, Charles had spent years in Parma, an inheritance from his mother, where he learned the principles of enlightened absolutism – the concept based on the idea that the mass of human beings were stupid and selfish, and, therefore, those who were most intelligent should make all decisions for them. Like modern authoritarians, Charles III had some successes and many failures. Most of all, he learned to dislike war. That was just as well, since he was not very good at it. On the positive side, he encouraged the excavations at Pompeii and Herculaneum, even though they were more large-scale digs for loot than an effort to understand the culture of imperial Rome.

Meanwhile, Anna's favourite general, Münnich, occupied all of Poland except Danzig, where Stanislas took refuge, then began a close siege of that great port city, driving back a French effort to bring in reinforcements by sea. When Danzig fell in 1734, Stanislas was already safely back in France. The tsarina then broke the impasse on the Rhine by sending an army west under Peter Lacy. When Prince Eugene led the combined imperial and Russian armies across the Rhine in the late summer of 1735, Fleury decided to get out of the war before Great Britain and Holland got in. The peace treaty resolved the Lorraine question by giving it to Louis XV and transferring Lorraine's last titular ruler, Francis Stephen (1708–65), to Florence. Since Francis was the husband of Charles VI's daughter, Maria Theresa, this provided an opportunity for them to demonstrate their capacity for government. She did very well, and he was first rate at carrying out her wishes.

Charles VI, whose own finances were now in tatters, was eager to avoid involving his empire in any conflict. Desperately, his ministers instructed the ambassadors to do everything they could to prevent Russia and Turkey from going to war. Because the tsar had come to the emperor's aid in Poland, it would be impossible for Charles VI to stay neutral without ruining imperial credibility. Moreover, the emperor's heir would need the tsar's aid – lacking a male heir, Charles VI had arranged for Maria Theresa to succeed him. Everyone had agreed to this 'Pragmatic Sanction', but everyone knew that it would be worthless unless Maria Theresa could defend her inheritance against those who would lay claims to various parts of it – the history of Poland had demonstrated that promises were worthless. Charles had already assumed that his daughter could never be elected Holy Roman emperor, and he understood how difficult it would be to force through the candidacy of her husband, whose principal ability seemed to be in impregnating her. He needed the Russian alliance.

Neighbouring rulers smiled at their promises to Charles VI, knowing that his death would provide an opportunity to extract territorial concessions – if Charles VI could not defend his lands, what chance would a woman have? Still, the Austrian army was strong, and until Eugene's death in 1736, it had a proven leader.

British Non-Involvement

Robert Walpole (1676–1745) had become prime minister a second time as a result of one of the great scandals of British financial history. By 1720 the government had such an accumulated war debt that the ministers worried about paying the interest. Financiers proposed to take advantage of a clause in the peace treaty, opening the Spanish colonies to British commerce by creating a joint stock company with a trade monopoly. Ignoring the severe limitations in the treaty and the unlikelihood of Spanish co-operation, the financiers agreed to accept government bonds in exchange for stock in this South Seas Company. The public, fearing that their bonds would be worthless anyway, rushed to obtain stock certificates, driving the price so high that more unscrupulous jobbers created new stock companies, promising incredible returns. When it became apparent that nothing stood behind the stocks except hope, the purchasers sought to sell, only to learn that so many early investors had withdrawn their money that the company was essentially bankrupt.

Walpole, a sceptic of the pyramid scheme all along, restored order and confidence in the currency. Henceforth, until 1742, he was the dominant figure in British politics. Refusing to involve Britain in the War of the Polish Succession, he could later boast, 'There are fifty thousand men slain this year in Europe, and not one Englishman.'

Russia and Austria Against Turkey – the Second Overlooked War

In 1736, the Polish war successfully concluded, the tsarina's advisors were ready to take on the sultan. The army – in tip-top condition, well-trained and experienced – was transferred to the east while Anna's ministers looked for an excuse to declare war. The tsarina's advisors found it when the sultan ordered the Tatar khan to take an army across the steppe to Dagestan, then to advance into Persia. Intricate negotiations followed, Biron and Ostermann being desperate to persuade the Austrians that the provocation merited a declaration of war. The outcome was foreordained – as Roider commented, 'Russia had come to collect its debt for the War of the Polish Succession.'

Charles VI understood that he could not renege on the promises he had made to his ally, but his army was exhausted. The toll of two hard years of combat, 1733–5, could not be made good immediately. There were reports of musketeers without food or shelter, and recruitment had failed to bring in anyone except boys too small to carry a musket, ne'er-do-wells and professional deserters. Charles delayed as much as he dared, using as an excuse the need to divide up the conquests along the Black Sea coast. Discussions were still underway in April 1736, when the tsarina declared war.

The Russian offensive, as was usually the case, moved much slower than expected – the vast spaces of the steppe could not be crossed quickly.

Although the siege of Azov was concluded successfully, Münnich's advance into the Crimea was frustrated by the Tatars' scorched-earth tactics. The tsarina had counted on the Persians to tie down significant numbers of Ottoman troops. Nader Shah, however, ignoring his promise to the Christians, had made peace in October 1736. That made it all the more important for Austria to enter the conflict.

In January 1737 Charles VI asked his advisors for their opinion. His army, he was told, though still weak, could handle the decrepit Ottoman forces easily. With Münnich pushing steadily southwards, the sultan would have to concentrate on stopping him. Moreover, once Anna's generals consolidated their conquests in the Caucasus and Crimean regions, Münnich would be able to march west and south into the Balkans where Orthodox peoples waited for their liberation – and the Austrians knew that Serbs and Romanians would rather be ruled by an Orthodox Russian tsarina than by a Catholic German emperor. Therefore, it would be best to occupy the Balkans before the Russians could.

Also, as Roider argues, Fleury, knowing that France could not afford another war, was friendly towards Austria – a welcome change from traditional French policy. However, Fleury was both aged and unwell, and there was no guarantee that his policy would not change as soon as the Austrian army was bogged down in the Balkans. That made it reasonable for Charles VI to make one last try at diplomacy, to ask the sultan to abandon every place of importance without bloodshed. This logical proposition would allow the sultan to concentrate his troops for the defence of Constantinople, and could lead to a quarrel between the tsarina and the emperor that would benefit the Turks, although the Austrian ambassador was afraid even to deliver the letter that contained the proposed treaty – Ottoman hospitality could not be counted on to overlook gross insults.[1]

It did not seem to matter. At least at first. Although the Austrian army had few units up to full strength, that was remedied by cannibalising every fourth battalion. Contributions from crown lands, royal monopolies and borrowing were sufficient to pay for a one-year campaign, and a special 'Turkish tax' brought in more, as did contributions from the pope and the Holy Roman Empire. As commander Charles VI selected Field Marshal Seckendorff, a noted Protestant in a court and army traditionally arch-Catholic.[2] As compensation to his many rivals, the Hofkriegsrat insisted on Seckendorff following their orders from afar, and the emperor made his son-in-law, Francis Stephen, an aide-de-camp to 'assist' him.

Seckendorff left for the front immediately, but found the army in such disarray that it was impossible to move south. Moreover, there were reports that the Danube was so flooded it would be impossible to approach the new Turkish stronghold at Vidin that he had been ordered to capture. As a result, when he finally managed to put the army in motion, he took even the Turks by surprise.

The first weeks of the campaign went well for Seckendorff, his army occupying the strategic town of Niś. From then on, however, everything went wrong. First of all, at Villeneuve's urging, the sultan gave increased authority to Bonneval, whose reorganisation of the artillery had proven effective; more importantly, the war had gone so badly that now the Ottoman commanders were willing to allow the foreigner to be blamed for what appeared to be certain defeat.

After the Ottomans managed to stall the Russian offensive, they poured men and materiel into the Balkans. Seckendorff did not recognise his danger quickly. When he heard of a minor Turkish victory in Bosnia, he divided his forces, dispatching men to suppress that danger: this left his main force too weak to meet an unexpected Turkish advance from Vidin. When he lost Niś, he was recalled. As Catholic fanatics screamed that God could not favour any army led by a heretic, and unfounded accusations of theft and embezzlement piled up, Charles VI put his commander-in-chief under house arrest.

Meanwhile, Cardinal Fleury had decided that France could not allow the Ottoman Empire to be weakened – it was too valuable for tying down Habsburg forces. He proposed an arbitrated end to the war, with France guiding the negotiations. Thus, at the very moment that Austrian and Russian armies were suffering reversals, the leaders of those nations had to fear renewed hostility from the most powerful nation in Europe – France, this time working with Britain, Holland and Sweden. Minor states began to negotiate their loyalty: Prussia, for example, demanding Russian assistance in gaining possession of territories along the Rhine. Fortunately for Charles VI, Fleury did not want the emperor weakened too much – the tsarina, holding Poland in thrall, was now considered a dangerous enemy, too. France's policy, though it did not involve acquiring more territories in Germany or Italy, was, naturally, for the benefit of France.

This was little help for Charles VI, who faced a more fundamental reckoning: the money he had raised for a one-year war was now gone. The conflict had not been concluded, much less concluded victoriously. How could he pay for a longer war?

Worse, the war was sure to become more intense. In December 1737 Yegen Muhammed, who had supervised the successful Bosnian campaign, became grand vizier.[3] He scorned all talk of peace, an attitude that had persuaded the sultan and his courtiers to put him in the place of his pessimistic predecessors. His armies, flush from the recent victories, took the field in 1738 ready to add to their fame.

Charles VI could not even raise an army equal to the previous year's inadequate force; moreover, unable to find a commander-in-chief that all factions would support, he finally named Francis Stephen to that post, while quietly entrusting Count Königsegg with the real responsibilities.[4] Both decisions were mistakes – Francis was too young and inexperienced, and Königsegg had recently made observers doubt his competence. Surprisingly, though, they did well at first, winning a notable combat in Serbia before retreating from a much larger Turkish army. This caution puzzled the emperor, who removed Königsegg, then reinstated him when Francis Stephen fell ill. With an epidemic running through the army, Königsegg wisely avoided any risk.

The Russian army was suffering similar losses among its troops, but the vast reverses of Russian manpower meant that setbacks were only temporary. Training men, of course, was more difficult than raising and equipping them – which was why the tsarina hired so many foreign officers. Still, this took time. As a result, Münnich's inactivity through the summer led many Austrians to believe that there was actually a Russian–Ottoman truce or an understanding that amounted to one. As a last, perhaps forlorn, hope, Charles VI asked the tsarina to send troops to Austria. To his surprise, she agreed.

Roider explains that Anna's advisors – most importantly, Biron – had heard rumours of a French–Swedish–Turkish alliance; the evidence was mostly hearsay, but there was a substantial French subsidy to build up the Swedish army. The hiring of new troops could not be kept secret long. Nor could the new, close relationship of France and Prussia be hidden.

Austria and Russia were not in agreement on many issues, but only three counted – to defeat Turkey, to keep Sweden and France out of the war, and to prevent the king of Prussia from adding to his possessions. Each depended on a speedy victory in the Balkans. That would be difficult once Augustus III announced he could not permit the Russian army to cross through Poland – the danger of an anti-Russian revolt was too great, and the chances were good that the rebels would join with the Swedes and French. Almost immediately, as if to provoke the king, a Russian army crossed a distant corner of the Commonwealth to besiege a Turkish fortress at Khotin.

War with Sweden almost broke out when Russian cavalry intercepted an obscure mercenary officer named Sinclair on the border of Silesia and Saxony. In his possession was a draft treaty of alliance between Sweden and Turkey. The horsemen murdered their captive, then bore his documents to Moscow.

The result was a diplomatic uproar. One just did not go about assassinating diplomats, even ones on a secret mission. Soldiers were expendable, but diplomats were often nobles – and just because this one was an almost anonymous Scot was no reason to violate the principle. It suddenly became very important for the Russians to make peace with Turkey – even if the peace meant returning important conquests.

The pressure on the Austrian court to get out of the war was also intense, but Charles VI was torn between abandoning all the posts on the Danube except Belgrade and praying that the sultan would yield to the war protestors in the Ottoman capital and to pleas from the Tatars to make peace. It seemed that his prayers had been answered when intriguers managed to remove Yegen Muhammed from office, but it was too late. With the arrival of spring both the Austrian and Ottoman armies were already in motion.

The Austrian commander was Oliver Wallis (1676–1752), one of eleven field marshals belonging to this prominent Irish–Austrian family founded in 1622 and ennobled twenty years later; Oliver's father had commanded the Wallis regiment, and he himself had served in the imperial army for forty years. Wallis was not hopeful of success, but he had always found that predictions of disaster warned off criticism of subsequent failures. That was not a good way to build up the troops' morale, but he was more concerned with retaining the emperor's favour. His method of avoiding objections to his plans was to keep them absolutely secret; there was also his ploy of demanding detailed instructions from the Hofkriegsrat, instructions that no intelligent committee would dare make so far from the front.

With reinforcements from various German states and many new recruits, Wallis managed to pull together an army of 45,000 men for the 1739 campaign. The fate of the Balkans was to be decided by one decisive combat – victoriously, the Austrians hoped, and swiftly, before the plague depleted the army's strength.

In July Wallis moved down the Danube from Belgrade, hoping to find the Turkish army on the march. Weather was bad for all concerned, but it hindered the Austrians more – while the Turkish light horse was not bothered by mud, Austrian cavalrymen had to dismount and lead their horses on foot; transport by wagon was slow and arduous. July was always hot in the Balkans, but the heat affected the Germans more than the Turks. When Wallis learned that the Turkish van had taken up a position in a wood near Grocka, he ordered a night march in the hope of taking the grand vizier by surprise. The cavalry went ahead to capture a pass, with the infantry to follow, but it took the wrong road and lost valuable time. The new grand vizier, similarly aware of the strategic value of Grocka, had meanwhile occupied the pass with his entire army.

When the Christian cavalry rode into the trap, the horsemen dismounted to conduct an ill-conceived attack on foot, then tried to retreat. The next unit up, the grenadiers, seeing Ottoman infantry on the surrounding cliffs, had moved onto the heights and exchanged murderous fire, but were unable to drive them away. When the cavalry attempted to ride out of the pass, it ran directly into oncoming Christian infantry, throwing them into disorder. By sundown, after Austrian reinforcements had driven the Ottomans out of the pass, Wallis's subordinates were urging him to follow the victory on the morrow, to destroy the Turkish army before it could rally – that was what Prince Eugene would have done. Wallis, however, having lost between a quarter and half of his entire force, had no stomach for further combat. He gave the order to withdraw to Belgrade. The grand vizier was unable or unwilling to follow the retreat, but it was clear that he had won the war.

Charles VI secured peace in September 1739 by surrendering Belgrade and all the lands south of the Sava River (i.e. all of the Balkans). The next year, when Charles VI died, it was obvious that the imperial army was not ready to fight another war to defend the rights of his twenty-three-year-old daughter, Maria Theresa. Frederick II of Prussia, after complaining about her father's personal insults to his father, proposed a very one-sided land swap and when she refused, he seized that sliver of land between Saxony and Poland known as Silesia. Frederick's legal claims were ludicrous, but this rich, flat plain of the Oder River valley was so valuable that its possession would largely determine which state would dominate the Holy Roman Empire – Austria or Prussia.

Austria's forces were battle-tested, but tired, while Prussia's army was the finest and best-drilled in Europe, and fresh. Maria Theresa had an alliance with the tsarina, but the Russian army was still fighting the Turks; moreover, many Hungarians were eager to be independent again. Prussia had an alliance with Bourbon France, which was tempted now by the prospect of crippling its ancient dynastic foe, the Habsburgs. When French troops supported a Bavarian invasion of Austria and Bohemia, Maria Theresa seemed doomed.

Russia Makes Peace, Too

As the Austrians had expected, Marshal Münnich had pushed into Moldavia, the first step towards Constantinople. Now, however, he faced a Turkish army that had been reinforced by troops from the Austrian front. He murmured that the Turks had been saved by Mohammed, the French and the Austrians. Negotiations at Belgrade, once more mediated by Villeneuve, who had remained in Turkey as an ambassador, resulted in a peace treaty by which all recent Russian conquests were returned to the sultan and the Tatar khan. Villeneuve returned home two years later and was rewarded handsomely for his services.

The sultan rewarded Louis XV with more favourable rights and privileges in the Ottoman realm than any Christian monarch had ever enjoyed before. The Ottomans remained at peace through the next two great wars that divided Christendom. Lord Kinross remarked in *The Ottoman Centuries* that this time should have been used to carry out essential reforms throughout society and especially in the military, but not even the energetic and far-seeing grand vizier, Raghib Pasha (1700–83) and the vocally warlike Mustafa III (1717–73) were able to achieve all that was necessary. Rhoads Murphey, in *Ottoman Warfare, 1500–1700*, agrees that this was the moment when Turkish self-isolation became self-immolation. Pragmatic and realistic assessments of proposed policies, especially of military preparedness, devolved into political wrangling. This was largely concealed from domestic observers and foreign commentators – Voltaire was still greatly impressed by the sultan's empire when he wrote *Candide* in 1751 – but when war came with Russia again in 1769, the Ottoman army was unready to take on the forces of Catherine the Great (1729–96). It was certainly not ready for the length of the conflict that followed. Murphey notes that even the legendary Turkish discipline and care for logistics were unable to compete successfully with the superior resources of the Russian state, not when mobilised by a single-minded autocrat who was willing to spend lives and treasure recklessly.

Austria was not such a state, either; nor were Maria Theresa and her sons willing to be so ruthless. Had it been up to the Habsburgs of the Enlightenment era and the sultans of the post-Tulip Age, there would have been no wars in the Balkans. Of course, there were always the Christian peoples of the region, who were ever less willing to tolerate the status quo; they heard the call of Orthodox propagandists and the seduction of proposed help by fellow Slavs. Modern ideas – especially Rousseau's exciting doctrine that people should be organised into states where everyone shared the same language, religion and national feelings – were undermining the eighteenth-century world of toleration based on mutual weakness.

Anna and Biron's reforms did not long outlast her death in 1740. The secret police might have continued to suppress nationalist resentment if Anna's health had been good, but when she realised that she was dying, she named an infant great-nephew as her successor, with Biron as regent. When Peter's daughter Elizabeth (1709–62) seized power in late 1741, she arrested Biron and banished him to Siberia, where he remained until his extreme old age, when he was made duke of Courland, a tiny land his dynasty ruled until 1795.

Münnich's reforms were abandoned, too. The new tsarina not only hated everything German, but she admired her father so greatly that she ordered a return to traditional forms. However, Peter the Great's common-sense instructions were transformed into a system of bewildering and complex regulations. Ostermann's policies were abandoned, too, after he was first sentenced to death, then banished to Siberia.

With the future of mercenaries in Russia turning unpromising, two of that empire's most successful young officers changed employers – word had gone out that the Austrian ruler was not happy with her commanders of the past war, and that she was eager to employ competent generals.[5]

Why were these the overlooked wars? First, because Great Britain was hardly involved, and Britons wrote the histories in the English-speaking world. Second, because there were no great victories for the great powers of the West. Only the Ottoman Turks and the Russians came away with triumphs – and almost nobody wished them well. Ethnocentrism? Yes, of course. But nobody ever said that history was impartial.

CHAPTER SIX

Great and Small Conflicts at Mid-Century

Reluctance to Make War

By 1740 many educated men and women in the West believed that warfare was an outdated byproduct of religious bigotry and dynastic ambition; they themselves would surely not be influenced by such base motives, and the universal interest in furthering commerce and culture would do the rest. Universal peace was at hand. Yes, there had been recent wars with the Turks, but they were only talking about peace between civilised nations, not with people who could not read Latin. Though this generation might have had less interest in advancing the cause of Christianity than their grandparents, they were equally sure that Christian civilisation – or the veneer that shone so brightly on its surface – was superior to that of lesser peoples. Anyway, only the Russians were interested in fighting the Turks again, and they were not quite Europeans. The occasional regional war could be dismissed as a disagreement over minor issues; even the Polish question had been resolved relatively quickly. The memory of past conflicts might not prevent war, but they would surely slow any decision to start one or join into it.

This pious belief was shaken in 1740 when Frederick II of Prussia seized Silesia. Christopher Clark says in *Iron Kingdom* that Frederick's behaviour at this time was spontaneous and reckless, while Dennis Showalter, in *The Wars of Frederick the Great*, points to evidence that he had made plans months ahead, apparently reasoning that Charles VI's daughter would inevitably be attacked from all sides. Showalter argues that unless Frederick used his main advantage – an army ready to fight immediately – he would miss his best chance. Should he fail to make Prussia stronger now, his kingdom would eventually suffer the fate of Brandenburg in the Thirty Years War – ravaged by all, respected by none. Silesia was a rich and populous region ruled by a distant woman who faced both internal and external enemies. Once Frederick acquired Silesia's men and crops, he could make good his claims to yet more territories; should he fail, his scattered western lands would remain vulnerable. A personal quirk might also have been important – Frederick despised women, and it appeared that Maria Theresa had no gifts beyond being a wife and mother.

Certainly, the Prussian king had neither historical claims on Silesia nor much of a common border, and nor was Habsburg possession of the province a danger. Silesia lay in the Oder River valley, extending from the Carpathian Mountains to Brandenburg, and had been part of the historic kingdom of Poland. Silesia separated the lands of Augustus III, elector of Saxony and king of Poland. Logically, if the distracted government of Russia had permitted – Anna had died in October and Elizabeth did not take power until December – he could have moved to annex Silesia first, but neither ancient rights nor modern motives were in play here. Augustus III could barely lift himself from his powerless throne; he might have united his two states, but he had no desire to replicate either his father's triumphs or his disasters.

Prussia was joined in this unjust war by France, Bavaria and Saxony (though not the elector's kingdom of Poland) and he was supported by Sweden, Spain and Naples. Austria survived largely through the personal qualities of Maria Theresa, who managed to rally public support – even that of the Hungarian nobility – but her natural ally, Russia, was unable to help because Anna Ivanova's death had been followed by a succession crisis. Only giving Frederick Silesia reduced her enemies to a manageable number.

Although Maria Theresa was Britain's most important ally on the continent, George II (1683–1760) remained neutral as late as 1742. Thomas Carlyle, whose books are as enthusiastic as they are occasionally unreadable, had this to say in his *History of Friedrich the Second Called Frederick the Great* about King George II's efforts to get his mercenary armies into the fray – by attacking France, he could make it difficult for Louis XV to support the Bavarian offensive:

Those laggard Dutch, dead to the Cause of Liberty, it is they again. Just as the hour was striking, they . . . plump down . . . into their mud again; cannot be hoisted by engineering . . . Tongue cannot tell what his poor little Majesty has suffered from those Dutch – checking one's noble rage, into mere zero, always; making of one's own glorious army a mere expensive Phantasm! Hannoverian, Hessian, British: 40,000 fighters standing in harness, year after year, at such cost; and not the killing of a French turkey to be had of them in return.

The next year Britain was not only in the war, but George II commanded the coalition army that invaded Bavaria and successfully fought the battle of Dettingen. Carlyle praises the king for 'not being easily put into flurry, into fear'. Instead, the king's troops 'tramp on, paying a minimum of attention to the cannon, ignorant of what is ahead, hoping only it may be breakfast, in some form, before the day quite terminate'. In the end, the king even spoke to his soldiers in English, 'Steady, my boys; fire, my brave boys, give them fire; they will soon run.' It might be wondered who could hear him at that moment. Carlyle's judgement was that the British–Austrian victory delayed the end of the war by two years, thereby dooming many men and much treasure to destruction.

The defeat of Austria raised doubts in British circles about how much assistance the Habsburgs could be in future wars with France. Most importantly, the question was now framed as 'How could Austria help defend Hanover, if its principal enemy was no longer France, but Prussia?' The 'Diplomatic Revolution' of 1756, when France, Austria and Russia agreed to crush Prussia and divide up Frederick's peripheral lands among themselves was a preview of the fate of Poland and a reminder of what Maria Theresa had narrowly avoided. Britons who worried about the growth of French power saw Frederick the Great as the only ruler on the continent who could help them significantly. Quite logically, their subsidies henceforth flowed into the Prussian treasury, while debts piled up in Britain.

As Austrian power declined, French influence grew. This revival of French greatness was associated with one field marshal we have already met, an illegitimate son of Augustus the Strong, born in 1696, who was, in the words of military historian Liddell Hart, 'a man built on a large scale – in his physique, in his intellect, in his outlook, and in his excesses'. He had nevertheless failed to make a career in Austria, Russia, Poland, Courland or Saxony. Only in France was he not perceived as a danger to the king, nobility and clergy.

Marshal de Saxe: Background and Upbringing

Everything about Maurice de Saxe was extraordinary, including his parentage. His father was Augustus, the 'Saxon Hercules', famous for feats of strength and his patronage of Dresden china. His mother, Aurora von Königsmarck, was the most notable woman of her era; or so said Voltaire, who knew her well. She was also one of the best educated. Swedish by birth, she also spoke German, French and Italian, and knew some Latin. She was good at poetry, music, knew her history and literature, and was completely at home in the most sumptuous courts of the north. She had to be. Orphaned young, she made her living by entertaining royalty and seducing nobility. When she and her almost equally talented sister appeared at the Saxon court with a letter from his relatives, the king and queen of Denmark, entreating Augustus to assist them in securing the inheritance of their late brother, Augustus was enchanted. Nay, he was captivated.

It was not as though Augustus had never seen a pretty woman before. According to Karl Ludwig, Freiherr von Pöllinitz, who wrote a tell-all book in 1732 (*La Saxe Galante or, the Amorous Adventures and Intrigues of Frederick–Augustus II*), on one of his educational travels he had been besieged by beautiful women all across Spain and Italy, and those who did not approach him rarely rejected his approaches. One conquest of a beautiful but reluctant countess had ended with his being assaulted by four assassins sent by the husband, who at the moment of the ambush stabbed his wife's mother, then forced his wife to drink poison. Augustus, with only a little help from an unimposing servant, killed three of his assailants and chased away the fourth. Remorse, if he had any, was but fleeting.

Soon afterwards Augustus returned to Saxony. His elder brother, who lacked the personality to govern an important minor state, had made an unsuitable choice as mistress and was unwilling to be parted from her long enough to honour the minimum obligations of an arranged marriage – Tony Sharp called her a 'teenaged nymphomaniac', while the young man was afflicted with the 'hereditary vice' of the Wettin dynasty, to wit: sex. In 1694, when the mistress died of smallpox, the deranged elector threw himself upon her body and refused to be dragged away; not surprisingly, he came down with the disease himself and perished. It was thus that Augustus became elector of Saxony.

Aurora came from a family of adventurers. Her grandfather had left Brandenburg to enter Swedish service in the Thirty Years War, and was in command of the Protestant troops burning the suburbs of Prague when the announcement of the peace treaty arrived. In the Polish wars he rose to become a Swedish field marshal, sufficiently high rank to marry his children into all the prominent military families of Livonia. Her father was a distinguished soldier who encountered a cannon ball prematurely, leaving four children to be reared by his brother, Otto Wilhelm von Königsmarck. This uncle was rarely at home, however – he had begun his military career in France, learning the arts of war from Turenne and rising to command of the Royal-Étranger regiment. He then entered Venetian service, commanding soldiers at the siege of Athens, during which the Parthenon was largely destroyed. His example was followed by Aurora's eldest brother, Karl Johann, who joined the Knights of Malta. In 1681 Karl took his younger brother, Philipp, to London. There he became a favourite of Charles II and lover of Lady Elizabeth Percy, a beautiful and rich widow of fifteen who was married to a womanising gambler of considerable wealth and influence, Thomas Thynne. (We might also hope that he was 'chynless', but the most we know is that he seldom, if ever, slept with his wife. Tom was not satisfied with his own annual income of 10,000 pounds, but began spending his wife's as well.) Karl twice challenged him to a duel, but after being set upon by six assassins, decided on more direct action. Three of his friends murdered Thynne in his carriage on Pall Mall. It did not take long to identify the drunken horsemen, all of whom were Swedes, and to hang them. Their fate was sealed because the victim was a close gambling and whoring friend of the duke of Monmouth (Charles's popular illegitimate son). Karl was charged with having been part of the plot, but was set free by the king on condition that he leave the country. He died shortly afterwards in Greece, fighting alongside his uncle. Philipp went to Hanover, where he seduced the wife of the future king of England, George I, then vanished in 1694 during an attempt to help her elope – it appears that he was lured to his lover's apartment and murdered, taking down perhaps four of his assailants before falling, but the truth may never be known. George I never forgave his wife, but kept her in what amounted to a prison without bars.

In 1695 the search for Philipp's body led Aurora to Augustus, who knew him from service in Flanders. Jon White reports in *Marshal of France* that

Augustus had earlier owed Philipp a huge gambling debt, but had been unable to pay him; instead, he had given him an honorary command in the Saxon army. Now that Augustus was elector and hoping to become king of Poland–Lithuania, he was rich; this seemed like the right moment to ask for her brother's money.

Aurora was reluctant to become Augustus's mistress. Although she was thirty-two and far from a virgin, she understood that her young admirer – handsome, immensely strong and recently married – was unable to concentrate on any one woman at a time. Giving in would have been, in the hunter's vocabulary, 'a one-night stand' – not the permanent arrangement she desired. Nevertheless, Augustus's discreetly delivered love letters and her sister's pleading wore her down to the extent of agreeing to attend a ball at the forest palace of Mauritzburg. She even agreed to wear the jewel-encrusted dress the elector sent to her.

Aurora was greeted by the ladies of the court (the most beautiful in all Europe, according to Pöllinitz), who were all dressed as Amazons. The hall was decorated with large paintings of myths surrounding Diana, and the ball-room floor opened up to allow a banquet to rise, while a Pan and other gods appeared to entertain the guests. A stag chased by huntsmen ran through the hall – perhaps a story known to every student of mythology, of how the virgin goddess Diana punished Actaeon for some unnamed transgression, perhaps seeing her nude while bathing, by turning him into a stag that was then hunted and killed by his own hounds. (How this related to Augustus is not clear, but such entertainments were common in high society, as was fox-tossing, a blood sport similar to bull-baiting and cock-fighting in which Augustus excelled.) Everyone who could mount a horse followed the hounds. At the pond they witnessed the death of the stag, then boarded boats to an island where a large Turkish tent (certainly recently captured by Saxon troops) was erected; they were then served refreshments by Turkish slaves. Returning to Mauritzburg, they changed their clothes for the theatre, then the dance (Aurora was the queen of the ball) until the two principals suddenly disappeared, retiring to her sumptuous bedroom where she 'gave him the most effectual Tokens of her Tendernefs'. Nine months later, Augustus named their son Maurice in honour of his conquest in the Mauritzburg.

When Augustus took his magnificent army into the Balkans to fight the Turks, he was more successful in overcoming the resistance of attractive women than that of ferocious Turks, but he had a new ambition – to become King Augustus II of Poland–Lithuania. Not only would that kingdom provide him the troops needed to be successful in the Balkans, should he be offered another command there, but he would acquire the people and resources to make himself into a great ruler. Any glance into a mirror, to admire his magnificent clothing and unsurpassed physique, was sufficient to make him believe he was irresistible. He left Aurora, moving on to younger and sometimes less-talented women (one of whom knew nothing beyond how to say 'yes' and 'no'; apparently, she did not say 'no' very often). According to Pöllinitz, all these characteristics passed down to his son.

Were the stories of Augustus II true? Yes, if you believe the sister of Frederick the Great of Prussia, Wilhelmine, duchess of Brandenburg-Bayreuth; in her *Memoires de ma vie* in 1748, she credited Augustus with not eight illegitimate children, but 355 – the number based on a list made by a Saxon finance minister late in the elector's life.

Marshal de Saxe: The Ultimate Mercenary

Maurice de Saxe began his military career as an aide to Eugene of Savoy at age twelve, then as an officer of Peter the Great and his own father in the campaign that drove Stanislas Leszczyński and the prince of Conti (François Louis de Bourbon, 1664–1709) out of Poland. He joined Prince Eugene again in 1717 at the siege of Belgrade, one of that commander's greatest triumphs, but returned home fazed neither by the epidemic diseases that struck down half the army nor the Turkish bullets that slew so many soldiers in the climactic battle. He went to France, rising quickly in the esteem of army commanders, but never fully mastering French. One would have thought that having the most brilliant actresses as his mistresses would have cured the latter problem.

Jon White recounts one scandal regarding Maurice and the cuckolded prince of Conti, who burst into his wife's bedroom, apparently moments after Maurice had hurriedly departed. His wife, a descendant of the Great Condé, shouted at her husband that if he thought she had a man in her room, he should have taken care to keep out! She left him the next day, while Maurice was seen to have a bad limp.[1] It was a *Marriage of Figaro* scene, except that Maurice was too old to have been Cherubino.

Maurice's career was not helped by Louis XV marrying the daughter of Stanislas Leszczyński, another failed candidate for the Polish crown. This would affect his efforts in 1725 to win for himself the duchy of Courland, an ambition encouraged by his father, who had once so coveted the land as to start the Great Northern War over it a quarter century earlier. Had Maurice been willing to marry Anna Ivanovna, the short, chubby sex-mad duchess who loved to ride wildly through her game-filled forests, he would have ended up in Russia as the tsarina's husband; but he held out for her younger and prettier cousin, Elizabeth, the daughter of Peter the Great and later tsarina too. He eventually won neither one, and his hurriedly assembled mercenary army was so inferior to the Russian forces sent by Peter's widow, Catherine I (1684–1727), that he advised his troops to surrender, then fled back to France. He came away bankrupt (with his lady friends and mother losing all their money, too), but he retained the document naming him 'duke-elect of Courland'. He had come close to achieving what every mercenary dreamed of – an independent state of his own – and he rarely failed to include that title alongside the 'comte de Saxe' that his father awarded him.

When the War of the Polish Succession began in 1733, Louis XV proposed that his father-in-law become king again; Stanislas was not enthusiastic, but he could not resist the king's entreaties. Geography was against them, however, since Austria and Russia were right on the spot to give the 'elective' crown to Maurice's half-brother, Augustus III. Stanislas managed to get to Poland, but when Russian armies overran the Commonwealth, he was on the run. The only significant fighting was on the Rhine, where Maurice was given a command (perhaps in order to keep him from joining the Saxon army).

Maurice found himself fighting his former mentor, Prince Eugene, but his commanders were too cautious to allow him to take advantage of his superior numbers. Louis XV, who had become king at the age of five, was too accustomed to giving in to his advisors; consequently, he left aged men in office far too long – men who did not trust upstarts like Maurice de Saxe. For Louis, life was good as long as women were willing, and so for him life was good. Warfare was boring.

Still, if it pleased Louis's generals and his wife, there must be war, no matter that Poland was already lost. When peace was finally made, his Habsburg rival had lost Naples and his father-in-law obtained Lorraine; therefore, it must have been a good war. Maurice, for his part, was ready for another.

In the second year of the War of the Austrian Succession, the example of Frederick the Great seizing Silesia proved contagious. Charles Albert of Bavaria invaded Austria with the assistance of a French army; this was to prepare the way for dismantling the Habsburg Empire, a task that would be easily done, everyone expected, once Charles was elected Holy Roman emperor (as happened the next year) – Maria Theresa was disqualified by her sex, her husband by his reputation as a good-natured lightweight. Minor players in this act of international robbery included Spain and Sweden, but not Russia, which was in disarray from its own succession crisis. Poland–Lithuania was no longer a player on the international scene, and the Turkish sultan chose to watch and wait – hence Maria Theresa was not hopelessly outnumbered. Still, although the way to Vienna was wide open to the French–Bavarian army, Charles Albert began to worry that the Saxon army would seize Bohemia before he could take it himself; therefore, he changed the direction of advance away from Vienna and towards Prague. Thus Maurice de Saxe was able to reach Prague at the same time as his three half-brothers (all by different mothers, but good soldiers) in the Saxon army. Together they hatched up a daring plan to take the strongly defended city, a plan that caught the Austrian governor, Karl Hermann Ogilvie, completely by surprise.

The feat was applauded by everyone, but the French garrison was soon besieged by a revived Austrian army. In late 1742 the garrison broke out of the city and fought its way home, losing most of the men and equipment; Bavaria fell the following spring after an overly confident French army lost the battle of Dettingen to a smaller British–Hanoverian force. Suddenly, France itself was under siege. Frederick the Great and Augustus III made peace, freeing the allied Habsburg and British armies to fall on the real enemy – a France that threatened to dominate everyone.

It was at this critical moment that Louis XV gave Maurice – a German and a Lutheran – command of the French army in the west. Maurice was immediately, if quietly, successful in preventing the Austrians from crossing the Rhine. It was more than anyone had expected.

Maurice augmented his forces with a private cavalry formation of Polish uhlans, raised with the permission of Augustus III. He saw that it had the

fanciest of uniforms, the finest of horses and the best of pay.[2] He had come
to appreciate the value of light cavalry, especially those drawn from the
frontiers of Europe – serving for pay, eager for booty and almost immune
to thoughts of discipline; these were dressed in spectacular costumes that
were more exotic than splendid.

The French army of this day contained more Frenchmen than foreigners
– an exception to the general practice. Villages conducted lotteries to see
who would serve in the militia, which was used to replace loses in the regular
army. The service was only six or seven years, less than the lifetime common
for other armies (however long a 'lifetime' might be), but unlucky men often
hired substitutes. Regulars were recruited, mostly through a combination
of alcohol, false friendship offered by a recruiter, and a sizeable enlistment
bonus. Swiss units were recruited from their native Catholic cantons, while
the German and Irish foreign regiments took pretty much anyone who was
willing to sign on. Though the soldiers were more suited for military duties
than ever, they were not well led. Officers were often poorly prepared for
their duties – their principal asset being a willingness to die, their weakness
being not knowing when to do so. The defeats in the early years of the
war – completely unexpected by the court and most officers – meant that
Maurice had a serious morale problem to correct.

One idea floated in 1744 was for Maurice to invade the Austrian
Netherlands, to tie down troops which would otherwise be available to
suppress an anticipated uprising in Scotland designed to put the ageing
Stuart claimant, the 'Old Pretender', on the throne. The uprising promised
to change everything – without British money, the anti-French alliance
would collapse. However, neither Louis XV's advisors nor Maurice were
under any illusions about the chances for success – James Stuart had
failed to inspire Scots earlier and now was more inclined to religious
devotions than to action; he was not as extreme a Catholic as his wife,
or his younger son, Henry, but even so Episcopalians and Presbyterians
were unlikely to welcome him. At best, the uprising would draw away a
few troops. While that might even the odds in the Netherlands, giving
Maurice a slightly better chance to occupy the region, for the Scots to
succeed, they would need substantial French support. The plan was
modified, allowing rumours of an uprising to distract George II, but
not permitting the Stuart prince to sail – that would have committed

Louis XV to provide an army, and no one imagined the Old Pretender to be a capable or charismatic leader. Instead, the king promoted Maurice to marshal and came in person, with a large retinue of courtiers and mistresses, to witness the anticipated victories in Flanders.

As expected, Maurice drew around him the British–Dutch–Hanoverian forces known as the Pragmatic army (from the Pragmatic Sanction that guaranteed Maria Theresa a trouble-free inheritance of her father's lands and titles). If Maurice's lieutenant had followed instructions to tie down the Austrian army, French victory would have been assured; as it was, the Austrians arrived, forcing Maurice onto the defensive. He was a daring commander, but he understood that the numbers were 2-to-1 against him.

It was at that moment that Frederick the Great rescued his French ally by invading Austria and Saxony, drawing the Habsburg army back into Bohemia and providing Maurice an opportunity to deal with his remaining foes. His most dangerous opponent was Jean-Louis Ligonier (1680–1770), a Huguenot who had fought under William III and Marlborough. In spite of his age, Ligonier was extraordinarily active, always leading troops personally and, surprisingly, never wounded. Right to the end of his long life he was a force in British military and social affairs. However, command was given to the twenty-four-year-old second son of George II, William (1721–65), the porcine duke of Cumberland. The boy-genius of the dynasty, William had fought well under his father's eye at Dettingen and only he had that aura of royal authority that would make a coalition army's commanders obey orders; better yet would have been the prince of Wales, but he was not allowed to endanger his life.

Winter followed, and in this quiet period Maurice, like much of his army, fell ill. His particular malady was dropsy, a kidney disease that produced terribly swollen legs; the only cure, and that only temporary, was to puncture the abdomen to drain off the excess liquid. Meanwhile, Charlie Edward Stuart (1720–88), the Old Pretender's handsome elder son, proposed raising a Jacobite revolt that could drive the Hanoverian dynasty from England and Scotland. 'Bonnie Prince Charlie' had the personality that his father lacked. Scottish exiles were instantly charmed. In their imagination, Scotland might yet be free.

Louis XV authorised the collection of a fleet to take de Saxe's army across the Channel once the British army went north to fight the Stuart prince,

but when the ships and barges were destroyed in a storm, that should have
been the end of the enterprise. There was more romance and myth to the
venture than Louis XV could easily appreciate; he could barely follow de
Saxe's reluctance to shed his troops' blood.

Maurice's ability to conduct a complicated campaign in the Netherlands
was facilitated by his attracting to his side Waldemar von Löwendahl
(1700–55), a Danish-born, Saxon-raised soldier-of-fortune. Löwendahl's
father had been a minister in Augustus II's Polish and Saxon cabinets, and
thus Maurice probably knew the family from those days. Löwendahl first
served in the Danish navy in 1715 against the Swedes, then with the imperial
army during the siege of Belgrade in 1717 (where he probably met Maurice
again); in 1719 he was with Austrian troops in Sicily, returning to Saxony in
1721. In 1724 he went to Italy, then served under the Prince of Württemberg
in suppressing a rebellion on Corsica. In the War of the Polish Succession
he fought in Poland, and subsequently on the Rhine (opposing Maurice);
the next year he was in Poland, then back to the Rhine again. When the
Russian war with Turkey broke out, he hurried to work for Anna Ivanova
as a lieutenant general, performing so well that when the war ended in 1740,
he was named governor of Estonia. That, however, became boring. With
Saxon approval he entered French service in 1744, his engineering skills as
much appreciated as his ability to lead troops.

Löwendahl was trusted with the second corps of the French army,
manoeuvring skilfully against the Pragmatic army with minimum direction
from Marshal de Saxe. He could be counted on to obey orders and to see
that whatever was necessary was done. This was not the case with the royal
bastards who were titular commanders of important units – and who
envied and hated Maurice de Saxe.

War in the Netherlands

In the spring of 1745 Maurice invaded the Austrian Netherlands, striking
before Austrian reinforcements could reach the scene of combat. He was
again opposed by Cumberland, whose imagination was as limited as his
concept of warfare was outdated. Maurice deceived his enemy until he could
pounce suddenly on Tournai, surrounding its Dutch garrison. Knowing that

Cumberland would have to come to the rescue, he set a trap at Fontenoy, a position much like that of Malplaquet, only more sophisticated. Maurice had spent years meditating on Villar's mistakes, writing out his conclusions in *Memoirs on the Art of War*. He put these into practice now – instead of digging trenches that became deathtraps if the attackers swarmed over them, thrusting their bayonets down, he constructed log barriers; he also built five redoubts that could fire into the flanks and rear of advancing troops; and he had much larger cavalry forces available. Alas, he also had the king and his girlfriends, and numerous civilian military 'experts' to deal with. On the other hand, Louis XV ordered his royal relatives not to give any orders themselves, but to obey those of Marshal de Saxe.[3]

British courage almost overcame every obstacle Maurice had devised. When Cumberland's attacks on the flanks failed, instead of bringing up his artillery, he sent his British troops at the French centre. The crossfire was terrible and the cannon fire worse, but redcoats kept coming on. They were funnelled by the terrain into an ever more narrow killing ground, but once they reached the blue-coated French Guard and the red-coated Swiss, they blew their enemies' front ranks apart and sent the rear ranks into wild flight. Only desperate counterattacks by the Irish 'Wild Geese', the Swiss Guard and the Household Cavalry saved the day.

Louis XV was appalled at the bloodshed, but Maurice, despite the terrible pain from his disease, simply told his majesty that this was what war was really like. Seven thousand or more Frenchmen had fallen, and more than ten thousand in the allied army. That made it, as far as Louis XV could see, a splendid victory; it had its frightening moments, but it provided anecdotes to enliven many a future conversation. Maurice went on to capture Tournai, then Ghent, and in the course of the summer, several more fortresses in the Austrian Netherlands. It helped that Cumberland was called home with the cream of his army to deal with the Jacobite rising in Scotland – the campaign that culminated in the battle at Culloden.

The allies in the Netherlands – Britain and Holland, now reinforced by the Austrians – decided that a new commander was needed. This was the unlucky Charles of Lorraine, Maria Theresa's brother-in-law twice over, whose fate was usually to lose against Frederick II of Prussia. Charles did much better through the summer of 1746, but that was partly because Maurice was handicapped by intrigues at court, disobedience by his officers

and his own poor health. In October the awkward position of the allies –
its extended lines and its difficulties in getting supplies past the strongholds
now in French hands – caused Charles to retreat. At once Maurice
pounced, moving on Liège, forcing the allies to come to its defence. In the
ensuing battle, named for the nearby village of Rocoux, he took advantage
of the almost total demoralisation of the Dutch who were nearest the
city on the left flank. He outnumbered the allies 120,000 to 80,000, but
more importantly, he was in place before the fighting started, whereas the
allies had no time to prepare a defensive position – indeed, the Dutch and
British were in an awkward half-circle that could be attacked from three
sides, while the Austrians were off at an angle to the right. The French were
rested, the allies exhausted. Maurice struck at the Dutch junction with the
British forces, while his cavalry sought to come in on their left. Since Liège
had surrendered before the fighting started, the Dutch were outflanked
and knew it; still, they fought well and managed to make a more orderly
retreat than anyone expected. As usual now, Ligonier formed his men into a
square and prevented the French from obtaining a complete victory. On the
right Charles stood on the defensive, failing to aid the British and Dutch –
though it is unclear exactly what he could have done to help them. Maurice
subsequently occupied most of the Austrian Netherlands.

Louis XV made de Saxe marshal-general, an honour so great that
in the memory of most men only Turenne had enjoyed it; appropriately
the king enjoined his new commander-in-chief to emulate Turenne in all
other respects – meaning to become a Roman Catholic and to die in battle.
Maurice promised only the latter. The king nevertheless made him formally
a Frenchman, an honour usually sufficient to inspire any foreigner to
great deeds. For those who held Maurice's ancestry and birth against him,
Maurice's revenge was to assist his Saxon niece to marry the dauphin. His
defence against accusations that he had allowed the British to escape the
battlefield intact – a treasonous action expected of a mercenary to keep the
war going so as to retain employment – was to advance so far into Holland
as to threaten that nation's existence.

Cumberland sought to drive the French back in 1747, but was tricked into
fighting in an awkward position at Laufeldt, near Maastricht. War, however,
makes up its own rules and is always ready with surprises. When Maurice
sent his incomparable troops forward against the British and Hessian part

of the line, they discovered that British troops had fortified themselves in small villages. Unable to halt long enough to clean out those improvised redoubts, his forces were shot to pieces. Maurice, with the king literally at his elbow, was reluctant to call the attack off – he understood that the king had been told repeatedly of his reluctance to destroy the enemy. The next units sent in were similarly massacred.

Such was the weight of the French infantry, however, that they eventually reached the opposing lines and drove the Hessians into flight, capturing their duke, Frederick II (1720–85), who is best remembered for renting his army to the British for service in America. Exultant, Maurice ordered the cavalry into the gap.

Cumberland, meanwhile, dithered. Ligonier, seeing the seriousness of the situation, charged forward, hitting the French horsemen in their flank and routing them. As he rounded up his men for a second charge, Cumberland sent word to halt. It took valuable minutes for Ligonier to persuade his superior that the day would become a disaster if the French were not halted. In that time the French cavalry had regrouped. Ligonier's second charge halted the French pursuit of the infantry, but, in what contemporaries considered the greatest cavalry battle of the era, his forces were defeated and he was captured – to be greeted graciously by Louis XV and invited to dinner.

As at Rocoux, at Laufeldt the Austrians refused to abandon their defensive works to come to the aid of the British and Dutch even when they saw the French forces massing against them. This would be remembered later, when the Diplomatic Revolution brought France, Austria and Russia into an alliance against Frederick II of Prussia. There was little nostalgia in Britain for the old ties to Austria.

If Rocoux was technically a French victory, it was an expensive one – 14,000 casualties against 2,000 British, 2,500 Hanoverian and 1,500 Hessians. Still, it enabled Marshal de Saxe to move into Holland and force his opponents to sue for peace. His capture of Maastricht in 1748 made little sense, the announcement of peace arriving just as he was commencing the final assault; Cumberland, seeing that de Saxe would not call off the attack and knowing that Maastricht would be returned to Holland, agreed to surrender the place rather than have more troops slaughtered. (This time 'Butcher Cumberland' did not live up to the nickname that was stuck on him after Culloden.) The

Peace of Aix-la-Chapelle (1748) returned most conquests to their original possessors (*status quo ante bellum*), causing many to wonder what the war had been all about. Silesia? That was left to Frederick II, but only temporarily if Maria Theresa of Austria had anything to say about it.

Maurice de Saxe died in 1750, still relatively young, but worn-out. What survived was a generation of officers trained in his offensive-minded style of warfare. Maurice de Saxe did not strike without a plan or careful preparation, but he was not a man to sit behind fortifications and wait for his enemy to act.[4]

Mes Rêveries

Maurice de Saxe had begun *Memoirs on the Art of War* in 1728 to record some of his thoughts about military tactics and human nature. Contemporaries found them provocative, and modern readers still find them interesting.

He wrote that soldiers should wear brass identifications on their shoulders, and like Indians have a tattoo on their right hand to discourage desertion. Non-commissioned officers should be recruited from veterans. Armour is good, he wrote, short hair is desirable, and discipline essential. Cavalrymen should be five foot six inches in height and slim; the horses large and fit – care being taken not to indulge them, as that makes them fat; constant exposure to combat makes the horses less liable to shy from noise and confusion.

He disliked volley fire, since to aim men have to stop moving forwards, and trying to fire while storming a breastwork was hardly better, because hurried men tended to fire without aiming, often discharging their weapons into the air. In such cases, the bayonet is the preferred weapon. Of course, when some obstacle prevents troops from closing with an enemy, it is necessary to shoot them down at a distance – meaning the other side of a hedge, ditch or stream. Units should not form a continuous line, but have gaps for the skirmishers to fall back through and for light artillery to be employed at close range. He did not like fortresses, but he appreciated the value of redoubts in breaking up an enemy attack. His training troops to march in step worked so well that everyone copied him: ranks were tightened up, drums determined the tempo and men who might have other thoughts on their minds could concentrate on remaining in step.

A commander should give few orders, but see that they are followed exactly. The punishments for stealing were too heavy – why condemn a hungry man to death for doing what is natural? Instead, as an example to others, thieves should be kept in chains and fed only bread and water until the eve of combat. He disliked the French gauntlet – running between lines of fellow soldiers, beaten by each, then being stripped of his clothes and turned out of the camp – this deprived the army of a man and the man of his last dignity.

Maurice employed the first truly effective general staff, distaining what he called the 'alphabet of the troops', the distractions of routine administration that kept commanders from more important tasks, especially from seeing the wider implications of strategy. He argued, in vain, for conscription and for opening the high ranks to men of talent.

A man must be born to war, he said, since war is like other 'sciences' such as painting and music, in which many can rise by training to the level of mediocrity, but few can master. Too many officers concerned themselves only with the mechanics of their business, which results in good colonels becoming bad generals. The required genius of the latter can be destroyed by the training imposed on the former.

Like any good Enlightenment thinker, he had ideas about ways to improve society. Noting that most women wasted their best child-bearing years waiting for a husband and that most marriages were unhappy, he proposed discouraging chastity, and argued that no marriage should last longer than five years, except perhaps for couples past the age of child bearing. Freeing women to choose their partners freely would eliminate debauchery, nuns, and (once women reach a sufficient number of offspring to qualify for a state pension) poverty. Would husbands willingly take on the children of other men? Certainly, since both peasants and artisans needed cheap and healthy workers. Also, kings needed more soldiers and taxpayers.

Maurice was reluctant to have his men slain in pitched battle; instead, he wore down his opponents slowly. The one time the marshal's army got out of control, in Löwendahl's capture of Bergen-op-Zoom, there was a universal public outcry of disapproval – according to the Enlightenment viewpoint, war should have as few casualties as possible and none among civilians.[5]

His contemporaries – other than the French toadies around royal favourites – considered him a good commander and a sound politician. Political observers considered Frederick the Great's notorious breaking of agreements and treaties far worse sins than the marshal's personal faults, many of which they themselves shared. They certainly did not approve of the way Frederick treated his wife, isolating her in Berlin with nothing to do except eat.

Carlyle, in his *History of Friedrich the Second*, reports that in his old age Frederick the Great gave a copy of de Saxe's book to Maria Theresa's heir. It was 'a strange Military Farrago, dictated, I should think, under opium'. The emperor kept it by his bedside his entire life; it was found there when he died, not a page read.

Scotland, 1745

The Scottish rising of 1745 was a dramatic episode, a source of romantic pride and almost a turning point in the country's history. The pretender's son, Charles Stuart, took the initiative – his father lacked the spirit and personality for such a venture. He had not consulted many knowledgeable men – no successful conspiracy can involve many people – and he had little support beyond drawing-room braggadocios and enthusiastic Highlanders, but the enterprise almost overthrew the Hanoverian dynasty. 'Bonnie Prince Charlie', the charming but impractical centrepiece of the enterprise, was all of twenty-five at the time. Alas for the conspirators, his behaviour was as unpredictable as his spelling. He was handsome, charming, chaste, quarrelsome and unlucky. When the prince slipped away from France with a self-financed army of exiles, one vessel with seven hundred men aboard had to turn back after an encounter with a British warship. Enthusiastically greeted by Highlanders – who couldn't understand why he wasn't sleeping with all the handsome women who were offering themselves – Charlie assured them that more French assistance would be forthcoming. Actually, he had done little more to secure this help than leave a note for Louis XV, asking for his help. Louis had once taken an interest in the project, thinking that it could, by distracting the Hanoverian forces into Scotland, allow de Saxe to ferry an army across the channel on flat-bottomed boats. Once that became impractical, he considered Charles's plans hare-brained.

In fact, the king was right. Everything had depended on the British army being overstretched – it could not be in Flanders, on the Channel coast and in Scotland at the same time – but if troops were withdrawn from the Low Countries, de Saxe should be able to gain some advantage. So it might be worth risking a few troops and some money. However, the French king remained cautious – he had not hit it off with the young prince, and he was distressed by his wild company while waiting for the fleet to be assembled; the royal mistress, Madame de Pompadour, saw that the prince was a snob and disliked him. In any case, sailing to Scotland with only a small force seemed insane. Moreover, why help put the pretender on the English throne? The Stuarts were not a dynasty that remembered favours for long. Lastly, Scotland would no longer complicate English plans.

Louis XV did belatedly send a thousand men from his Scots Regiment, commanded by James Drummond,[6] to join Charles's army; and he enquired among his allies about providing mercenary troops, but time was too short to hire them.

Charles behaved better than expected, and at first his advisors were both competent and lucky. His Highlanders marched five hundred miles into the heart of England, within striking distance of London, before Charles's commanders – perhaps deceived by spies – informed him that the promised uprising of Jabobite supporters was not happening, and the three armies surrounding them were too numerous to overcome. Even a victory would have left him too weak to seize London, the one place in England well disposed towards him. Charles was appalled at the decision to retreat – perhaps rightly so – but he lacked sufficient understanding of warfare to persuade his officers that the risk was reasonable, and he did not have the personality to force them to yield. As his army retreated north, Scots flocked to join the colours – unfortunately, the colours were those of the Union Jack, not the Stuart flag.

In April 1746, when the Jacobite army reached the Highlands, where the British redcoats would be at a maximum disadvantage, Charles took personal command. It was a disastrous decision – instead of fighting in rugged country, he chose the moor at Culloden – perfect for redcoats and British cavalry. The confrontation was more a massacre than a battle – only the Scots Regiment was allowed to surrender with honours. The rest of the Jacobite soldiers were hunted down or harried out of the kingdom. Meanwhile, according to the Tombses in *That Sweet Enemy*, Louis XV sent 3,500 men to Canada – enough to have made the difference in Charles's campaign – in hope of recapturing Louisbourg. That expedition failed after most of the army died of scurvy.

Charles managed to hide in hovels and swamps through what passed as summer in the far north, warming himself with whisky so often that by the time a French warship rescued him in September, he was on the way to becoming a hopeless alcoholic. Meanwhile, the combination of redcoats and loyalist Scots dealt the Jacobite party and the Highland culture fatal blows. Once Charles was safely in exile again, the crisis was over. The Hanoverian dynasty could now entrust the government to new men, leaving the most important Whigs in the opposition. The irreconcilables, even Flora MacDonald, who had saved Charlie, left the country – many to America. Nor was the expedient of voluntary exile confined to Scotland.

De Saxe was unable to take advantage of the English difficulties.

Ulster Empties Itself into America

One hundred thousand Scots-Irish[7] left Ulster for America between 1718 and 1775. There were numerous reasons – though each successive government prided itself on settling Protestants in Ireland, their church was still persecuted, they were hardly represented in the Irish parliament, and the economy remained weak. Most Scots were renters, much like the native Irish, their land owned by absentee English lords; Swift's 'Modest Proposal' (to eat surplus children) applied to Ulster as well as the Catholic counties. When the favourable contracts offered to immigrants expired, the landlords raised the rents. The crops failed, the demand for linen declined, Lowland immigrants from Scotland crowded the labour market and there was little enough work for any of them. There was too little hard currency to sustain the economy, much less to pay taxes. In time, thanks to a tax exemption designed to benefit England, the linen industry provided more jobs, eventually becoming more important than food production. But it was all too little, too late. It was better for Scots-Irish to flee into the Pennsylvania wilderness, with its forty years of hardship, than to endure pharaoh's slavery forever.

Protestant Scots and Catholic Irish made few efforts to bridge the cultural–theological–linguistic chasms between them. Both were 'ultras' in religion, disagreeing loudly with other Protestants and Catholics, insisting on their traditional practices and interpretations, and both were against extending toleration to the other party. Thus, the solution to the Irish question most acceptable to the modern mind – everybody trying to get along with the others – was unacceptable to eighteenth-century Scots, Irish and many English immigrants.[8]

Although the Scots-Irish had been second-class citizens in Northern Ireland, most had been able to pay their passage across the Atlantic rather than become indentured servants. The convicts and indentured servants who went to the West Indies did far less well, most of them dying of heat and disease.

Pennsylvania, the goal of many Ulster migrants, was indeed a new world. It had been established only in the 1680s to pay off royal debts and get as many troublesome Quakers as possible out of the country. There followed a rich array of newcomers. First there were Huguenot refugees from France, then Protestant Germans fleeing Louis XIV's armies – so many that some feared the English language would be overwhelmed. Ulster Scots were so numerous that even Benjamin Franklin wondered if potential immigrants could be frightened away by advertising the fact that smallpox was common in America. Happily for coastal residents, however, the Scots moved inland, where there were many more taverns than courthouses. Corn (maize) was too heavy to transport, but it could be made into whisky. Thus yet another product of Scotland and Ireland, modified to the local crops, made its way into America.

The rugged hills and lurking dangers of the frontier country in America reminded the newcomers of family tales from Scotland; there were few neighbours to complain about their lack of fine manners or their readiness to settle quarrels with violence. The Native Americans – whom Americans called Indians – quickly moved away. They knew that American settlements were disease-ridden, alcohol was too available, and young men and women were too easily corrupted; even the deer left the vicinity of men armed with the new and more accurate Pennsylvania rifles. By moving into the interior, however, the Indians left behind a stretch of seemingly empty land that was quickly filled by adventurous Scots-Irish eager at last to have land of their own. Established Americans were often deterred from moving over the mountains by stories of skulking Indians, but not the Scots-Irish – they had been schooled in the religious wars of Ulster.

The frontier had a levelling effect at first, the new Americans becoming more like Indians, the Indians becoming more like Americans; intermarriage, in fact, was fairly common, especially with leaders of those southern tribes most willing to accept European practices – including slavery.[9]

With the established churches and government offices confined to the 'tidewater', Americans in the mountains learned to fend for themselves. European crops gave way to Indian corn, trapping and hunting; European habits such as judging people by their social class became less important – even dress and speech became less formal. As these frontiersmen moved slowly westwards – without any planning from above and usually against the wishes of governors – they encountered French trappers and soldiers who were offering the Indians alliances to keep Americans from crossing the mountains into the rich interior they regarding as their own fur-trapping ground. (The Indians had as little appreciation of the differences between the English colonists as the colonists did understanding what made one Indian tribe different from the rest.) Indians who saw traditional rivals join the French asked for English aid.

As the French and English colonies divided the Indians into hostile camps, the way was prepared for a great war. Whatever the Scots-Irish had been before the conflict of 1754–64, afterwards most of them were Americans.

The British Army

Although a third of the officers in the British army were Ulster Scots, there had been few efforts to recruit Catholic soldiers in Ireland until the Seven Years War, when the manpower shortage became acute. Afterwards, according to Kevin Kenny in *Ireland and the British Empire*, Anglo-Irish officers were among the most vehement enforcers of British imperialism, while Catholic Irishmen, enlisting largely for economic reasons, were mainly cannon-fodder. This was not surprising, he says, because it was not unusual for one colonial people to help oppress another, or even co-operate in governing their own.

There was much ambiguity in the situation. Irish-born Protestant soldiers and officers were not mercenaries in the sense that they would flit from army to army, but some of their ancestors had served in the British army in the hope of obtaining lands in Ireland, or, perhaps reluctantly, had accepted farms in lieu of back pay; some served now for the same reasons. Many owed rents to friends of the king, local elites and absentee landlords. But Protestants remained a minority on the island. What should they do about Catholic willingness to aid England's enemies? How should they deal with local terrorism? Were there any compromise solutions possible? Questions like these complicated every discussion of Ireland's future.

Ireland, like Scotland, was just too close for English monarchs to ignore. It was too small to defend its independence, and it would be a dangerous base for Spanish or French armies. In the years following William of Orange's conquest, Irish Catholic exiles made up a disproportionately large number of the professional mercenaries in France, all hoping to return home someday and drive the English and Scots out. When the union of 1707 opened the English market to Scottish goods and talents, Ireland did not similarly benefit. That had to wait until 1801. Meanwhile, memory of the 'flight of the earls' to Spain in 1607 and the 'Wild Geese' flying to France in 1691 suggested that English fears were not imagined.

It was very different in Scotland. The mutually beneficial relationship of the Royal Army and Navy with the British economy lasted until the American War for Independence. Whenever the army needed uniforms or cannons, there were entrepreneurs ready to provide them, and manufacturing provided jobs. The workers went to the taverns, where their beer was taxed, thereby eventually paying for the uniforms and guns. It was a stimulus package that benefited everyone in one way or another, and relatively few workers were hauled off to military service (though God help those caught by recruiting gangs and forced on board warships or troopships).

Soldiers and officers of this era were no models of Victorian-era rectitude. Too many fell into that broad category of 'losers' who would otherwise have filled the poorhouses and prisons; too many drank too much, swore too heartily and suffered from venereal diseases. No householder was happy about having troops 'quartered' in his home, with little to do through the winter except eye the daughters and seduce the maids. And what were they to do with the women who legally or illegally followed the troops? Too many of the troopers' wives and daughters were involved in prostitution, too many were left behind in destitution when the men were sent abroad; many lost their looks through household labour and bearing children, others through too much drink and too little personal hygiene. Officers created busy work for their men such as polishing brass buttons – which were notoriously difficult to bring to a shine. Awkwardly for the host communities, the better the soldiers looked, the more attractive their daughters found them. If soldiers lacked good prospects for supporting a wife, they were at least not dull like the village boys; they understood that women, like fortresses, succumbed more readily to storming than to pleas for surrender.

It is sometimes said that Scots built the British Empire. The statement by itself is an exaggeration, but some exaggerations are truisms. Statistics tell the story – Scots were represented in India far beyond their percentage of the population in the British Isles. But it was the ordinary Englishman (being more numerous than the Scots, Welsh and Irish) who paid the excise taxes that paid the bondholders whose loans made the empire possible. With every draught of beer, with every pipe of tobacco and cup of tea, pennies went into the Exchequer to pay for the armies in Asia and America. Indian taxpayers and consumers, too, contributed to its maintenance.

By 1789 Scots were engineers, missionaries and doctors, teachers and administrators, and less often soldiers. The age of the military mercenary was dying, but Scots still enlisted in armies for the traditional reasons of honour, adventure, poverty, opportunity, family tradition, politics, dynastic loyalty and, of course, money. However, the emphasis was now on the British Empire, in far-flung climes among unfamiliar peoples, not on employment on the continent.

James Miller concludes *Swords for Hire* by saying that Scottish achievements as merchants and scholars should be as celebrated as much as their not-entirely enviable reputation as soldiers.

The Seven Years War

Frederick II of Prussia was a warrior by training, not by inclination. His famous quarrel with his hard-nosed royal father ruined him for family life forever – he married as instructed, but he may never have slept with his wife. He spent much time with his army, in a raucous masculine world, with jesting that went beyond bawdy; in his appropriately named palace of Sans Souci in Potsdam, well outside Berlin, he pursued music, art and philosophy. In his old age he preferred the conversation of intelligent men, playing the flute and supervising the economic and cultural development of his capital and country. In *Iron Kingdom* Christopher Clark investigated as much as possible the question of Frederick's sexual preferences – a question that could be raised about several great generals of this era – without getting past gossip or plausible reasons why he would greet his wife after years of separation, 'Madame has grown fatter.'

It was quite different when he was young. Frederick had gone to war voluntarily in 1740. Newly become king, he had seized an opportunity that might never come again, to steal Silesia from Maria Theresa. Only a few decades before no one could imagine that Prussia would dare to challenge Austria, certainly not the Austrians. The Habsburg domains may have been much smaller than France, but they were much larger and richer than Prussia. However, the Austrian army had performed poorly in recent wars against France and Turkey, and now several neighbouring rulers saw the succession crisis as an opportunity to help themselves to parts of the Austrian Empire.

Frederick had a fine army and a full treasury, but he still found it difficult to occupy Silesia swiftly. Dennis Showalter, in *The Wars of Frederick the Great*, blames this partly on the king's lamentable lack of experience, his army having been at peace for a quarter century, and on his father's habit of calling off manoeuvres whenever bad weather struck – Frederick William had been so determined to avoid buying new uniforms that the army found itself almost unable to march and fight in snow, rain and mud. Moreover, the Austrians refused to admit defeat. Frederick managed to win the war, but when the Seven Years War began in 1756 he faced the unlikely combination of Austria, Russia and France, each attacking one part of his wide-flung state.

The Prussian 'miracle' – surviving this onslaught – was due partly to Frederick's military genius, and partly to the awkward alliances allied against him. Each monarch may have wanted to see the Prussian king humbled, but each wanted someone else's army to do the job. In the end, credit has to be given to the military system the king's father and grandfather had created. Prussia simply had the best army in Europe.[10]

This was important for the government of William Pitt, which understood that unless there was a coalition to tie down French troops in Europe, those regiments would be sent to Canada and India, and even against Hanover. With Austria now a French ally, the only German state that could put substantial numbers of troops on the French frontier was Prussia. Consequently, Pitt provided subsidies and prayers, together with the small Hanoverian army, in the hope that some miracle would save both of them. It worked.

In 1762 Pitt claimed that he had won America on the Rhine, but his opponents were already noticing that whereas previously the government had rented armies, now it was providing subsidies to allies in peacetime or just to keep them neutral. The difference seemed small even then, but it was significant. Moreover, mercenary allies, reckoning that British money had rented only their soldiers, refused to sacrifice themselves for British interests. Certainly Pitt trusted Frederick only to do what was in both their interests. Nobody trusted the Prussian king, except his soldiers, and for good reason. Frederick was out for his own kingdom, a cause that interested the British taxpayer not at all.

The split became final with Pitt's fall from power. The subsidies ceased, the funds diverted to defend Portugal against Spain. But it did not matter. With the death of the Russian tsarina, Elizabeth, her heir withdrew the troops from the Austrian alliance, then loaned them to Frederick. Prussian and Hanoverian armies then drove the French out of the war, so that not even the palace coup in St Petersburg had a significant impact on the balance of power. Prussia and Austria, left alone to fight it out, were too exhausted for either to achieve a decisive victory. The French were ready for peace, with England also ready to concede almost every contested point except the Atlantic fisheries. Only Pitt had stood in the way, insisting that all the interconnected wars be resolved at the same time and that Britain retain every conquest won by British arms. In 1761 the Tories, no longer suspected of wanting to place a Stuart on the throne, won over young George III (1738–1820) to making concessions in return for peace. With Pitt gone, the king's party was able to replace the Whigs, who had been so long in office that their intellectual infirmities seemed on a par with Pitt's physical ones.[11] As it happened, the new government led by Bute not only failed to make peace, but found itself at war with Spain as well.[12]

A Portuguese Side-Show

Spain had wisely sat out the Seven Years War until now, when intervention seemed likely to bring significant rewards. The late king, Ferdinand (1713–59), had been neither mentally nor physically sound, but his instincts were good: he had understood better than his ministers how difficult it would be to combine the Spanish and French fleets effectively. Not so his successor, Charles III (1716–88), who abandoned Naples for the richer Iberian kingdom. Charles was a man in a hurry – he saw the potential for capturing Gibraltar and the kingdom of Portugal, where the incompetent king, Joseph I (1714–77), had given his minister, Pombal, complete control of the government, then, after the terrible earthquake at Lisbon in 1755, moved into a complex of tents and never spent another night under a roof. When Charles III invaded Portugal in 1762, only British troops prevented the kingdom from collapsing immediately. The Spanish army, once checked, proved to be poorly prepared for war. Many of its troops deserted, including Irish and German mercenaries who were soon drawn into Portuguese service. Then the Portuguese army began to disintegrate as well, suffering from the extreme heat, from hunger, from a lack of clothing and an inability to devise a strategy. The British army had to take the matter in hand.

The first commander was Lord Tyrawley, a professional soldier from County Mayo in Ireland. Hurriedly recruiting a battalion of Irish Catholics, thanks to a relaxation of the anti-Catholic regulations – which suggests both the lessened importance of religion in the politics of the day at home and an awareness of Iberian suspicions of Protestants – he hurried to Portugal. However, Tyrawley's men lacked motivation to fight, while the Portuguese remained not only totally disorganised, but also unhappy at being treated as mere puppets.[13]

To correct the situation, the Portuguese hired as commander-in-chief William von der Lippe-Bückeburgh (1724–77). This famed artillery officer had been born in London to the count of Schaumburg-Lippe, a minor prince who had gladly rented his troops to the British government. Walpole complained in a private letter about giving the command to a German who was almost a Portuguese rather than to a Briton, inadvertently confirming that the count of Lippe, who had been ambassador in Lisbon, knew the country well. After Tyrawley returned home in disgust, the count of Lippe went on to organise victory.

Among other generals to serve with distinction in the war was John Burgoyne (1722–92), one of the handsomest and most notorious officers of the era, and one of the most competent; in Portugal he brilliantly cut to pieces the Spanish forces opposed to him, using effectively a figure who was to become famous fighting against the British in the American Revolution, Charles Lee.

Elsewhere British troops captured Manila and Havana, territories that they exchanged in the peace treaty for Florida.[14] The French, embarrassed for their ally, gave them as compensation the huge but largely useless territory of Louisiana.

The question raised by Lawrence Henry Gipson is relevant here – was this long conflict a 'war for the empire', that is, essentially defensive? Or was it a 'war for empire', little more than a land grab? The answer is, unhappily, complicated. If British policy was imperialism run amok, in the years to follow the principal architect of the Whig triumph, William Pitt, was among the foremost defenders of American constitutional arguments against the new taxes that Tory ministers had cooked up to repay loans Pitt had taken out. Awkwardly, Americans approved of empire when it meant expansion into the interior of their continent, but not when government policy was to keep them from going there.

London was concerned with keeping its Native American allies happy, while Americans, who were experiencing a demographic explosion at the very moment that Indian numbers were declining swiftly, wanted land. Moreover, since Indian raids on frontiersmen, in the words of Wayne Lee, in *Barbarians and Brothers*, were 'terrifying, frequent and unpredictable', it was not a matter that Americans were willing to ignore.

The British Army of the Future

No military establishment has ever found it easy to keep pace with challenges and change. That would be easy if one had a clear vision of what the future would require, if old methods, even old weapons, were indeed obsolete, and if new ones would work as well as hoped. But no aspect of military life was more difficult to change than the means used to supply and pay troops.

This was true for numerous reasons, most of which seemed good or necessary when the system was implemented, and it continued partly because it was familiar, partly because it worked, and partly to discourage parliamentary or royal oversight. Edward Curtis, in *The British Army in the American Revolution*, noted that a parliamentary inquiry in 1780 abandoned its efforts at reform because the members could not figure out how the system actually worked.

Each regiment in the British army had six fictitious soldiers on its rolls. The pay of two went to a fund for widows of regimental officers; the pay of the remaining four went to the colonel, to allow him to clothe recaptured deserters, to cover costs of recruiting, and to provide an allowance for himself and his agent. In addition, each company of foot had 'contingent men', whose pay went to the captain for expenses.

Pay was not much and was rarely raised, not even to compensate for inflation. Curtis cites one estimate that a tailor lived on his wages better than a colonel, and a common soldier barely had anything left after deductions. The soldier's pay was divided into two parts: first, 'subsistence', which was insufficient to begin with, less after deductions were made for shoes, medicine and medical care and repairs to his weapons; second, 'gross off-reckoning', meaning a kick-back to the paymaster, a contribution to the Chelsea Hospital, a payment to the regimental agent, and the cost of clothing.

In spite of this, officers continued to buy commissions and soldiers enlisted. In spite of the 1711 order forbidding infants to hold commissions, it was still done; and some officers were too old to carry out any duties effectively. Clearly, the officers loved their work – Curtis notes that many would forgo marriage in order to devote themselves totally to their regiments. It was a 'gentleman's occupation' and all the officers of a regiment became family.

Their morals did not rise above those of their age. Drunkenness was common, mistresses were winked at (probably in more than one sense) and severe punishments had to be inflicted (though this was often moderated or avoided) despite the tender feelings of the officers towards their men.

Weapons improved, but only slowly. In 1776 Major Patrick Ferguson demonstrated a breech-loading musket that could dependably fire four to six shots a minute, resisted water and was extremely accurate. But few were manufactured and only a few were used in combat. The standard weapon remained the fourteen-pound 'Brown Bess'. It was not a bad weapon, but haste in loading often meant insufficient ramming, which lowered the muzzle velocity significantly; the fourteen-inch bayonet impeded swift loading, so that only two to three shots could be fired per minute. Those shots were seldom well aimed, so that it was occasionally joked that it took a man's weight in bullets to shoot him down. The flints were not reliable, either. No wonder soldiers preferred to use the bayonet!

This preference was borne out in confrontations with elite American units armed with long-barrelled Pennsylvania rifles. The riflemen were deadly even at long distance – more than three hundred yards – but they could not fire rapidly and their weapons could not be fitted with bayonets. Therefore, rather than stand fast against a bayonet charge, they withdrew quickly – very quickly.

Age of the Enlightenment

From time to time it had seemed that the age of great wars was past. Opinion, not only of what might cautiously be called the public, or even of philosophers and rulers, expressed doubts that any gains likely to be achieved were worth the sacrifices demanded by Mars.[15] Mankind – at least the European minority – had left the brutalities of the past behind (except in dealing with the suddenly overmatched peoples in Africa, Asia and the Americas).

There were, nevertheless, reasons for wars, and of all the religious groups preaching peace, only the Quakers were getting much beyond pious words. Their doctrine of simplicity was pushing them towards abandoning practices that supported war and slavery (products requiring sugar and dye), that encouraged luxury and idleness (literature, the fine arts, music) and stimulated the senses (coffee, tea, tobacco, rum, brandy). They were fundamentally opposed to military service, and open to the plight of peoples whose lifestyles emphasised simplicity and honesty (such as the Indians of North America and Bengal); they were equally open to recognising that the Jew and the Turk had insights into the relationship of God and man equal to their own.

This made little difference to most Britons. The rich liked luxuries and the distractions of society; commoners liked their dram and their smoke.

The rich appreciated Georgian architecture, hunts and walks in the country; commoners coveted the servants' jobs. The rich liked the show of high church or Catholic services; commoners were attracted to the preachers of the Great Awakening and its periodic revivals. The rich made the grand tour, concentrating on great cities and society, and visited churches only to see the art; the gentry were beginning those hikes across Europe, especially over the mountains, that marked the beginning of the Romantic movement; the poor stayed home. Quakers became known as honest and sincere, but impractical people – pirates may be good people, really, but they still wanted your ships. Pressed to declare war on the Indians, the Quakers in Pennsylvania chose to give up control of the government and withdrew into Quietism. Their once fully filled large meeting houses in London and Dublin slowly began to echo with the sound of silent worship.

Crowds did occasionally flock to these meeting houses to hear speakers attack slavery, propose women's rights and advocate universal peace. However, it often happens that one generation has to die off before the next can be persuaded of any argument. Those who are in a hurry for social or political change are almost bound to be disappointed; the passion of a crowd is best maintained by hammering weekly at problems that never go away – like sin. However, Jonathan Swift was wrong in asserting that the Irish had only two interests in life – food and sex – they were also enthusiastic about horse-racing.

Philosophical concerns, however, hardly touched on one basic fact – that even before the Industrial Revolution began, the technological advances that made warfare so deadly were pushing forward rapidly. Specialists (we could almost call them scientists now) were studying the chemistry of gunpowder, the mathematics of artillery and ballistics, and new means of producing weapons of war in greater quantities and more cheaply. Germans, Britons and Frenchmen vied and co-operated in these ventures, making steady progress, while Austrians, Italians, Poles, Spaniards and Russians fell behind. The efforts could be justified on grounds of pure science, of making nations safe against attack, and of making war so terrible that no one would lightly start one again.[16]

At the same time, thinking men and women understood that nature (by then as important a concept as God) provides an endless supply of dolts and madmen (making an argument against hereditary kings and nobles), also that crowds are dangerous and unpredictable (making an argument against democracy) and that clerics are narrow-minded and corrupt (making an argument against popes, priests and Protestants). While progress may have seemed inevitable, there were disciples of Voltaire ready to warn against undue optimism. Candide may have thought that life consisted of scientific experiments with the duke of Thunder-ten-tronckh's daughter, but the Bulgar army was just on the other side of the border.

CHAPTER SEVEN

The Race Towards Enlightenment and Destruction

By mid-century all the great European rulers, and some not so great, were adherents of Enlightenment philosophy. They had failed to outlaw war, but they still believed that, given the power they were gathering into their hands, they could make the lives of their citizens happier and more prosperous. They were certain that their education and experience (and that of their advisors) made them better prepared to chart the course of society, economics and politics than any of their citizens individually or collectively – a position still held by despots and armchair essayists today. Nowadays we can see that the Enlightened despots did much that was good, but they had many failures. Partly, this was because they came to imagine themselves so wise that whatever seemed to be to their advantage also seemed to be best for humanity as a whole. Their great visions often proved impractical, and sometimes when they were right – at least in our eyes – they were too far ahead of what people would accept.

Nowhere was this pride and self-confidence clearer than in the great wars of mid-century. Though the efficiency of armies made them into killing machines, each of the most powerful rulers saw logical reasons for making war – Prussia could become a great power only if Austria was humbled, Austria could survive only by crushing Prussia, France was willing to risk overseas colonies for tiny parcels of Germany, and Russia was reluctantly ready to gobble up Polish and Tatar lands. Poland would disappear between 1772 and 1795 – victim of a belief that if it refrained from threatening anyone, it would be left alone – and the Ottoman Empire survived mainly because Austria and Russia were too busy carving up Poland to finish it off. Then, in 1789, there was the French Revolution, which was first the culmination, then the disappointing end of the intellectuals' belief that they could reform society and even states without much difficulty. Enlightenment self-confidence was never the same again, but while it lasted, it was powerful.

Religion supported such willing suspension of doubt, and philosophy did too, much of the time – in *Candide* Voltaire satirised the belief that 'everything was for the best'. As for the lower classes, intellectuals had an exaggerated hope for their future improvement that coexisted with despair over their present habits, morals and superstition. As for improving anyone's mind, the educated elite were as appalled with the Catholic crowds in Vienna making the British ambassador bow towards the host when he encountered a procession bearing it through the streets as they were of anti-Catholic rabble-rousers in Scotland. Scoffing was in vogue, especially when talking about the military, except in the presence of officers.

When we try to visualise an army before the age of Bismarck and Napoleon III, we usually call up a mental picture of the 1700s. Even the storm of the French Revolution did not change the uniforms and weaponry significantly. There were changes in the size of the armies, the motivations of the soldiery, the origins of the officer corps, but even so, as the French say, 'Plus ça change, plus c'est la même chose' (the more things change, the more they remain the same).

The soldier, ram-rod straight (the necessary posture to keep the mitred hat from falling off) with his heavy cloak, the bullet pouch over his left shoulder, his bayonet sheath, his knapsack and, of course, his heavy musket. The artillerymen pushing their weapon into place by the spokes, the caisson nearby, their comrades ready with powder bags, shot and ram. The cavalryman, gorgeous in his braids and sashes, his steed pawing the earth, his moustache the envy of men and the object of female admiration.

The reality was different. Warriors looked less handsome away from the parade ground, especially after a few weeks of heat and rain, with few opportunities to wash or even to eat properly. Infirmaries filled up, and the guard house too.

This was especially true in the decadent Holy Roman Empire, where so many mercenaries were once recruited, and where conscription was becoming more common. Austrians and Germans began to think longingly of home, of family, of the neighbourhood *Stube* (a word conveying a much more comfy and welcoming atmosphere than the English word 'tavern', much less the American 'bar'. Germans were, in fact, not considered military by nature. *Gemütlichkeit*, with its connotations of relaxed comfort, was more to their liking. At least, so we are led to think by intellectuals, visitors and generals when they had a bit more wine and brandy than was wise.

Madame de Staël

Anne Louise Germaine de Staël (1766–1817) was a Swiss traveller, writer and conversationalist, and among the most quoted personalities of her era. Her father was the famed economist Necker, whose advice could have saved the head of the French king, Louis XVI, had it been heeded; her mother ran one of the most influential salons in Paris. At age twenty she married a slightly older Swedish diplomat with whom she was not close. She attracted most of the important people of the revolutionary and Napoleonic eras to her salon; she travelled widely with gentleman friends, became acquainted with the minds (and more) of some of the great men of the era, and her marvellously passionate and exaggerated novels began the Romantic movement in France.

Her books attracted a wide readership, partly because of her style, but mostly because her observations reflected what others had seen. When she said that 'Germany was not a nation', heads were certain to nod in agreement. Who, after all, was not aware of the jealousies and ambitions of German princelings? She noted that the north of Germany was different in almost every way from the south – climate, geography, crops, language and customs – and yet everyone thought it was possible to speak about 'Germans'. Admittedly, German philosophers were Europe's best. Yet their theories rose into the air, incomprehensible and without effect on even their closest neighbours. The ruins of castles contrasted with mud hovels, all covered with snow month after month. Yet there was a colour and variety to life – from murals painted on stucco walls to flowers in maidens' hair. Honesty and morality were spoken of more commonly than elsewhere, though Frenchmen suggested that this was as much due to the slowness of their minds, which applied imagination to literature rather than to action. 'It is impossible' was a phrase travellers encountered every day, in every place. But how they could sing! Workers sang, worshippers sang, soldiers sang;

everywhere one heard musical instruments – harps played by shepherds in their fields, horns by soldiers in theirs.

In this society, marked as it was by strong contrasts, nature and civilisation not yet quite synchronised, de Staël, in *Germany*, observed:

> Stoves, beer, and the smoke of tobacco, surround all the common people of Germany with a thick and hot atmosphere, from which they are never inclined to escape. This atmosphere is injurious to activity, which is of no less importance in war than courage itself; resolutions are slow, discouragement is easy, because an existence, void of pleasure in general, inspires no great confidence in the gifts of fortune. The habit of a peaceable and regular mode of life is so bad a preparation for the multiplied chances of hazard, that even death, coming in a regular way, appears preferable to a life of adventure.

These were the men that Prussian kings were making into the finest army in Europe. The French disagreed, of course, believing that everything was better in France; and even Germans had a proverb, 'Leben wie Gott in Frankreich' that suggested luxurious prosperity. Contemporaries would have been shocked by the twentieth-century belief that Germans were the best soldiers in the world. The facts simply did not support that. Not in the eighteenth century, except in Prussia.

The Prussian army employed special means to make farm boys into soldiers. While discipline was firm, it could not be so brutal that no one would enlist – and recruiting mercenaries from other German states was very important for keeping the numbers of troops high without depriving the countryside of agricultural labour.

In 1733 Frederick II's father had divided Prussia into cantons, each of which was to select sturdy young peasants for military service, exempting students, apprentices and skilled workers, ministers and nobles.[1] These were pious Lutherans for the most part, though Showalter is probably correct in *The Wars of Frederick the Great* in suggesting that they sang hymns while marching mostly because they knew the tunes; most likely they improvised bawdy lyrics to suit their moods – as has almost every army in the history of the world.

There were mercenaries among their number and, in wartime, prisoners and deserters were dragooned into their ranks. The soldiers took care to see that such men behaved, much as they punished those who were stupid, lazy or thieves. Performing the intricate drills and remaining steady under fire was important for each man – that was the best way to survive battle – as well as to retain the pride that each had in his unit, his army and his king.

The conscripts had to be healthier than the mercenaries, who would often have been older and whose bodies showed the effects of hard service – poor food, hard marches, nights in the open, diseases (especially venereal diseases) and wounds – and who probably spent much time between wars in poorhouses and jails. But conscripts could not be trained for combat nearly as quickly, and they would have been more liable to become confused and frightened in combat.

In *The Army of Maria Theresa* Christopher Duffy notes that the Austrians continued to recruit by regiments, each getting permission from regional administrators or being assigned areas. When wartime pressure to fill the ranks frustrated all efforts to attract the very best men, recruiters welcomed deserters and foreigners, even 'shady characters' (but not Frenchmen, Jews, Turks and Gypsies). More humane treatment was more significant than the bounty, much of which disappeared in deductions for uniforms and side arms; on the other hand, like other professions of the day, service was for life (that is, till death or so many years, whichever came first).

Conscripts and mercenaries in all armies were indoctrinated so that their primary loyalty came to be to their comrades and commanders. Regimental pride was fostered by encouraging soldiers to see themselves as an extended family; flashy uniforms, marching songs and band music and ceremonies honouring past suffering and triumphs emphasised the male bonding. Medals and sashes, titles and promotions became as important as bonuses and land grants – which could not have been afforded anyway. Garrison towns became the troops' homes, and retirement homes for veterans, with hospitals for invalids, became centres of regimental activities.

Chesterfield, Johnson and Casanova

Philip Stanhope, the earl of Chesterfield (1694–1773), was regarded as the greatest wit of an era known for quotable men and women. A career of twenty-five years in diplomacy followed by almost three decades as a literary lion made his essays required reading by the sophisticated set. His Tory views happily prevented too deep an immersion into politics; his quips kept him from even wading. Tory in those days meant a point of view – stability in society, in church, in literature – that contrasted strongly with the Whig emphasis on election victories, commerce and social climbing. Chesterfield emphasised manners, those principles of behaviour that could be mastered only by early training and emulation – hence difficult for anyone but nobility and gentlemen to acquire.

Even so, Chesterfield understood that politics was less concerned with groups than with individuals. The prince and the minister were influenced by wives and mistresses, who were each influenced by friends, lovers and ladies-in-waiting, who were in turn subject to influence by maids and servants. The chain, as he called it, was long, but whoever wished to have a voice in politics could not break any link. Negotiations were long and stressful, but anything worth doing at all was worth doing well. His arrangement of the marriage of the prince of Orange to a daughter of George II was masterful. The prince was deformed and unlikely to become king; the princess was fat. However, she was the only royal match available, and he was the only likely husband. On such common ground Chesterfield could always find a way to the bedroom.

He was such a master of French that he was warned to avoid putting French writers to shame, and such a master of the telling retort – usually coming completely 'out of the blue' that the victim was left speechless. If the victim tried to protest, it would have helped little – the anecdote would be repeated instantly by the circles of gossip that passed for society, and, in any case, Chesterfield would have written up his own very quotable version of the event.

Upon meeting Montesquieu (1689–1755), he immediately invited him to spend the winter at his home on St James's Square, brought him to London on his yacht and arranged for his election into the Royal Society. When Montesquieu published his *De l'Esprit des Lois*, he acknowledged his debt to his English friend. The translation of this classic analysis of government – most importantly the usefulness of a separation of powers between administrative, legislative and judicial branches – was read closely by those who created the future American Republic.

When war with Spain broke out in 1739, followed by the Prussian attack on Austria, Chesterfield was called to serve the new government – his task being to bring the Dutch into a new coalition against France. The Dutch may have regretted this after the disastrous battle of Fontenoy, but French expansionism was blunted; Chesterfield was rewarded with the office of Lord Lieutenant of Ireland, a post that was seemingly insignificant, but became critical for the survival of the Hanoverian dynasty in 1745 when Charles Stuart landed in Scotland. That there was no rising in Ireland was due largely to Chesterfield's skilful handling of potential rebels and fearful loyalists; his letters of wise counsel regarding the war turned the king's ancient enmity into favour. Unfortunately for Chesterfield, he profited little from this – increasing deafness (a sad affliction for a famed conversationalist) and injuries from a riding accident caused him to withdraw from public life.

Shortly after the conclusion of peace in 1748, he sent his teenage son on a grand tour of Europe – a long, leisurely journey to visit the major cities of Italy, France and Germany – but with such detailed instructions about what to see and how to behave that his son's widow made of them a posthumous book, the infamous *Letters to his Son*. When the young man reached Paris, Chesterfield advised him not to worry about the number of mistresses – the more, the better – as long as they did not harm his health or character (elsewhere he wrote that he should not lose his nose or his character, implying that a cultivated woman was safer than a prostitute). Awkwardly, his son was not only illegitimate (a fact that hampered his entry into society), but also socially inept. Instead of embarking on social conquests and a brilliant career, the boy secretly married a young woman of undistinguished background; his diplomatic career in Germany was marked by competent but mediocre performance; subsequently he died young. Chesterfield's heir, a nephew, was a similar plodder.

More important for the future, Chesterfield met a penniless but proud writer named Samuel Johnson (1709–84), who had an idea for a *Dictionary of the English Language*. Chesterfield encouraged him, even gave him a small sum of money for the project, then forgot about it until 1754, when he learned that the publication was almost completed. As it turned out, Dr Johnson was to be as quotable in his own ways as Chesterfield, though much less agreeable. When Johnson wrote a very rude letter, criticising the earl for having been a poor patron when he needed one most, Chesterfield admired the style, then wrote two essays praising the dictionary highly. For Chesterfield, manners mattered. His was a dying breed.

In Chesterfield's last days, almost blind as well as deaf, he opposed the government's attempt to impose the stamp tax on Americans as unenforceable and unlikely to bring in appreciable income. By that time, however, he had far less influence than Dr Johnson, whose intimate circle of intellectuals mimicked a Parisian salon, only without the rustle of petticoats. The choleric Dr Johnson (it is difficult to think of Samuel Johnson without his academic title, *honoris causa*) had an opinion on everything – why women should not speak in public, on the evils of the American Revolution (and the traitors who supported them), about the shortcomings of Scotland and Scots – but he was eminently readable and funny. To be insulted by Dr Johnson was an honour – and almost unavoidable.

Casanova (1725–98) was the anti-Johnson. Reared in Venice, then famous for its carnival and its vices (and thus an essential stop on every nobleman's grand tour), he entered the church, left the church, went to Paris, London, etc., everywhere enchanting kings, popes and habitués of salons with his wit and his anecdotes. He claimed to have visited Bonneval in Constantinople, and did converse with Voltaire in Geneva and Catherine II in St Petersburg. Part raconteur (about the places he had seen, the people he had known and his escape from the doge's prison in Venice), part con-man (quack, alchemist, Rosicrucian, Freemason, fortune-teller, forger), part adventurer (soldier, spy, organiser of state lotteries) and part just good company (musician, gambler, spendthrift), he advertised himself as the greatest lover in Western history – a pose that undoubtedly aided his amatory efforts in an era when flirtations and affairs were expected of people in society. But in truth the total of his conquests – lovingly detailed in his multi-volume *Mémoires* (*Histoire de ma vie*) – was not that extraordinary, certainly far short of Augustus the Strong and Maurice de Saxe. The value of the *Mémoires* today lies not in its erotica, which is too mild for the modern porn market, but in the people and places he described, and his advice on how to please (then seduce) anyone. A better description of society – high and low – can hardly be found, though a reader might have difficulty explaining this to those who ask why he (occasionally she) is reading *that* book.

Society was becoming porous. Intellectual adventurers like Voltaire and Rousseau were now welcomed into the best salons, their books were read by minds of varying levels of seriousness and they became invited guests of the greatest kings of Europe. Everyone was expected to dabble in science, philosophy and gossip. The effect was even felt in distant America, where Benjamin Franklin's experiments with electricity alone made him famous. When Franklin (1706–90) came to Paris as a diplomat during the American War for Independence, he quickly established himself as a highly desired guest in the most important salons and, despite his age, an impressive favourite of the ladies; a noted humorist and wit, there was also a bit of the con-man in Franklin.

The salon culture was evidence that the world was changing. The old nobility of birth was losing control: a new aristocracy of talent was coming in. This was demonstrated in 1740 when a strange mixture of intellectual and political genius – the king of Prussia, an adventurer equal to Casanova, dedicated not to Venus, but Mars and Apollo – challenged the ancient authority of Habsburg Austria, and won. The world would have been better off, perhaps, had Frederick the Great confined himself to his father's hobby of collecting tall grenadiers or even slept once with his wife, but that is to agree with the Austrian judgement that Berlin was filled with soldiers, while Vienna had musicians. Neither city, it might be noted, was famed for its salons. Vienna did have its coffeehouses, but they only drank *Kaffee mit Schlag*. Maybe a bit of cinnamon too, or chocolate, or both. And something sweet to snack on.

As for the English, the Gin Act of 1751 changed drinking habits forever. Some frugal Britons returned to ale, while John Wesley's preaching persuaded others to forgo alcoholic beverages altogether. William Hogarth's *Gin Lane* was replaced by *Beer Alley*, and everyone was healthier for the change – except the rich, of course, who could still afford gin. As for the poor, who were said to have only two joys in life – sex and alcohol, with the latter providing a more lasting experience – popular religion offered itself as a substitute for both.

For those who preferred to hold onto tradition, there was always military service. War was changing, but not the habits of warriors.

Changes in Warfare

Frederick II had been an amateur at the beginning of the War of the Austrian Succession. He was at first prone to panic and misjudgements, but by its end he had learned to manoeuvre linear formations effectively, marching his well-drilled troops out of sight to appear suddenly on one flank of the enemy line. This 'oblique attack' was more suited to the alternately open and wooded lands of central Europe than to the Low Countries or Italy. His troops could fire more balls per minute than anyone else's, and his cavalry was more determined in its attack. Artillery was becoming lighter, hence more mobile. Prussian determination to win remained impressive even as casualty lists lengthened.

Only disciplined troops excelled in this kind of warfare. Young men attracted by the pay and the promise of adventure quickly learned the reality of army life. And much of the famed limitations on pillage and plunder were aimed not at protecting civilians, but at depriving the troops of opportunities to desert, 'the outcasts of half central Europe', as Showalter characterised the many mercenaries in the army, were needed to replace the well-drilled troops slaughtered in the battles and ambushes in Bohemia and Saxony, and with the value of Prussian coins dropping rapidly, it could not have been easy for the recruiters to meet their quotas; there were reports of young men promised officers' commissions who ended up carrying a musket. However, as the Prussian army ravaged wide districts of Saxony and Bohemia, not only to support itself, but to deprive the imperial armies of supplies, poverty drove many desperate men to accept enlistment bonuses. In making a choice between armies, many must have preferred to serve in one with a tradition of winning: the chances of surviving were better, and veterans always preferred to boast of victories than to explain that their regiment had made a good fight of it.

The young king was not uniformly victorious, and he often ignored the advice of his most experienced generals (who were more often right than wrong), but he learned. Most of all, he was a fighter. The troops loved that. Any particularly battle might seem lost, but if they persisted, 'Old Fritz' would find a way to win.

After the first Silesian war (1740–2), Frederick reorganised his cavalry and artillery. Neither had been particularly effective, and military theory now yielded to bitter experience. The smart ranks of soldiers on parade under the eyes of drill masters were less impressive strung out across muddy fields or climbing steep hills; sleek fat horses looked good on the paved streets of Berlin, but scrawny nags performed better on campaign. Stirrups were raised so cavalrymen could stand to deliver a more deadly blow – and sabres were replaced by a straight sword that could be thrust, thus gaining vital inches in reach and discouraging any tendency to engage in a time-wasting mêlée. Troops had to be ready, not only to march off to war, but to fight effectively – against enemies who were improving steadily.

Frederick could rely on the support of his Junker nobles (minor aristocracy, whose name derives from *Jung Herr*), but they were not the sole origin of his officer corps – an important minority were foreign-born. Nor were the peasants as cruelly oppressed as historians have portrayed them, a situation that Clark in *Iron Kingdom* calls the 'black legend of Junker tyranny'. The king hired as many mercenaries as possible in order to avoid weakening his nation's economic base – men were more useful on the farms than in the army – and employed many soldiers in agriculture during the summer. He encouraged his foreign soldiers to marry, thus binding them more closely to Prussian service, and families lived together in the barracks, making the soldiers' lives less divorced from society's norms than was later the case.

In *The Wars of Frederick the Great* Showalter praises Prussia's careful preparation of the economy for war. If Prussia was not completely the case of an army having a state rather than the other way around, it was as good an example of such as we have from that era.

The king did not love war, but he saw it as the only way to make Prussia a great state; perhaps even the only way for his kingdom to survive in a contest with the regional superpowers – Russia, Austria and France were fighting over Poland, with Sweden waiting for an opportunity to recover its lost greatness. Brauer and van Tuyll argue in *Castles, Battles and Bombs* that Frederick's aggressiveness was a logical choice, given that he was outnumbered so badly that unless he used his well-trained army to strike down his enemies decisively, he would have been worn down by their superior resources. Of his eleven battles, he attacked in nine and accepted combat eagerly in the other two. He sought decisive victories and, after he learned his craft fully, never despaired, no matter how hopeless the situation appeared. His soldiers, of course, loved his will to prevail, identifying him with the by-word '*Durchhalten!*', meaning 'persevere'. Also, he was lucky, as all great commanders were.

Most importantly, Brauer and van Tuyll argue, he was not a mere general, who would be held accountable for errors and failures. As a monarch he could afford to take risks that would cost any subordinate his job.

Frederick the Great's Maxims

Frederick II had learned much from his first experiences in command, 1740–5. He summarised these lessons in his manual of war, a small book designed to acquaint his officers with his principles and expectations. Every army had such a manual, but some were little more than a description of drills and regulations – Frederick also offered wise advice.

Illustrative was his chapter on 'Sutlers, Beer, and Brandy'. He advised the commissary to collect all the beer and brandy available locally in the very first days of any campaign: they were essential for making the soldiers happy. This was especially important when invading another state, because the brewers and distillers might shut down or sell off their stores; should they seek to suspend production, they must be put back to work, for the soldier could not do without his daily dram.

Officers must protect the sutlers, who were responsible for buying or requisitioning food and fodder. This is especially important when there is nothing left for sale; in such cases rough methods are justified. Sutlers and camp-followers should bring in vegetables and cattle, and reasonable prices should be guaranteed.[2]

He also advised how to deal with the Austrians' irregular troops. Hussars and skirmishers are not to be overly feared, he wrote, because their bravery is great only when they see a prospect of plunder, or when they can inflict damage without fear of retaliation; they are troublesome only for convoys and baggage, and against retreating troops. Prussians should have little concern in encountering them, though they do inflict some losses, because it took too much time to drive them away.

He counselled officers retreating over open country to drive hussars away with a few shots from cannon, and skirmishers by using dragoons and hussars – they dread Prussian cavalry. In wooded and mountainous regions, send an advance guard to seize the heights along the route; detach troops to protect the flanks and protect the rear; keep a cavalry reserve for emergencies and expect to take casualties. Never, ever stop. Keep moving, because, once halted, a force will inevitably be surrounded, then outnumbered and finally destroyed.

When abandoning heights, move quickly, because skirmishers can occupy them quickly, then lie down behind cover and pick off every man still in range. Neither cannon fire nor musketry is of much use against them, because there are so few of them and they are so well concealed.

The best of these skirmishers were the Pandours. Croats, the most numer-ous of these free companies, had been trained in the hard school of war against the Turks. They were the most famous mercenaries of the era, feared for their marksmanship, ingenuity and courage. Peasants feared them for their lack of scruples, but sutlers loved them – when nobody else could find cattle or stores, the Croats could. They were the best light infantry in Europe.[3]

The king himself refused to weaken the numbers of his heavy infantry by creating units of skirmishers. There were many times that his men wished he had taken the problem more seriously.

Although Frederick won the war he had started in 1740, it took him five years; afterwards, Prussian dominance of culturally superior Saxony was taken for granted. However, he understood that possession of no land could ever be assured, and his spies informed him that Maria Theresa was determined to humiliate him and his army, then recover Silesia.

Frederick's *Maxims* illustrate his familiarity with de Saxe's short book, *Memoirs on the Art of War*. Certainly, he took to heart de Saxe's admonitions. The marshal had described the three main qualifications of a commander as courage, genius and health. A commander should also be discerning, calm, merciless when necessary and ready for anything. This would render him 'beloved, feared, and without doubt, obeyed'.[4]

The Diplomatic Revolution

Until 1756 one could count on the French and the Austrians being on opposite sides of any conflict, and that the British would be opposed to France and its allies, which usually meant Prussia. One could also assume that the Russians had a plan – maybe a bad plan, but at least a plan – before becoming involved in any conflict in central Europe. That rule of thumb no longer applied. This Seven Years War began as an act of revenge – Maria Theresa wanted Silesia back and Frederick of Prussia punished, and she had as allies two women who hated Frederick too – Elizabeth of Russia and (more controversially) Madame de Pompadour of France.

Maximilian Browne, commander of the Austrian army in Bohemia, had followed closely the diplomatic moves that hammered out the great alliance of Russia–Austria–France that was to strike simultaneously and by surprise. Browne was not especially happy to be fighting as a French ally against his British friends, but he was a loyal subject, and he sent repeated warnings to Maria Theresa that the Prussians were stirring. As he expected, Frederick II did not co-operatively await the onslaught, but struck at neutral Saxony to prevent its entry into the war on the Habsburg side; the Prussian army surrounded the Saxon forces at Pirna, a fortress not far from Leipzig on the west bank of the Elbe. Saving those fifteen thousand soldiers became Browne's primary mission – if they surrendered, they would surely be forced to serve in the Prussian army.

Nothing could be done, however, until more troops were collected – Browne sorely missed his trusted Hungarian and Croatian light cavalry, which could have hindered Prussian movements and disrupted their supply lines. Meanwhile, he began an elaborate series of deceptions that fixed Prussian attention westwards; as forces came up, he prepared them for a swift, if difficult, march up the east bank of the Elbe, to meet the Saxons as they crossed the river and hurried south.

This plan was disrupted by a Prussian invasion overrunning northern Bohemia. Browne drew up his forces behind morasses and ponds at Lobositz, with the Elbe River protecting his right flank, then sent his cavalry forwards. This drew the Prussian attack in that direction, and only slowly did the Prussian king understand the nature of the trap – though the Austrian superiority in cavalry soon made itself apparent. Up to ten thousand horsemen were soon involved in a gigantic mêlée; fifteen minutes later the Prussians fled.

It now became an infantry battle. As Browne watched from a distance Lacy's Croats being overwhelmed, there was nothing he could do: he had to count on the officers nearest to the fighting to take personal initiative and enter the fray. Unfortunately, all his past efforts to develop sound judgement among his subordinates proved to have been in vain – his officers were willing to die bravely, as long as they did not have to think. Lacy was wounded, and his formation collapsed.

The day was not lost, however. Browne's well-prepared defences else-where repulsed the Prussians with terrible casualties, slaughtering so many men that Frederick decided to withdraw himself quietly, leaving it to Jacob Keith to break off the action as gracefully as possible. Subsequently, Browne, who had suffered fewer casualties, surprised Frederick by retreating. But it was less a retreat than preparing to rescue the garrison at Pirna. Unfortunately for him, just at the moment that Browne needed to give all his attention to the offensive, his health collapsed – he was spitting up blood, probably from tuberculosis; he used his last strength to regain control over his Croats, who were robbing everyone and threatening to kill their officers.

Then the Saxons lost their nerve – the pontoon bridge had not arrived, the Prussians had recognised what was afoot, and rain came. The attempted flight up the west bank became entangled in the woods and hills of Saxon Switzerland, as the rough hills along the border with Bohemia were called; there was no way to get across the Elbe River to the waiting Austrians at Schandau, just above the great fortress at Königstein. Browne, once he saw that the Saxons could not escape, ordered his troops to march quickly back to Bohemia before the Prussians could trap them too. Not long afterwards, he put his men into winter quarters.

Browne, unwilling to allow the Prussians similar rest, sent his light troops out to attack their convoys and quarters. Meanwhile, the tsarina of Russia and king of France had concluded that Frederick could be beaten. They declared war in early 1757, and their armies were readied to move as soon as the weather allowed.

Once again Frederick II did not wait – he invaded Bohemia, easily intimidating the new Austrian commander, Charles Alexander of Lorraine; this oft-beaten general may have been privately aware of his many shortcomings, but he defended himself stoutly in public. Three great Prussian columns crossed the mountains from Saxony and Silesia weeks before the Habsburg high command had believed the snow would be sufficiently melted to allow the passage of armies. Charles Alexander ordered a retreat, much to Browne's dismay, who pointed out that once the Prussian armies combined, they would be too strong to defeat.

Browne was right. The Austrian army fell back on Prague, to await reinforcements from other units, most importantly the army of Marshal Leopold Joseph Daun (1705–66). To prevent being trapped inside the city, Browne took up a strong position on the hills east of the old city; if Daun's army arrived, the combined forces should be strong enough to drive the Prussians out of Bohemia. Frederick, of course, went on the attack immediately, confusing the defenders by attacking both to the east and west of the city. Browne was slain in the fighting, but his men performed so well that the Prussians marvelled – these were not the Austrians they had been fighting earlier. Charles Alexander cautiously withdrew the rest of the battered army into the city.

Frederick had too little time to take Prague by siege – Daun's army was approaching. Indeed, had Daun's lead elements marched to the sound of gunfire instead of cautiously taking up a defensive position, they would have come in on the Prussian flank. Frederick understood that his only chance for victory lay in audacity – to paralyse his enemies with doubt and fear, then strike them down with swift and daring blows.

This was no longer easy. Frederick might be admired (best at a distance), but his opponent, Maria Theresa, was beloved. Moreover, she now knew as much about war as many of her generals. Her soldiers' love may not always have kept them in line when the bullets began to fly, but it was important in getting them to the battlefield.

The Battle of Kolin

Frederick had only 32,000 men at his disposal, while Daun had at least 44,000 men, perhaps as many as 60,000. Under the circumstances, one would expect that Daun would be on the offensive, trying to break through to the besieged city. But Daun was cautious, both by nature and because he was facing Frederick the Great, who had encamped somewhat to his northwest. Also he had lost Browne, the one commander he could rely upon for initiative and daring. He dug his army in along the ridges of two rolling hills, most of his army facing north, where a road ran parallel to their lines, the rest protecting the left flank. There he awaited the Prussian attack. He could not imagine the Prussian king remaining inactive. Not with Russian and French armies closing in on ancestral lands in Prussia and on the Rhineland.

Frederick did not disappoint him. Moreover, his tactics could be easily anticipated – a flank attack. But on which flank? The left was closest, which was the reason Daun had put so many reserves there. Seeing this, Frederick led his blue-coated men up the road eastward past that position. Was this a feint? Daun watched from the most pronounced height, Przerovsky hill, as the Prussians moved across his front to face him, while Frederick, having called a halt for his men to recover from the heat, went to the upper story of a scruffy inn named Novi Mesto (New Town) and studied Daun's position with a telescope. The Austrian right wing seemed vulnerable perhaps. Although the village of Krzeczor had strong earthworks dating from the time of Gustavus Adolphus, there seemed to be nobody there or on the high hill behind it. If Frederick could get past Krzeczor, he could outflank the whole position and roll up Daun's line. Carlyle wrote of this decisive location: 'That easternmost Village of this is spelt "Krzeczhorz" (unpronounceable to mankind), a dirty little place; in and round which the Battle had its hinge or cardinal point: the others, as abstruse of spelling, all but equally impossible to the human organs, we will forbear to name, except in case of necessity.'[5]

As it happened, Frederick's van turned towards the Austrians too soon – causing some units to charge straight up towards prepared positions on Przerovsky hill held by more numerous forces, rather than outflanking Daun's trenches. This may have been the result of harassment by Croatian skirmishers, so that the Prussian cavalry could not reconnoitre the battlefield properly, but it may have been Frederick's having seen dust from behind Daun's lines – dust caused, in fact, by troops hurrying from the left flank towards Krzeczor hill. Carlyle, with his usual Olympian overview of events, florid language and Presbyterian certainty, called it a mistake and put the blame squarely on the king.

Frederick had dispatched cavalry to drive the Austrians away, thereby allowing infantry to move swiftly up the hill, but as they reached the summit, they found their white-coated enemies waiting. The Austrians were exhausted, but they drove the Prussians back. Following the retreating blue coats too incautiously, they lost contact with the cavalry on their right and became the victim of a crushing flank attack.

Daun, who had led military exercises on this very ground the previous autumn, was not rattled. He sent reinforcements – among them the Botta and Deutschmeister (Teutonic Knights) regiments – to Krzeczor hill. The main Austrian cavalry force was still fighting a fluid combat with the Prussians, but Serbelloni[6] hurried forward to guard the right flank; his cavalrymen held their positions through a hail of cannonballs and canister shot, then made repeated devastating charges until almost his entire command had been killed.

Meanwhile, the outnumbered Austrians on the hill refused to flee even after exhausting their ammunition – they fixed their bayonets and fought on. Through a long and hot afternoon their numbers diminished steadily, but not their courage. Daun shifted every unengaged regiment to that flank, and Frederick did the same. The confusion of battle was almost beyond description: charges and counter-charges, entire units shot to pieces, units retreating and reforming, new regiments thrown into the slaughter. Artillery pieces were taken and lost, ammunition was distributed in the very middle of combat; second lines moved up to give the front lines momentary relief, but the rattle of musket and artillery fire never slackened. Late in the afternoon Prussian cavalry almost broke the Austrian lines. Just as many Habsburg regiments began melting away, an order arrived for the others to retreat. That would have led to the dissolution of the army, but most of Daun's men ignored the command. Their lines held.

Elsewhere on the battlefield, on Przerovsky hill, Prussian infantry staggered back repeatedly from the concentrated musket fire out of hilltop trenches; Hungarian hussars broke through the line and took the Prussian camp – the need to loot, however, stopped what could have been a decisive envelopment of Frederick's army, and Prussian cavalry, arriving at the battlefield at the last instant, managed to restore order. At one point Frederick pointed his sword at the Austrian position and started forward, alone, until his staff stopped him.

The story that Frederick yelled at his retreating troops, 'Rucker, wollt ihr ewig leben?' (Cowards, do you want to live forever?) may be true, but not the commander's response, 'Fritz, for eight Groschen, this day there has been enough.' Carlyle's quote implies that if you want men to die for you, you should pay them better.

There was still a chance for victory on Krzeczor hill, where a Prussian column was moving straight into a gap in the Austrian lines. Units from the Austrian Netherlands and Saxony fired into the flanks of the Prussians while Serbelloni led a cavalry charge that reduced every formation to momentary chaos. It almost became a massacre, but the unthinking discipline of the Prussian army made it possible to form a new line – totally ragged and thoroughly un-Prussian – until they ran out of ammunition. Then they turned on their heels and marched away. The Austrians did not follow the retreating blue coats, but only watched in amazement.

As the end of the long summer day approached, both armies were totally exhausted; dead and dying lay everywhere – men and animals screamed in pain. Prussian soldiers ceased to go forward again to certain death; nor did their officers ask them to. Even Frederick left the battlefield, believing that the day was irretrievably lost.

Daun let them leave. There was no serious pursuit until the next day. Not only were the Austrians exhausted, but they had too much respect for the Prussian soldiers and their king to take the slightest risk. Fortunately for Frederick, there were no television cameras to show that he had fallen into such a deep depression that he could not even issue orders.

At this point most historians heap criticism on the Austrian commander, but Brauer and van Tuyll do not. They argue that Daun had to preserve the Austrian army at all cost, because Prussia was not the only enemy in the field. Therefore, fighting Frederick to a draw was an accomplishment worthy both of high praise and of the compliments that the Prussians themselves grudgingly conceded. The Austrians were not as well trained as the Prussians, but they were courageous and competently led.

Frederick, having lost fourteen thousand men to Daun's nine thousand, withdrew from Bohemia in near despair, knowing that his other enemies were closing in on him.

The empress's joy was expressed through her creating the Order of Maria Theresa, Austria's highest decoration for valour. As other rulers were recognising that they could inspire officers to perform acts of patriotic valour by means other than a pay rise, they began awarding gaudy but relatively inexpensive medals and sashes instead of estates and titles.

The Battles at Rossbach and Leuthen

By early November 1757 Frederick's situation seemed desperate: the Swedes were moving down from the north, a French army had overrun Hanover, a Russian army had occupied East Prussia, while an Austrian force was moving through Silesia. Worse, a combined French and Austrian army under Charles Alexander was crossing Saxony into Brandenburg, an army with almost twice the 35,000 men at Frederick's disposal.

Just as most onlookers deemed the king's position hopeless, Frederick struck at the Austro-French army while it was strung out on the roads to the south. At Rossbach he came in on the flank with charging cavalry, routing the van – mostly French – then following up so relentlessly with infantry that observers considered the Austrian commander's success in rallying his forces a miracle of sorts.

When Charles Alexander established a line of field fortifications at Leuthen in December, Fredrick saw a weakness that nobody else detected. Frederick knew that most of the 65,000 Austrian and French troops had not yet seen combat, and although they could defend trenches effectively, they lacked the self-confidence of Prussian troops. No wonder this: they knew that their commander had been beaten often.

Frederick noticed that the allied lines were not formed up exactly opposite his, but overlapped his left considerably. Others might have worried that this would allow a flanking movement, but the king had assessed his opponents perfectly – knowing that the Austrians and French would remain behind their fortifications, he ordered a feint on the left (actually more towards the centre), then, his march hidden behind a ridgeline, struck hard on the right. The concentrated weight of his artillery and infantry drove the Austrians out of their prepared positions, after which his cavalry swept them from the field. Though Charles Alexander skilfully formed a new line of battle, repeatedly charges of Prussian infantry broke his formations, after which cavalry completed the rout. Frederick had lost almost 6,400 men, but his army had slain 10,000 Austrians and captured 12,000.

Leuthen was Frederick's most famous use of a concentration on one wing, then attacking in echelon. It is widely cited in military textbooks, including Clausewitz's *Art of War*, as an example of great generalship. Whether he could have achieved the same success against a more daring Austrian general is not clear – the empress gave better men little opportunity to demonstrate their skills.[7]

Charles Alexander reformed what remained of his army, but kept it well out of Prussian striking range, leaving Frederick free to concentrate on other opponents. The Prussian king was not uniformly victorious, but the chief defect of any alliance – a reluctance to risk casualties – worked to his advantage. Otherwise, being at the end of his resources, he would have gone down. Replacing his well-trained veterans with newly hired mercenaries was possible only because of the British subsidies and his exploiting the lands his armies occupied. Neither were dependable resources.

Drill and More Drill

Frederick the Great's successes were studied, then lessons drawn from them. What contemporaries saw was an army that worked like a finely tuned machine. In practice, it wasn't quite so perfect, but it had beaten all that France, Austria and Russia could send against him. All of those states soon introduced similar drills, hoping to match the quality of the Prussian soldier; all increased the size of their armies, on the principle that two or three such soldiers are more likely to prevail over one Prussian than relying on their generals to match up to the Prussian king.

The implications of this for mercenaries are obvious: military duty was coming to resemble a form of servitude rather than service. Since larger armies could not be manned by recruitment, the state relied on conscription rather than on voluntary enlistments. Prisoners of war were enticed or coerced into service, but those who refused were often exchanged in order to fill the depleted ranks with trained men. While conscription was a good way to acquire cannon-fodder, it could not provide competent officers. Unhappy with the prospect of bringing retired officers back into service, of summoning failed officers from garrison duty where they normally could do little harm, or calling up teenage cadets from military academies, they sent out word that there were opportunities for foreign officers. Frederick the Great offered both employment and promotions.

War ministers who paid attention to Prussian innovations such as field exercises, better maps and requiring officers to spend time with their troops found that their armies improved. Minor German princes with such armies could rent them out profitably.

Mercenaries or Exiles?

Christopher Duffy, in the very middle of *The Wild Goose and the Eagle*, reminds us that foreign officers and men were not always what we think of as mercenaries; rather they were exiles who yearned to return home. To return to a country purged of its hereditary oppressors, one might add. While they rarely changed from one army to a recent enemy, their employers failed to appreciate fully either their loyalty or their deeds, but treated them as mercenaries. Duffy does not agree with this, but acknowledges that there *is* a question about how to classify them. Perhaps looking at them case by case would help.

Maximilian von Browne made the transition from Irish to Austrian successfully; he was buried with honours in the Capuchin church in Vienna – where tourists can visit his monument today. His sons both rose to high rank in the army, partly because he had personally supervised their military training, employing them as aides. He had hoped to place the youngest, Joseph Ulysses Maria Browne, as commander of the *Deutschmeister* regiment in 1752, but budget cut-backs led to intense infighting for the few commands remaining, and Browne, though powerful at court, learned that there were others yet more influential. Joseph Browne was wounded in the foot at the battle of Hochkirch in 1758, where 80,000 Austrians overwhelmed Frederick the Great's 31,000 Prussians; he was seemingly making a good recovery when he was overcome by a sudden fever and died. The elder son, Philip George Browne, distinguished himself at Hochkirch – receiving both the Order of Maria Theresa and a promotion – but after the conclusion of peace in 1763, he retired to his estates and married. He was among the Irish officers invited to a St Patrick's Day celebration in Vienna by the Spanish ambassador, a splendid occasion with the entire court wearing the Irish cross in honour of the guests. When Philip died in 1803, the Browne line – then three generations long – expired too.[8]

Some mercenaries, of course, were less noble. Some were poor souls drafted or kidnapped into service, and some were simply criminals. Trevelyan described this later class in *The American Revolution*:

> As always during a long peace, Europe swarmed with a nomad population of mercenaries. The tramps and vagrants of military life, they would serve one month in Turin, and another at Munich, and the next at Stuttgart; taking to the fields at the first opportunity which offered itself as soon as they had secured a bounty. They played this game in France, in Austria, in Holland, and (much more cautiously, and only as a desperate resource) in Prussia.

This was the most generous of his more extended comments!

Changing Values in Russia

The complicated war with Sweden that broke out in 1741 saw some of Peter Lacy's most brilliant victories. Although Swedish machinations had assisted in overthrowing Anna's choice as her successor – Ivan VI (then only eight months old, with his mother, Anna Leopoldovna, quickly replacing Biron as regent) – the new tsarina, Elizabeth, refused to give up the Baltic states and sent Peter Lacy to drive the Swedes away from St Petersburg.[9] With the conclusion of a victorious peace, Lacy returned to his quiet governorship, while Elizabeth grew ever more hostile to Frederick the Great. Soon, opposition to all things German, cultural and political, was imperial policy;[10] French language, culture and political influence increased (even as did a surge of enthusiasm for authentic Russian culture). Of course, enthusiasm for French culture was not a Russian phenomenon alone; it did mean that fewer Germans were recruited for service in the Russian army.

Elizabeth's determination to remove German officers from high command gave opportunities to two native Russians to demonstrate their talents. The most famous was Alexander Suvorov (1729–1800), who fought the Turks in 1773–4 and the French in Italy in 1799, but contemporaries considered Peter Alexandrovich Rumyantsev (1725–96) more important. Rumyantsev was the son of one of Peter the Great's favourites and a well-travelled mother who was a society favourite wherever she went. Indeed, there were rumours that he was actually the tsar's son. Rumyantsev fought in the most desperate battles of the Seven Years War, once opening the way for Russian armies to occupy Berlin.

The tsarina's anti-Prussian policy became more pronounced in the last years of her declining health; after her death the youthful Peter III abandoned the alliance with Austria and sided with his hero, Frederick of Prussia. Most historians consider this a foolish decision, made without any effort to negotiate for advantages, but Showalter, in *The Wars of Frederick the Great*, says that Peter's assessment of the situation was correct – that Prussia was no danger to Russia. Hence, there had been no good reason to join in the war to begin with. However, in abandoning it just as victory was at hand, Peter made a fatal mistake – his officers and courtiers, thinking he was a foolish boy in a feeble man's body, replaced him with his obviously more intelligent wife, Catherine II.

There was no danger of the generals, nobles or churchmen objecting that no woman could govern Holy Mother Russia – that principle was now well established. But traditionalists observed that she was German by birth, Protestant by upbringing and eventually had four illegitimate children by three different men. Turning her back on both Elizabeth's and Peter's policies, Catherine remained neutral in the Seven Years War. Why risk a defeat? Then she surrounded herself with Russian generals who had proven their ability.

The best of these, Rumyantsev, took his father's place as governor of the Ukraine, one of the most difficult assignments any man could receive. The vast steppe was populated lightly by runaway serfs, Cossacks, Tatars and other steppe peoples. His efforts to bring order to the region have been assessed a number of times, especially his policy of discouraging runaways from coming south by immediately placing them in serfdom again.

Towards the Partition of Poland and Turkey

When Augustus III of Poland died in 1763, it was clear that the tsarina's choice of a successor was sure to prevail in the end, no matter how many Poles wanted to argue the matter; in fact, the Diet was not even easily brought together, much less quickly persuaded to vote for her candidate. Not a patient woman, Catherine sent in her army to make Stanislas Poniatowski king.[11] Not unsurprisingly, Polish patriots resisted. The nobility, after decades of bowing to the superiority of foreign armies, had been insulted once too often. They may have become accustomed to Saxon kings, but to accept the lover of the tsarina, even if he was Polish, was too much. That was to admit that the long conflict with Russia had ended in total defeat. Or so they thought. They had no idea yet how total defeat could be.

The Polish army was courageous, but the Russian army was larger and ready for war. Thus, it was not a fair match. After the Russian victory, some Polish officers and men fled into Turkey and persuaded the sultan's officials that a similar fate awaited them. The Ottoman sultan, Mustafa III (1717–74), had already begun to reform the Ottoman army by bringing in foreign officers and introducing modern weapons; most importantly, the sultan had hired a French officer, Baron Tott, to manage the artillery.[12] Turkey was not yet ready for war, but when Catherine annexed the Crimea and large parts of eastern Poland–Lithuania, including the Ukraine, the sultan was persuaded that the balance of power was being tipped. In 1768, when Polish patriots rose against the Russian army of occupation, Mustafa, with French encouragement, declared war.

This conflict finally brought the Romanov dynasty the victories which had eluded Catherine's predecessors. Rumyantsev abandoned linear tactics in favour of columns, which could quickly form large squares to repel the swarms of Turkish and Tatar horsemen. His mobile artillery tore holes in the janissaries' lines, after which bayonet charges swept them from the field. He captured Azov (again) in 1768, then crossed into Moldavia (modern Romania). By 1770 Russian armies were on the Danube; meanwhile, a Russian fleet had sailed out of the Baltic, around Europe and destroyed the Turkish fleet in the Aegean.

Russia and Austria had earlier agreed that they should profit equally from the dismemberment of the Ottoman Empire. Now, however, Maria Theresa's army was unprepared to join in; consequently, she could not profit when Mustafa's janissaries revolted, dealing a final blow to his frail health. Mustafa's successor was his gentle and naive brother, Abdul Hamid (1725–89), a man with no experience in government and totally incapable of rising to the Russian military challenge. The decisive battle was fought in the rain in the Crimea in June 1774. The Russian infantry kept their cartridges in leather pouches, not in cloth ones as the janissaries did, and consequently had dry powder. Presumably both sides had praised God, but not equally effectively. Tott lost twenty-five cannon, the battle and the war.

This was Rumyantsev's last major command. He had already roused the jealousy of Catherine's latest lover, Potemkin, who had passed on his recommendations as if they were his own, then taken over many of his offices.[13] Rumyantsev suspected Potemkin of denying him needed supplies during the Turkish war, but that may have simply been a breakdown of transport over the long distances from the Russian heartland. Uprising in 1773 was seen as a major event, but it was actually the moment when Cossack power was finally broken for good, never to revive. As usual, the Cossack timing was incredibly bad.

The Russian advance southwards had alarmed both Frederick the Great and Maria Theresa, who believed that a tsarina occupying both Poland and the Balkans would be just too powerful. By annexing small territories in Poland, these two monarchs sent a message that the Russian army should stop its advance and that the tsarina should start negotiations for peace. The problem was how to persuade Catherine to go back on her announcement that she would rescue the Orthodox Christians from persecution; the answer, agreed upon in 1772, was to allow her to rescue only those in the eastern reaches of the Commonwealth who were complaining about Polish Catholic oppression. By dividing one-third of Poland–Lithuania between Russia, Prussia and Austria, Catherine could remove that kingdom as a danger to Russia forever, Frederick could make his eastern lands a contiguous territory, and Maria Theresa would take Poland's rich southern provinces. The remainder, with the cities of Cracow, Warsaw and Vilnius, was left to Catherine's protégé.

Norman Davies, in *God's Playground*, observes that this was not the first time in world history that a nation had been cannibalised, but it was scandalous that European princes had eaten a fellow European.

The sultan saved himself in a similar way – territorial concessions. In 1775 he surrendered Bukovina to Maria Theresa, bringing her empire closer to the Black Sea. It would have been wiser for the sultan to have given her even more land, putting Austria right across the most direct Russian route to Constantinople, but few statesmen are capable of persuading foreign patriots to abandon an inch of national patrimony. Even fewer have the imagination to present their enemies such a poisoned pill. As a result, it was easy for Catherine to raise new demands later.

The Dismemberment of Poland–Lithuania

The decrepit condition of Poland–Lithuania in this era has been bemoaned by generations of Polish patriots and political philosophers. The combination of an elective kingship, nobles overly zealous of protecting their rights, clergy fearful of competition and heresy, Lithuanians fearful for their language and culture, and powerful, aggressive neighbours doomed this far-flung and culturally rich state.

The problems were widely recognised at the time, even in the Commonwealth itself. But often the defects were considered virtues: as neighbouring states moved away from what Germans called a *Ständestaat* (government by estates, meaning sharing power between the king, the nobles, the gentry, the clergy and the cities) towards more royal authority, Poles prided themselves on having retained their ancient liberties; as serfdom disappeared in the west, Poles defended it as necessary for nobles, like ancient Romans, to devote themselves to politics and war; when foreign parliaments adopted majority rule, Poles insisted that every decision be unanimous. As would-be kings bargained away their few remaining rights to win elections, foreign powers learned to bribe powerful nobles and factions. In 1717 Peter the Great had used bayonets to force the nobles and clergy to silently assent to his wishes. His successors kept the Polish military budget absurdly low so that there could be no resistance to their dictates – and they rejected quiet proposals to divide up the nation mainly because they saw no reason to share what they could perhaps take over in its entirety.

The Polish nobility, seeing that their role in government had become as much a mockery as the king's pretences at leadership, withdrew to their country estates and ignored the nation's slide into impotent irrelevance. Rather too late the French realised that their intrigues had only contributed to the crisis leading to the partition. On the principle that 'one's neighbour is an enemy, the neighbour's neighbour is a friend', France had always been seen by Poland as a potential ally against the Habsburgs. The Seven Years War had violated this principle; afterwards France could not count on Prussia offsetting Habsburg and Romanov ambitions. What future Polish king could turn the situation around? That was the question raised by the insurgents in the Confederacy of Bar (1768–72), who sought to replace Stanislas Poniatowski with anyone who had more to contribute to Poland than a reputation for having seduced the tsarina.[14]

Among the many princes who hoped against hope for election was Frederick II of Hesse-Kassel, who might seem both strong enough and weak enough to satisfy all parties; his conversion to Catholicism was an obvious imitation of Augustus the Strong seven decades earlier, and was plausible enough that a delegation from Poland visited him in 1770. He similarly emulated Augustus's contemporary, Frederick the Great's grandfather, in recruiting an elite unit of tall, handsome guardsmen whom he paid double the wages of common soldiers. But the Russian army ended all discussion of possible alternative futures for Poland, crushing resistance and driving the insurgent leaders into exile.

The pattern set in 1772 was followed easily by a second (1793) and third partition (1794–5), occurring as they did while Western Europe was distracted by the French Revolution. The Poles fought back, but their valour was unequal to the mercenary armies of the three black eagles (the symbols of Austria, Russia and Prussia); Poland's white eagle succumbed.

Henceforth, political philosophers used the Polish–Lithuanian Commonwealth as an example of why representative government could not work. Since demagogues would work on popular feelings to prevent the passage of necessary legislation and would hinder generals in defending the nation, power had to be kept in the hands of kings and their close advisors.

Austria and Russia Attack Turkey

Russia began the war in 1787, followed – as per agreement – by Austria's attack. The Russians were momentarily distracted by a minor war with Sweden, but soon Suvorov was pushing south relentlessly, winning victories that forced the sultan to concede defeat. While population increase had made Russian armies irresistible, McNeill wrote in *The Pursuit of Power* that the immediate effect in Russia was to confirm traditional practices, unlike the transformative effect that population growth had in the West. If the Russian peasant was terribly poor, he was either too ignorant or too clever to complain. In the short run (decades) Russia could copy Western successes while avoiding the inevitable failures that accompany experimentation; since state-run armaments industries could never go bankrupt, there were weapons in abundance. In the long run, the system was fatally flawed – control from the top made administrators at the bottom cautious. However, since Russia's principal enemy, Ottoman Turkey, was even less innovative, Russian arms were more than good enough.

Nevertheless, Western experts were repeatedly frustrated by their inability to employ their skills fully. Intrigues crippled the ambitions of the American naval hero, John Paul Jones, who joined Catherine's navy in 1788.[15] His successes aroused Potemkin's jealousy, so that he was recalled to St Petersburg and dismissed, his sole reward being the medal of St Anne. Jones returned to France, then in the throes of its great revolution, and died in Paris before he could find employment.

The Austrians did well against the Turks at first, Count Franz Lacy (1725–1801) taking Belgrade. Then rebellions broke out in the Austrian Netherlands and Hungary, and the Prussian king began to rattle his sabre. Equally importantly, the French Revolution had begun. With the Austrian army in the Balkans, there was no way that either Austrian emperor, Joseph II (died 1790) or Leopold II, could go to the rescue of their sister, Marie Antoinette, the queen of France.

In 1789, when the French Revolution began, royalist supporters confidently expected to crush the revolutionaries because so many of the officers had fled the country. France was a weakened state, much like Poland earlier. As Simms notes in *Three Victories and a Defeat*, feckless royal policies had cost the kingdom much – its German allies made into enemies, Poland partly dismembered and Sweden and Turkey weakened too, its colonies lost and the nation bankrupted. Now who could lead the French armies? With the king a prisoner, who could unify the nation to fight the armies of foreign kings?

Consequently, it came as a surprise to most Europeans that the army of the French Republic did, in fact, defend the frontiers. This was partly because each king in the royal coalition was ready to hold back and allow the others to shed the blood of their soldiers, weakening them, so that when traditional politics returned, the king with the most intact army would prevail. It was partly because the French officer corps was replaced relatively quickly, thanks to the royal military schools having trained many talented young men who, under normal circumstances, would have spent their careers as mid-level officers.

Lynn, in *Battle*, provocatively suggests that reforms designed to open military careers to talent actually cemented the aristocrats' control of the officer corps. Old families with few resources were being replaced by wealthy upstart newcomers, but once commanders had state money to spend, aristocrats with ancient lineage but little money brought their influence at court to bear to gain the coveted posts; moreover, they could afford to live in great luxury again, more lavishly than they could at home – a practice that confirmed their status as great lords.

Revolutionary Armies

Max Boot argues that the 'levy en masse' of the French Revolution was less revolutionary than we customarily believe. First, both population and industry had grown to the point that nations could provide soldiers for larger armies and equip them without destroying the economy; second, Enlightenment thought had opened the way to new ideas in every aspect of human activity, including the military; third, discussions about recent battles and campaigns had resulted in proposals for sweeping reforms. Also, it is in the nature of human affairs that defeated nations are most open to new ideas, and the French had lost three major wars in a row.

French officers were talking about the armies once again living off the land rather than moving from fortress to fortress: this would increase the speed of advance and manoeuvre. A new combination of arms – the division – allowed officers to co-ordinate attacks more effectively. The value of shock – especially a charge by masses of men and horse – was becoming more appreciated. Artillery became more mobile and effective. There was reluctant awareness that men of the lower orders could be effective commanders – resulting in Napoleon Bonaparte, a lowly Corsican, being trained as an artillerist at the French military academy. The importance of numbers was stressed, using half-trained troops in 'columns' rather than lines of battle. The columns were often masses of men rather than marching units, but that hardly mattered – speed and numbers were more important than smartness, and if the enemy line melted away before the massed bayonets reached them, all the better.

Still, as Black reminds us in *Warfare in the Eighteenth Century*, the old system was not swept away entirely. Patriotic determination was necessary for effective shock tactics, and talented officers were needed to direct the new formations – lacking those, there was no point to changing a system that worked fairly well. The problem may have been, as Christopher Clark suggests in *Iron Kingdom*, that the Prussian army simply failed to keep abreast of the developments in warfare; instead, it had concentrated on drills that sent the troops marching impressively into a French killing machine based on the employment of combined arms. But this might have been unavoidable. At Frederick the Great's death, 110,000 of his 195,000 men were foreigners; such troops were less motivated, more unruly and more likely to desert. Therefore, the Prussian army hesitated to use its jägers aggressively, and the artillery was still a separate branch of the service.

Napoleon's army dominated the battlefield for years, and Leo Tolstoy could argue in *War and Peace* (1869) that its commander was essentially irrelevant once he had brought the army to the battlefield. From that point on, he argued, the lower ranks of officers and the common soldier fought almost without direction. While Tolstoy's insight had some merit, it was fundamentally wrong to think that officers had no role in determining the outcome of battles. Nevertheless, that idea appealed to Marxists who were looking for additional reasons to declare the ruling class obsolete – reasons other than the fact that the nobility's roles in society and government were diminishing decade by decade.

Soldiers' behaviour did reflect the routine of training and discipline, not an instinctive understanding of what had to be done, but only officers could direct the troops' fury against the right part of the enemy formations, or order the regiments to adjust to new threats and opportunities. In one sense it was certainly true that the most essential challenge was to train an army, motivate it, then get it to the right battlefield at the right moment, but there were decisive differences between the ways similarly armed forces performed – for example, those armies led by Frederick the Great and those commanded by Daun. One difference was leadership. Another was morale. Yet another luck. Not every general is lucky.

Daun was not a bad commander, but he was not a king. Frederick did not have to explain his failures to anyone. Daun would have to face Maria Theresa.

Proven ability was so highly valued that rulers continued to look for successful officers from abroad. Foreigners who had demonstrated their ability to lead and were also obviously lucky were more likely to win battles than home-grown officers whose sole luck seemed to have been in being born into the right families and not dying of childhood diseases or in epidemics. Nevertheless, Showalter notes that Frederick removed most of his middle-class officers as soon as he could. The reason seemed to be that, not having the class connections to save them from blame for minor mistakes, they tended to avoid taking unnecessary risks. Nobles may have been idiots, but they were self-confident idiots.

CHAPTER EIGHT

Hessians in America

It seems almost impossible today to imagine how professional soldiers from central Germany could have been sent to fight in Britain's North American colonies; it seemed impossible at the time, too, until shortly before they disembarked on Staten Island in New York harbour. They were the best-dressed assistant tax-collectors Americans had ever seen, more resplendent even than the redcoats who had failed to keep order in Boston.

In retrospect, one can see how one British policy after another led Americans first to peaceful resistance to new taxes, then, in 1775, to take up arms against the king. It was not just that the prime ministers and their cabinets were incompetent or corrupt — they were perhaps little worse in these respects than their predecessors. However, they misjudged the situation, and they misjudged their own power. Business as usual meant treating outsiders and rivals with contempt, rewarding themselves and their friends, and mistaking conversational brilliance for good ideas. Most of all, they thought of Americans much like they thought of the Irish and Scots — as somewhat less than Englishmen. Nor was it only British noblemen, government officers and petty bureaucrats who considered themselves superior to every colonist; but ordinary Britons did as well.

The complexity of British politics is often obscured by imagining that the Whigs and Tories were modern parties. It would be more accurate to say that the division was between Whigs in power and Whigs out; the Tories had essentially sailed their vessel onto the rocks of Jacobinism and sunk, seemingly forever. However, because George III (for a variety of reasons, good and bad) hated the leading Whig politicians personally, he called to office a new group known as the king's party; historians have traditionally called this government Tory, and the opposition Whig, and it is best to leave it at that. As Lewis Namier remarked in *England in the Age of the American Revolution*, there was a distinct Whig and Tory mentality, but in practice the political game was played by humans whose actions confounded logic. The same might well be said of Britons across the sea, that is, Americans.

Americans had long considered themselves loyal subjects of the crown, equal in every way to true-born Englishmen. George Washington (1732–99), though among the richest plantation owners in Virginia, would happily have joined the royal army, but colonials were not good enough. And if no colonial could buy a commission, what were the chances of any ever being awarded a peerage?

The question of taxes – how they were raised and why – had become serious after the end of the Seven Years War. As Ferguson notes in *Empire*, the average Briton paid twenty-six shillings a year in taxes, while the average American paid one; not surprisingly, Parliament and the British public believed that Americans should pay more. In response, Americans pointed to their charters, granting colonists the sole right to tax themselves directly – customs duties were something else, something an inventive smuggler could evade easily – and to the contributions they had made in what they called the French and Indian War (1754–63). Britons soon followed Dr Johnson in mocking American declarations of liberty while holding slaves. Americans responded that Britons were complicit in the slave trade and that what went on in the West Indies was worse than anything seen in Virginia or the Carolinas. Mutual insults grew louder and more common. Family quarrels are often vicious.

Americans resisted with boycotts of British goods – eventually learning to drink coffee instead of tea – and by forming 'Committees of Correspondence' to co-ordinate efforts to appeal over the heads of the Tory governments to King George III, and over the head of the king to the British people and the Whig opposition. Only the latter effort was successful – so successful that the parliamentary majority became angrier than before. Who were these colonials – unmilitary, whining tax-evaders – to challenge the judgement of their betters? Then they actually met together in Philadelphia, in a laughable assembly grandly called the Continental Congress. What a joke!

Where did these colonials get such ideas? It was well known that God was an Englishman. That is, there was no other explanation for the string of British victories against enemies more numerous and inherently richer, except perhaps the tradition of British liberty. And *there* was the problem. If the Tory government had forgotten the lessons of the Whig revolution that brought William III to the throne in 1688–9, Americans had not. The principle of self-government was 'self-evident', that is, governments are instituted to secure rights of the people and if the government failed in that duty, the people had the right to change the government. The heart of the American argument concerned John Locke's 'contract theory', in that the royal charters had established basic rights that the government was attempting to revoke. The short version of the proper relationship was 'No taxation without representation': the British government should either not impose taxes other than customs duties or give the colonists seats in Parliament. The American plaints were familiar in Ireland, where the interests of the common people were hardly taken into consideration; there only the landowners – many the beneficiaries of William III's grants – counted, and even their powers, represented in the Irish parliament, had been weakened by royal appointments, parliamentary law and Tory policies.

Nevertheless, at the start of the American crisis in 1765 some colonial leaders suggested that an American parliament on the Irish model would resolve both the constitutional question and the disputes over taxes. Whatever the limitations of an Irish-style parliament, they could not imagine a country as rich as America filled with starving people – as Ireland was. Had the king's party been sufficiently far-sighted to make such an offer, or to give one or two seats in Parliament to each colony in the New World, events might have played out differently. However, the king's party understood that a compromise with Americans might be followed by demands to reform the entire system at home, top to bottom, and neither they nor the Whig opposition welcomed that idea. They thought small – personal reputations, a bribe here and there and royal patronage – and acted small. They believed that the budget crisis could be solved most easily by appointing governors themselves and by raising taxes on peoples who had no legal means of resisting them. Their disdain of American interests was expressed by heaping insults and scorn on Dr Franklin, a wealthy retired publisher, inventor, philanthropist and internationally famed scientist from Philadelphia, who had come to London to represent Pennsylvania's interests in these matters. His assistance during the French and Indian War was forgotten. When he went home, he vowed that British insolence would eventually be repaid, with interest.

British officers had returned from the recent war thoroughly disgusted with Americans. They could not understand their subjects' insistence on the contractual details of their service, their lax discipline, their insistence that their officers were equal to any Briton of the same rank, and their taking cover when shot at by Indians. Colonialists, in turn, learned that British officers and troops looked down on them, and that they had little respect for the rights listed in colonial charters.[1]

New taxes were necessary, the king's ministers insisted, to pay for the recent war, which they said Britons had fought to defend America against the French. Americans, who knew well how few British troops had been sent to their aid, rejected that argument – the war was over British interests in Europe, and the debt had accumulated because of subsidies paid to Prussia. Americans understood that British nobles paid few taxes, and that the lower tax on tea, as well as giving the East India Company a monopoly in America, were deceitful methods of rescuing their party's investors. They were insulted that the government expected them to be so eager for cheap tea that they would abandon constitutional principles. Lastly, when redcoats were sent to America, they were not stationed on the frontier, to protect them against the Indians, but in the cities, where it appeared they would be used to collect taxes.

Parliament's response was to treat Americans as they would protestors in Ireland or Scotland. But the king's party had forgotten, if they even knew, how many Irish and Scots they had transported to America, or who had been forced by poverty to emigrate – but those men and women had not forgotten, much less forgiven, the British for the injustices they had suffered. Nor were Americans of English descent any less worried. These memories and fears were reinforced when it was learned that the British government had hired German troops to suppress colonial resistance and restore royal authority.

So obvious was this that sometimes it comes as a surprise to find that half of Americans were either in agreement with royal policies, or willing to make concessions, or did not care. Parliament could have worked with this large block of citizens, but failed to do so.

Memories of the French and Indian War

Parliament's decision to employ mercenaries in America was partly based on bitter experiences in the recent war in America. Casualties had been high among the forces involved, Indian tactics disconcerting, and the endless forests daunting – in the first great battle, in July 1755, General Braddock's Highlanders and redcoats were cut to pieces in western Pennsylvania, with over five hundred men lost. Braddock had expected to drive the French from Fort Duquesne easily, then from the Ohio country, but he was ambushed just short of his goal. The regulars had fired volleys blindly into the woods, cutting down many colonial auxiliaries who were between them and the howling Indians, then fled, panic-stricken, from the scene of combat. It was not only a disaster, it was embarrassing; worse, it was a lesson for Americans that Britons were not all-wise and all-conquering. Two future American officers were eyewitnesses of the debacle – Washington and Gates. Walter Borneman notes in *The French and Indian War* that George Howe, the younger brother of the two British commanders assigned in 1776 to put down the rebellion, modelled the first British Light Infantry on an American unit of frontiersmen, Roger's Rangers, in order to prevent such ambushes in the future; however, he died in 1758, fighting the French north of Albany in New York.

A second campaign, conducted by Henry Bouquet, a Swiss soldier in a British uniform, reached Fort Duquesne in 1758 only hours after the French had burned it and withdrawn. In *The British Empire Before the American Revolution*, Lawrence Henry Gipson reported that when Scottish troops, approaching the smouldering fort, saw the road lined with heads on spikes, trophies taken from Braddock's men, with their kilts draped underneath, they were ready to kill any Native American they encountered. Fort Pitt, which Bouquet erected on its ruins, was soon besieged by frightening savages from Ohio who seemed to lurk everywhere in the surrounding wilderness.

This was more nerve-wracking than dangerous, because Indians would never assault a fort directly. As a result, some European observers came to consider their skulking foe cowards. This was a profound misunderstanding of the Indians' demographic problems – their numbers were declining rapidly, mostly from disease. Warriors could not risk leaving their families without a hunter and protector – Indian society, generous though it was, lacked the infrastructure to care for widows and orphans. Tribes, lacking any taxation system at all and limiting the authority of chiefs, could not pay those who went to war or even compel warriors to go. Moreover, Americans were not the only enemies – the competition with other tribes was fierce; many tribes had been displaced repeatedly in recent decades, and every warrior lost would weaken a tribe's ability to defend itself against both ancient enemies and new ones. Still, they had no doubt that land-hungry Americans would move across the mountains unless frightened away. For all these reasons they employed tactics that minimised casualties and maximised the number of prisoners who could be adopted into the tribe. Whenever a British general proposed a pitched battle, the warriors usually went home, ignoring appeals to their long-term self-interest.

When the Indians found that they could not sustain the siege of Fort Pitt and would soon be subjected to attack, they signed the 1758 'Easton Treaty' with Bouquet, then withdrew from the war. Gipson noted that Indians did not trust the British government to honour Bouquet's pledge to stop Americans from migrating across the Allegheny Mountains, but it was better than no treaty at all.

Britons and Frenchmen alike began to wonder what they were fighting over, if they were to abandon the interior to the dwindling numbers of native peoples. No wonder that many protested, as did one of Voltaire's characters in *Candide*, that men and money were being sacrificed for a few acres of snow (*quelques arpents de neige*), with each nation spending more money than the land was worth. Only the Americans would profit. Let them pay for it.

Canada, in particular, seemed worthless. French policy had limited immigration and restricted the rights of colonists – mostly in an effort to protect the Native Americans, whose numbers were nevertheless plummeting from the effects of disease and wars among the tribes over control of the fur-producing interior. French explorers, trappers and a few army posts stretched up the Saint Lawrence River to the Great Lakes, then over easy portages to great rivers leading to New Orleans in Louisiana. It was an empire of great promise, but of little immediate profit.

The real prize was the sugar islands of the West Indies. However, there was a price to be paid there, too. The heat and humidity were more than even African slaves were accustomed to; they were deadly to Irishmen and Scots who were transported there or enticed into immigrating. Malaria, yellow fever and scurvy cut down many, then piracy, storms and shipwreck took another share; 40 per cent of any regiment sent to the Caribbean died from disease.

Even the mainland colonies were deadly to newcomers – America had such swings of temperature that any one location could be, according to season, both hotter and colder than Europe, and few towns had either good water or adequate housing. Pay was slow, proper clothing unavailable and prices high. This provoked mutinies among those few troops stationed on the frontier in isolated garrisons. Alcoholism and desertion became serious problems, and even peace in 1763 did not bring an end to hostilities, since Pontiac's Rebellion occurred later that year, requiring the government to send back troops that had been preparing to return home. Pontiac, it might be noted, was an important chief in what is today Michigan, far in the interior, an indication of problems to come in dealing with the various Indian nations. As Colin Calloway notes in *The Scratch of a Pen*, the country, the climate and the enemy had no counterparts in Western Europe.

The commander-in-chief from 1758 on, Jeffrey Amherst (1717–97), performed brilliantly in capturing the French fortress at Louisbourg near the mouth of the Saint Lawrence River. It helped that one French regiment, composed of Germans raised to fight Prussia, had been stranded four years at that god-forsaken northern base; they actually yearned to be freed from starvation and cold. With only such troops at the French commander's disposal, one understands his not sending them out to oppose the landing. Amherst captured the fortress, and with it much of the fleet that had been sent to protect Canada.

In 1759 Amherst was ordered to capture Quebec, a fortress overlooking the Saint Lawrence River that was widely thought to be impregnable; moreover, its commander, the marquis de Montcalm, was highly regarded. The French Canadian troops – almost more Indian than the Indians – included Scottish Jacobites like James Johnstone (1719–1800), who was second-in-command. He had been to Russia to visit two of his uncles in tsarist service, but his father would not allow him to become an officer there; over his father's objections he had served as an aide to Bonnie

Prince Charlie in 1745–6. Surviving the battle of Culloden unhurt, he was smuggled by Jacobite friends to London, then to Holland and finally to France, where he enlisted in the French army, then sent to Louisbourg. He was luckily transferred to Quebec before Amherst arrived.

Amherst had been greatly impressed by his own second-in-command at Louisbourg, General James Wolfe (1727–59), who at an early age had fought at Dettingen and Culloden. He had recently come to Pitt's attention for his initiative in a raid on a French port, and sent to America. Amherst appointed him to command the land forces for the attack on Quebec, and provided him strong naval support.

Wolfe was lucky – as most successful officers are – as well as skilful and resourceful. His daring plan to scale the cliffs to the rear of the fortress almost became a disaster, his men still being on the water when a French watchman spotted their boats, but a reply in French by Simon Fraser (1729–77, in command of the 78th Highlanders) satisfied the soldier's curiosity. William Howe (1729–1814) then led a volunteer force up the cliffs to clear away the pickets, permitting the army to use the road to the summit.

Montcalm made a series of mistakes when he discovered that Wolfe's army was just outside his walls. Apparently doubting the willingness of his men to withstand a siege, he led them out to fight before the British force could be reinforced. Charging at run, his lines lost cohesion, after which his men fired too soon, making their volley ineffective. The redcoats and Highlanders kept fire discipline – the first shots at a hundred yards, then a deadly volley at thirty. It was the beginning of the end for French Canada.[2]

In all these campaigns Amherst had the full backing of the secretary of state, William Pitt, who was determined to finish off the French colonial empire, thereby guaranteeing peace for many years to come. When Pitt was replaced by the earl of Bute, Amherst received orders to impose a more direct rule on the Indians (thus prefiguring royal policies towards the colonists) and to save money in every way possible, most specifically by eliminating traditional gifts to chiefs. Amherst applied this economy even to the sale of rum, which he believed only enflamed their child-like animal nature; when he informed William Johnson (1715–74), the agent to the Iroquois and the most important Indian expert in the colonies, that he would not bribe the Indians into good behaviour, Johnson tried to persuade him that friendly Indians needed gunpowder – they could not go back to bows and arrows.

But Amherst had his orders, and he limited Indian supplies to only the amount needed for hunting, as if the forest was now at peace.

The reality was very different. Indians needed goods for commerce with interior tribes, goods they had formerly been able to obtain from the French; English promises to provide these now proved as false as guarantees that no settlers would be allowed to enter the Ohio country – the promise was, in a technical sense, sincere, but colonial farmers and hunters had not waited for permission, and orders to commanders to drive the interlopers out were impossible to enforce. Indian spokesmen had always insisted that they would not fight for hire, and now they learned that they would not receive the traditional gifts for assisting voluntarily or remaining neutral.

Amherst did not even deign to flatter the chiefs. The consumption of tobacco and alcohol was part of the process of diplomacy (only more formal among the Indians than among Europeans, and consumed sitting cross-legged on the ground, a posture that overweight Britons found painful and embarrassing). Amherst negotiated even with British Americans only reluctantly; Indians were far beneath his dignity.

Although gifts were theoretically an exchange, Indians viewed them much as European princes did subsidies – a payment not for services rendered, but as security for an agreement to provide troops when requested. Bute had suspended the subsidy to Prussia as an economy measure, and he almost returned Canada to France in exchange for more profitable sugar islands. Neither Amherst nor Bute saw much advantage to possessing the interior of America or securing the friendship of its native warriors, but they did not want the French back there either.

This stinginess provoked Pontiac's Rebellion in 1763. A frustrated Amherst then enquired of Henry Bouquet – on his way back to beleaguered Fort Pitt – whether smallpox could be employed against the insurgents. Nothing came of this directly, perhaps because of the fear of infecting the Iroquois, but most likely on practical grounds – it would not have been easy to carry out such a plan. Indians were not stupid. Although no action was taken by either Amherst or Bouquet, the acting commander of Fort Pitt, Simon Ecuyer, had already done so on his own. When two Indian chiefs came to demand the fort's surrender, he sent two traders who knew the chiefs' language out to negotiate; when the chiefs insisted on being given gifts, Ecuyer provided the traders with two fine blankets and two linen and silk handkerchiefs out of the smallpox hospital. Ecuyer was, like Bouquet, Swiss; his associates regarded him as a brave and capable officer, not a genocidal maniac.

The siege could not have been too arduous – men in the fort wrote more about the beauty of the women at the balls than about the Indians. It is not clear who instigated the effort at germ warfare: Alexander McKee (the acting deputy superintendent of Indian affairs), William Trent (the merchant) or Ecuyer. In any case, the infected items do not seem to have had the desired effect. Smallpox was already raging through both American settlements and Indian villages; the epidemic could have originated as far back as Montcalm's siege of Fort William Henry in 1757 (featured in Cooper's novel *The Last of the Mohicans* and the movie based on it). The French army at that siege had included 2,700 regulars from the Royal Roussillon (Catalan grenadiers), Languedoc (commanded by the Saxon Baron Dieskau) and other prominent regiments, but Montcalm allowed the British garrison to march away freely with the troops' personal possessions. Some Indians were so disgusted by this that they attacked the camp, massacring the invalids, then fell on the rear of the column marching south under French protection. Montcalm did what he could to protect the prisoners and even to ransom those captured by the Indians. But thereafter the Indians would not fight for Montcalm, and he would not ask them to do so. That was a mistake of the greatest importance – it tipped the balance of power in favour of the British.

For the Indians the mistake had been to loot the hospital, even to dig up the corpses of smallpox victims, unaware that the clothing was still infectious. Who could imagine that the dead could kill as well as the living? As a result, the warriors hurrying west carried with them a disease that soon killed vast numbers of both kinsmen and trading partners.

So prevalent were smallpox outbreaks in these years that it was no surprise that the disease was present at Fort Pitt, nor was it strange that those Americans and Britons who had fallen ill were placed in a hospital outside the fort so as to not infect the soldiers and crowds of refugees inside the walls. In any case, the siege was not lifted because of disease, but because a relief column came to the rescue.

When word arrived that Fort Pitt was under siege, Bouquet had been in Philadelphia. He quickly raised about five hundred Germans, Highlanders and Englishmen and led them west along a new road. Ambushed near Fort Pitt and facing the destruction of his entire force, he abandoned the traditional hollow square in favour of taking cover behind the supplies in the baggage train. The next day he lured the Indians into pursuing a feigned retreat, then closed in with a co-ordinated bayonet charge. He made it to Fort Pitt only to discover that his victory had not been decisive. After a further nine months of siege, with smallpox decimating both the garrison and the civilians who had fled to the fort for protection, he led an expedition into the Ohio country that resulted in the Indians releasing all their white captives. Disgusted at the brutal methods of the frontiersmen in revenging themselves upon the defeated Indians, Bouquet applied for transfer to Pensacola in Florida, where he died of yellow fever in 1765.

The cost of this unnecessary war – known inaccurately as Pontiac's Rebellion from that chief's capture of Detroit – was added to the already heavy debt and the ongoing expense of maintaining hundreds of redcoats in the interior. General Gage, Amherst's successor, thought himself the victor in the campaign, but he had prevailed only by distributing lavish gifts and resuming the trade in rum and gunpowder.[3] The Indians thought themselves the winners, and prepared to act on the principle that a bit of violence now and then would pay off handsomely.

The British government, distressed by the great costs of the campaigns in the wilderness, again promised the Indians that it would forbid migration across the mountains. Having thus laid the basis for peace on the frontier, the government began to withdraw the troops needed to enforce the proclamation; this false economy soon provoked a crisis. Since Indians lacked institutions capable of recruiting and paying border guards, they could not prevent Americans from moving west whenever it seemed safe; the most the tribes could do was to kill any intruders who were not watchful, but even that was not effective – the Americans continued to come. As frontiersmen asked where the redcoats were now that they needed them, they learned that the western lands had been assigned to Quebec, thus closing them out from trade that was allowed to French Canadians.

To make matters worse, at the very moment that the Grenville government was abdicating its authority west of the mountains, it was devising new taxes for the Americans on the pretext that the incomes were needed to pay troops defending the frontier, when they were actually being stationed at half-pay in towns along the coast. Within a year it became an article of faith among colonists that the new taxes were not designed to protect them, nor to pay off loans from the recent war, but were part of a deeper plot to deprive them of their traditional rights and liberties – in short, to make them subjects, not citizens, of a state that thought of them as ignorant, backward and unwarlike. This was very much the attitude that professional officers and soldiers had displayed towards Americans during the war: since Americans lacked the qualities and aptitudes of regular troops, surely there would be no effective resistance to any firmly pressed government policy. America, Ireland, parts of Scotland, India – it was all the same: an empire could not be ruled by weakness and conciliation, an empire needed an army, and armies were expensive.

Tradition put the king at the head of the military and he, not Parliament, entrusted this authority to the secretary of war. At the time this was Lord Barrington, a very capable administrator. Among Barrington's subordinates was the paymaster-general, who was able to pocket large sums legally, and whose subordinates made all contracts for military expenditures for equipment, installations and manpower. The 'system' was elaborate, chaotic and impossible to manage well. Yet, given the geographic dispersion of resources and responsibilities, more central control was impossible.

The Origin of Britain's American Difficulties

The Tory government that struggled with Britain's debts in the years following the victory of 1763 faced three problems.[4] First, somehow they had to pay the creditors (sometimes themselves, often their friends); second, they had to do so without asking the nobles to contribute; and third, they had to answer the mocking comments of Whig critics. Asking colonists to pay their share seemed like a logical and just way to do this. American money would not cover all the needs, but every shilling would help.

The problem was that Americans did not see the matter as the government ministers did, and many Whigs in the opposition supported the Americans. Americans had made extraordinary efforts to raise troops for every campaign, and though Pitt's subsidies and the presence of British troops had injected much money into their cash-starved economy, they were offended by slurs on their martial ability and courage, and they quickly saw that British policy was designed to increase government authority over them in order to impose taxes. Within a decade the government had to send troops to Boston, where tax resistance was strongest. From that moment on, the relationship of colonies and mother country became ever more sour.

Americans saw redcoats as a threat to their rights as Englishmen, and they considered the concept of 'virtual representation' a cruel joke.[5] The government explained that most Englishmen and Scots were not represented either, but members of Parliament represented all Britons, not just their own districts. So just shut up and pay.

British policy towards the American colonies rested on several inaccurate assumptions. The most important was that the colonists would accept new taxes if they were imposed in clever ways, such as reducing previously uncollectible taxes to levels that would make smuggling unprofitable, then stepping up enforcement. Or imposing a stamp tax similar to that being introduced all across Europe. As resistance to the new taxes became violent, a second theory arose – that Americans would not fight. They had not resisted when the king had replaced elected governors with royal appointees, and the effort to strengthen the Anglican Church had resulted only in boycotts on British goods. The British army was the best in the world. Surely the mere display of force would make the colonials back down.

Keegan, in *Fields of Battle*, gives reasons to believe this – after 1763 colonial militias saw little reason to drill and officers were content to enjoy their social prestige and what little royal favour came their way. To oppose the British army in Boston the rebels created the minutemen, who could respond quicker than the militia, and began moving arms and ammunition from government arsenals into the interior. With British troops and officers making jibes at colonial customs and courage, by 1775 trouble was inevitable. Moreover, Americans possessed the opposite spirit of the mercenaries – they might not fight effectively, but they had passion and purpose. When the British government ordered General Thomas Gage to arrest the most prominent troublemakers and to disarm all rebels, he sent seven hundred regulars to seize the supplies at Concord.

The confused clash of arms there was followed by the redcoats' costly retreat, being shot to pieces by units of minutemen; exhausted from heat and the long march, hungry and thirsty and almost leaderless, the British troops were ready to surrender when a rescue force appeared.

The battle of Bunker Hill was the next British embarrassment. When Gage saw militiamen on a nearby promontory, he ordered William Howe to drive them away. Howe's misjudgement, based on the popular belief that militiamen would run away when confronted with bayonets, was to take his men up the slope straight at the entrenchments – the regular troops, including the crack Scottish unit, the Black Watch, were shot down in rows. Had the militiamen possessed more powder, bayonets and a bit more confidence, the disaster might have been total. As it was, Howe's last attack succeeded in taking the hill, but his men failed to catch the retreating rebels. From Howe's report the war cabinet learned that it would take more troops to subdue the rebels and from the Ministry of War it heard that there were not enough trained regiments in the British army to do the job. Britons may have scoffed at the 'Continental army' besieging Boston, but the professional soldiers had learned that half-trained militiamen could defend field fortifications tenaciously.

Thomas Paine (1737–1809), who had come from England only in 1774, had been initially struck by the fervent loyalist sentiment in pacifist Pennsylvania. Two years later, as the patriot party gained the upper hand, he penned the most important single pamphlet in American history, *Common Sense*, explaining why America should be an independent nation, not a continent subject to an island. Philadelphia, Pennsylvania's capital and the largest city in the colonies, was chosen to be the seat of the Continental Congress. When Washington's eight-month siege of Boston ended with a precipitous withdrawal of all British troops and about a thousand loyalists by sea, Washington hurried with his army to defend New York City against a new army collecting in Halifax. He reported that British troop ships were arriving daily – ultimately twice the number of fighting men as had been in the Spanish Armada. In July 1776 the Continental Congress voted for independence.

It was now a real war, but it was also a civil war – while many Americans were unhappy with king and Parliament, most held back from taking up arms, so that the number enlisting in the Continental army were small and the larger numbers in the militia were unwilling to serve outside the boundaries of what they began to call their 'states'; loyalties were local, not national. With the divisions in the patriot party and the presence of numerous loyalists, British experts on colonial affairs were confident they could bring the rebellion to an end peacefully or with minimum bloodshed and destruction of property.

The key, they said, was intimidation through overwhelming force, and so they instructed Howe, now commander-in-chief. The Royal Navy could keep the island colonies quiet, but only large numbers of troops could restore order on the mainland. Raising new units was not easy. Recruitment went slowly in England and failed almost entirely in Ireland. Only Scots enlisted in significant numbers, perhaps the result of landlords' enclosures depriving clansmen of their small plots. As sheep replaced people, people moved to cities, to England, to the colonies, or into the army. *Johnson's England* offers a vivid description of how uniformed British lads were transported over the seas to America. Anyone who has seen the woodcut of slaves pressed together in the dark bowels of wooden ships can imagine what it was like for the soldiers, except that no uprising was feared – without the need for shackles, the captain could pack even more men below decks. On fair days the soldiers had some hours in the sun, but storms must have been uncomfortable and frightening. Seasickness was combined with poor food (mouldy salt pork), weevil-infected biscuits and bad water, outbreaks of disease (diarrhoea probably being worse than smallpox, in the sense that it was more common), and the unpredictable length of the voyage. Navigational aids were primitive, so only God knew where the ship might actually make land – or break up at sea or on some rocky outcropping.

Stories of these horrors usually precipitated desertions when word of an overseas posting spread. Too many colonial garrisons were in unhealthy locations, either too hot or very cold, and the only entertainment was drinking and fighting. The prospect of loot made the privations of European campaigns bearable, but there would be little of that in the American wilderness, especially if the policy was to avoid driving neutrals into the rebels' arms. Officers went on half-pay rather than serve in America, potential recruits shunned every entreaty.

It had come as a shock to many Britons that Americans were resisting, and that they could embarrass regulars. One of the lessons of the previous war was that Americans were dirty, shiftless and cowardly – partly a result of colonial militias having sent their most useless men to assist the royal army against the French. Still, the Irish had fought earlier, too, but

British and foreign regiments had prevailed. Moreover, each Irish rebellion had provided excuses to confiscate land and treasure. However long the American war lasted – and surely it would not last long – Great Britain was certain to win, and in winning assure itself ample rewards. In America, one paper proclaimed, there were neither honest men nor virgins – perhaps prompting jokes that there would be even fewer of both soon. In another, cited by Troy Bickham in *Making Headlines*, all the departing troops would have to do was witness the surrender of the men, kiss the pretty girls and come home.

That seemed the lesson of the Americans' plans to capture Montreal, then Quebec, before reinforcements arrived. The commander, Richard Montgomery, was the perfect man to lead the expedition, but his men lacked experience; when the expected uprising of the French inhabitants did not happen, Montgomery faced the prospect of a siege lasting through the oncoming winter. Knowing that victory would come only if he achieved it quickly, his daring attack led to his death and the wounding of his dashing second-in-command, Benedict Arnold.[6] If a handful of redcoats could do that well against the best the colonials had to offer, what could a proper army do?

Such optimism was not widespread, at least not to the soldiers on the transports. Moreover, America was a big land, and occupying it would not be easy. Whig politicians like Pitt – the hero of the Seven Years War – proclaimed themselves supporters of the rebels. Still, most bets were on the British army. America had few officers and men who had ever served in a real army. Washington, to be sure, had fought on the frontier and had rescued what remained of Braddock's army after its ambush, but he had never commanded a large body of troops in the field. Moreover, American militiamen were notoriously undisciplined. It was fortunate that Washington not only had the personality and character necessary to inspire loyalty among those who served under him, but his tall, straight, athletic figure, his strength and vitality and his courage under fire kept his army together through some very dark days when the combination of his inexperience and the troops' unsteadiness produced one defeat after another. Some prominent politicians and officers advocated removing Washington in favour of one of those many officers who lacked his humility and his awareness of personal shortcomings.

One potential rival was Lord Sterling (William Alexander, 1726–83), whose claim to Scottish lands was upheld by a jury in Edinburgh, but was overturned by the House of Lords, which had not forgotten his ancestor's role in the 1715 rebellion, nor forgiven his escape to America. The excuse was that he could not prove his descent, but the reality was probably that he would be able to claim vast stretches of American land. However, Sterling, believing that Washington was the young nation's best hope, was content to serve as a major general.

Others wanted to disband the army and trust to guerrilla warfare – a policy Washington strongly opposed, knowing that the British army would react as it did in Ireland – or any European army would, once it concluded that farmers and villagers were the unseen enemy – by burning their homes and fields. He employed bands of cavalry to harass British supply lines, but he made certain that the enemy kept their eyes on his main force.[7]

The quality of this American army varied so greatly as to almost defy description. Some soldiers were enthusiastic volunteers, some were coerced into service, some were hired substitutes; all had enlistments so limited in terms of time that just as a unit became reasonably competent, its men went home. Militiamen were good with shovels, but rarely stood long when faced by co-ordinated volleys and shining bayonets; most did not have bayonets themselves, that not being a useful weapon in fighting Indians. Most mocked drills as foolish and as an unworthy imposition on the dignity of free men: certainly nothing they should perform without proper clothing and equipment or even pay. They let their elected officers understand how quickly they could remove them. And no militia company would accept an officer from another state. The best one could say is that most of the men were acquainted with firearms, though the targets had been far more often squirrels than Indians or Frenchmen.

Revolutionaries, Loyalists, Redcoats and Mercenaries

The British government had been angered and embarrassed by the debacle at Boston, first by the slaughter at Bunker Hill, then by Washington's surprise seizure of Dorchester Heights, whence cannon could rake the town and much of the harbour. After Howe hurriedly evacuated Boston, he gathered a gigantic flotilla to seize New York City, thereby separating rebellious New England from the supposedly less radical colonies to the south, while simultaneously rescuing the many loyalists of that once Dutch town. Overall command was given to William Howe, and the navy to his brother Richard (1726–99). William was considered the best officer in the army, but he could be, in McCulloch's words in 1776, 'slow-moving, procrastinating, negligent'. He had purchased his commission in 1746, subsequently serving in Flanders, and later in America. Richard was so silent that no one was certain what his opinions were, but many believed that he was less than enthusiastic about this war. Old hands knew when action was imminent, because that was the only time that 'Black Dick' was ever known to smile. London gossip was that their mother was an illegitimate daughter of George I; certainly she was important at the courts of both George II and George III. It was hoped that this sibling tandem would be less subject to the rivalry between army and navy that had so crippled other expeditions. And this was no ordinary expedition, but the greatest in his nation's history – four hundred ships with 32,000 troops

It was fortunate for America that there were so many loyalists in the colonies. Otherwise, the policy advocated by General James Grant (1720–1806) – to use the fleet to fall on one coastal town after another, burning them until the colonials surrendered – might have prevailed. In McCulloch's words, Grant was 'a grossly fat, highly opinionated Scot' who despised Americans. In contrast, Howe's policy was reconciliation – he wanted to defeat the colonial army without angering the neutrals and loyalists. In this sense, Howe's war was to be the most limited of any in the era of limited war.

Wars, however, do not easily lend themselves to civilised behaviour. The first sign of a departure from efforts at reconciliation was the use of mercenary soldiers: Germans known collectively but inaccurately as Hessians.

Every American schoolchild has read the Declaration of Independence, but few get beyond the stirring first lines of that document to the list of abuses committed by the English king, George III:

> He has plundered our seas, ravaged our coasts, burned our towns, and destroyed the lives of our people.
> He is at this time transporting large armies of foreign mercenaries to complete the works of death, desolation, and tyranny already begun with

circumstances of cruelty and perfidy scarcely paralleled in the most barbarous ages, and totally unworthy the head of a civilized nation . . .

Americans had some confidence that they could rely on British officers and most British soldiers to respect their rights and persons, but they were certain that Germans – with whom few outside rural Pennsylvania could communicate – would live up to their dreadful continental reputation.

The only surprise was that George III did not bring over soldiers from Hanover, since he was the ruler of that north German state, or Prussians, since England and Prussia were close allies in the recent Seven Years War. Instead, the government hired soldiers from recent allies in the Seven Years War.

The Hessians

Frederick II of Hesse-Kassel lived in the rolling hills of central Germany. He had the usual expenses of a minor prince who desired to acquire for himself everything he had seen in Paris and London: a beautiful capital with an opera house, a university and a public museum; a large private library; the still-impressive garden in Kassel; the company of famous Italian and French 'intellectuals'; and the services of beautiful mistresses. Goethe and other German intellectuals admired what he achieved, especially in the arts (poets tend to appreciate the generosity of patrons). However, Frederick also wanted his country to recover from the brutal treatment it had suffered during the Seven Years War. Like his ancestors, he found it expedient to rent out his army to neighbours to cover the expenses of rebuilding. And recently the British subsidy had come to an end.

Hessian troops had served in Italy and the Low Countries, and often fought for the British crown – Frederick himself had served as a British mercenary in 1741 in Westphalia. When he led Hessian troops into Scotland in 1746 to put down the uprising of Bonnie Prince Charlie, the citizens of Sterling had conferred honorary citizenship upon him. His first wife was George III's aunt, but she had left him (after bearing four sons) when Frederick became a convert to Catholicism. Subsequently, he took up with a bevy of mistresses and, according to rumour, sired more than a hundred children. His motives in becoming a Catholic were obscure; he may have intended only to annoy his father, but that also made him eligible for election as king of Poland. In all respects, he was besotted with France – he spoke French, supported a French theatre, insisted that his court represent French manners and culture, encouraged art, science and education (as any Enlightenment ruler should) and, of course, was determined to have a respectable palace. All this was more than he could afford from tax revenues. But he had quite a few impoverished subjects who would not object to seeing the world. Of course, they had no idea how much of the New World they would see between 1776 and 1783.

The British government had originally hoped to suppress the rebellion cheaply. There had been a slight chance of getting a Scottish regiment back from Holland, but the negotiations for that soon failed. Five battalions from Hanover freed British troops in Gibraltar for service in America, but that was it. There was an effort to recruit twenty thousand Russians, who would have been much cheaper and unlikely to feel sympathy towards the American rebels – while few soldiers anywhere had read much written by Enlightenment *philosophes*, why take the chance? Russians would have no idea what was going on, but Catherine had said no. Negotiations were opened with German princes; the price was high.

Frederick had a standing army of twelve thousand men – renting their services to Great Britain would reduce his expenses considerably; in addition, the men sent to America would earn him three million pounds sterling. Moreover, he believed that the experience would be good for his soldiers, most of whom were volunteers, many undoubtedly seeking to escape the poverty of rural life. Two years after a massive crop failure in 1770–1, the duke had forbidden further subdivision of peasant holdings. With primogeniture the law, younger sons saw no future in staying at home. In the end he sent about seventeen thousand soldiers to America – fifteen infantry regiments of 650 officers and men, four grenadier regiments, two jäger companies equipped with rifles, and two field artillery companies. They had been trained in Prussian methods and were considered to be among Europe's best soldiers.

Friedrich was not alone in hurrying to rent out troops. His own estranged son, Wilhelm, count of Hanau, east of Frankfurt, did so too, as did the count of Hesse-Hanau and Karl I of Brunswick (Braunschweig), whose son had married George III's sister. Friedrich von Waldeck, Karl Alexander of Anspach-Bayreuth (in Bavaria, but a branch of Frederick the Great's Hohenzollern family), and Friedrich Augustus of Anhalt-Zerbst joined in.

There was some immediate consternation when it was learned that the army would be transported overseas. Everyone, including Duke Frederick, seems to have initially assumed that the troops would be employed on the Rhine, anticipating that Louis XVI would attempt to invade Hanover; when it was learned that the troops would be sent to North America, Frederick insisted on British promises that they would be employed only there and not in any region known for heat and disease. Hard bargaining won him a British subsidy so generous that he could increase his troops' wages from one and a half thalers a month to five. Since this was less than Hanover was offering without an overseas posting, Frederick offered a sizeable enlistment bounty that brought deserters from other German armies to Hesse, and some militiamen exempt from service volunteered for service in America. Some soldiers took their families with them, but since common soldiers were forbidden to marry, most of these were officers or militia troops doing garrison duty.

European intellectuals, including Frederick's friend, Voltaire, were appalled by this cynical deal. Many assumed that America was an Enlightenment paradise, and readily believed that the worst of Old World evils were being transported to the New World. Ingrao reports in *The Hessian Mercenary State* that the negotiations to hire the armies had begun in the winter of 1774–5, but the British had been reluctant to meet the German demands until after battle of Bunker Hill. Benjamin Franklin later circulated a forged letter attributed to the prince, complaining that so few of his men had died, because he needed the money; however, there was nothing in the contract about payment for dead or wounded soldiers. As for the concept of liberty, Trevelyan commented in *The American Revolution* that the French nobility 'thought it a fine thing that all men should be born free and equal so long as it was not in their own hemisphere'.

The Hessian officers were highly respected. Johann Gottlieb Rall (1726–76) had served in the War of the Austrian Succession – in Bavaria, Holland and even Scotland – and in the Seven Years War; in 1771–2 he had been in the Russian army fighting the Turks. Baron Wilhelm Reichsfreiherr zu Innhausen und Knyphausen (1716–1800) was born to the military – his father had served in the Prussian army and had fought under Marlborough. Knyphausen had trained in Berlin and earned a fine reputation for both administrative and combat skills. The Hessian troops boarded ship near Bremen and disembarked four months later. It was a terrible voyage, with seasickness so awful that death might well have come as a welcome relief. On shore they learned how hot an American summer could be.

The officers and soldiers had neither fear of nor respect for the Americans. They could not understand anyone not paying taxes for protection against the French – they had personal experience with French armies. Having an indirect representative system at home, they could not see the constitutional issues as colonials did. Nor could they sympathise with slave-holding, which made them see Americans as base hypocrites. They could easily have quoted Dr Johnson, 'How is it that we hear the loudest *yelps* for liberty among the drivers of negroes?'

A number of black runaways joined the Hessian army, most as drummers. A few survived the war to return to Germany and serve in the duke's elite guard.

Washington's Need for Experienced Officers

Although the battle at Bunker Hill had persuaded many Americans that their militiamen were real soldiers, cooler minds knew otherwise. George Washington had fought alongside British regulars. He knew both their shortcomings in the forests and their ferocity in pitched battle. Not wanting the American Revolution to degenerate into a guerrilla war, he argued against retreating into the wilderness; instead, he wanted a regular army that could protect towns and villages. He believed that properly trained Americans could stand up to regulars, if well-led, but he was aware that he had precious few officers who understood the business of war.

It was no accident that Washington had been named commander-in-chief. First of all, he was well known from his exploits in the recent war. Second, he was a Virginian, and New Englanders wanted Virginia committed to the cause. Next, he was a man of property, not a demagogue – the plantations he had inherited or acquired by marriage put him among the most prominent and progressive landowners in the South. Lastly, he looked, talked and acted like a leader. An accomplished horseman and dancer, he was a natural aristocrat who had trained himself in manners and self-control to compensate for his rural upbringing and fiery temper. Only

one of his officers ever slapped him on the back. He did that on a bet, and
he never did it again.

Washington looked first to former officers of the British army – Lord
Sterling, Charles Lee (1731–82), Horatio Gates (1727–1806) and Richard
Montgomery. Lee had fought alongside Washington in Braddock's defeat,
then settled in Virginia. A true eccentric, he married a Seneca Indian
woman, fought with the British in Spain, then in the Polish army. He had
a good military mind, courage and sufficient opinions for several men, but
his poor conduct at the battle of Monmouth would cause Washington to
remove him from command, after which the Continental Congress would
dismiss him from the service altogether. Gates had been a British general
and served in the French and Indian War. Originally named adjutant
general of the Continental army, he spent much of the war conspiring
against Washington, trying to persuade Congress that only he could lead
the army to victory. Although the contention by Lee and Gates that they
understood warfare better than George Washington eventually proved
wrong, at the beginning of the conflict they appeared to be correct.

The Campaign of 1776

The British plan, once Howe had evacuated Boston, was to co-ordinate an
attack on New York City.[8] After rallying the loyalists there, he planned to
sever New England from the other colonies, then prevent its fishermen and
merchants from going to sea; eventually, he reasoned, the economic stran-
glehold would bring the rebels to their senses. This seemed likely, because
the forces of William Howe, Lord Richard Howe and Henry Clinton
(1738–95) faced only poorly equipped American units eager for a winner-
take-all engagement that would allow them to go home soon. That was
what the British commanders wanted, too – a quick clean, decisive victory
that would destroy the rebels' morale. The Howe brothers disembarked the
redcoats on Staten Island to await the arrival of the Hessians.

The Germans were pleased to see the end of their long and uncomfortable
ocean voyage. While the soldiers recovered their land legs, their commanders
viewed the disposition of Washington's units and assessed the quality of
his men. Although they were not impressed, they later found the colonial
fortifications more formidable than they had expected – Americans knew

how to dig in. While their men suffered from the heat, they learned that the Americans had more illness and more desertions. This was not surprising – how would a Hessian get off Staten Island and where would he go?

Washington had an impossible task – to defend an island and a peninsula against naval assault. The almost daily arrival of more British troopships made his task ever more difficult. The safest strategy would have been to withdraw to the mainland while there was still time. However, Congress had instructed him to defend New York City, and he did not believe that anyone was fit to command who was not also ready to obey.

If New York was the key to the colonies, Manhattan was the key to New York, and Long Island the key to Manhattan – Brooklyn Heights overlooked the city a mile away, across the East River. Washington had to defend the heights to hold the city. That, or abandon the city altogether. Such a setback so soon after the Declaration of Independence might prove politically fatal. Loyalists, of whom there were many, would rally to the crown, and those many undecided citizens, who were always ready to say they had secretly wished the victors well, might tip the balance in what was becoming a civil war in community after community. Unhappily for Washington, Long Island had all the appearances of a trap where his army could be cut off and forced to surrender. For this reason he placed batteries to hinder warships from sailing up the Hudson River and isolating him from the mainland. Surprisingly, when vessels did make their way successfully past the guns, neither he nor the Howe brothers seemed to understand that their plans should be quickly revised.

When Washington placed about half of his forces on Brooklyn Heights, he determined the British strategy. William Howe was convinced that he could capture the entire army in a few days, whereas if the Continental army withdrew into the city, reducing it by siege might take months. Moreover, the loyalist citizenry would suffer and his operations might be interrupted by troops from farther away coming to the rescue. Lastly, he did not want New York City destroyed – he would need it as a base for future campaigns.

The battle of Long Island (22 August) was not a bloody affair, though it could have been. Howe sent a force on a long night march eastwards past the fortifications, then around the almost unguarded flank – as much a fault of Washington as of the local commanders – and feints by redcoats and Hessians kept the outnumbered Americans' attention to their front until it was too late. Only two miracles saved Washington's army – first a storm that kept the Royal Navy from blocking the East River, then a well-executed escape through night-time fog to Manhattan.

Only another miracle allowed Washington to escape north after his defeat at Harlem Heights on 16 September – Howe's lack of initiative perhaps reflected a hope that Washington would sue for terms. The performance of American troops had not been impressive, but they had been sufficiently competent to remind Howe not to attack their trenches head-on. British and Hessian letters home indicated that the Americans were learning.

The battle of White Plains on 28 October, however, indicated that neither side was learning quickly enough. Howe sent into battle newly arrived British and Hessian units, pinning down Washington's men behind their fortifications, while directing the main assault on a flanking height. Colonel Rall led the charge up the hill overlooking Washington's entrenchments, driving back hastily dispatched militia units, but suffering 250 casualties, twice the American losses. As Howe waited for reinforcements, rain came. It was Howe's best chance to trap the entire rebel army, but he was unwilling to send troops into a killing zone if there was any possibility of defeating Washington by manoeuvre and offers of reconciliation. The next day Washington was gone.

Howe then turned to Fort Washington, sending an overwhelming force against the garrison of 2,800 troops, capturing most of them. Many of those who surrendered died in prison ships – crowded together in conditions seen only in the slave trade – but before their surrender to Knyphausen, they had killed or wounded 458 attackers (mostly Germans) at the cost of only fifty-three men. Angry Hessians murdered some captured riflemen.

Howe pursued Washington across New Jersey, then gave up as winter approached. He looked across the Delaware River towards Philadelphia, noting that Washington had taken every boat and barge from the east bank to the west and put his troops into winter quarters. Howe stationed a crack unit of Hessians at Trenton, the most important position along the river, housing them in hastily built barracks. British troops were then withdrawn to New York City, where the officers could be more comfortable. A large contingent of Hessians was stationed there, too.

Meanwhile, General Charles Lee had been moving slowly across New Jersey, not co-operating with George Washington or even keeping him informed of his plans. It was no secret that he thought Washington incompetent, and that he was telling congressmen and army officers that supreme command should be given to him – both in military and civil matters. His eccentricities both enhanced and hurt his reputation – some expected military geniuses to be 'different', while others feared that such individuals would be ambitious to rule. Lee's hounds and extravagant dress were both present the morning of 13 December 1776, when he awoke at an isolated inn, several miles from his troops, then put on his dressing gown and leisurely began to answer his correspondence. Out of nowhere, it seemed, a small British scouting party swept down on the inn, scattered his guards and carried him away, still in his dressing gown. The captor was Tarleton, a dashing cavalryman whose name would later become synonymous with British cruelty.[9]

According to McCullough, in 1776, the British believed they had won the war – they had captured the only American general whose competence they had respected. In reality, they had guaranteed that Washington henceforth only had as a rival Horatio Gates, who was too fat to be either eccentric or effective.

This success probably made General Howe comfortable with his decision to put the army into winter quarters. With ice forming across the Delaware River, he would have been reluctant in any case to take his army on to Philadelphia. And there was his charming mistress waiting in New York, and her co-operative loyalist husband, who was making a fortune feeding rebel prisoners as little as possible. The Germans in Trenton could keep an eye on General Washington, whose army was, in any case, disintegrating.

Or so they believed. Actually, Washington had been reinforced by troops from Lee's army and by Gates. Still, even that knowledge would not have changed the mind of James Grant, who denied a request that more troops be stationed along the Delaware River and in Trenton – Americans, he contended, were too cowardly to be dangerous.

The Battle of Trenton

The fourteen hundred Hessians at Trenton were commanded by Colonel Rall. His experience fighting American troops had led him to despise them, but it was more the ice-filled river and the heavy snow storm that caused him to believe that Washington would keep his men in Pennsylvania. If somehow colonial troops did appear, he would order an attack with the bayonet – a weapon few patriots had and the one they most feared. A spy sent him a written warning that rebels had crossed the Delaware, but the colonel was playing cards; he glanced at the outside of the note briefly, then put it aside. His dying words reflected his memory of that fatal moment, 'Hätte ich es gelesen, läge ich jetzt nicht hier' (If I had read it, I wouldn't be lying here now.)

Neither Rall nor his men had been drinking, celebrating Christmas Day, as later mythology had it. Nor were they unaware of the American threat. In fact, they may have been too aware – they were exhausted from a week of patrols and alarms (they had just returned from one night-time reconnaissance) and were trying to sleep in full battle gear. However, with the heavy snow and high winds, it did not seem likely that there was any reality behind the warnings that Washington was moving about. Surely now they dared to relax, at least to sleep.

On 26 December Washington made his crossing of the Delaware, a daring move in every respect. It was almost an act of desperation, since many enlistments would expire in five days. But thanks to skilled sailors in his command, his gamble succeeded. The troops then marched to Trenton through the snow, occasionally leaving bloody footprints, and overwhelmed the surprised outposts. Knox's cannon swept the streets when the Hessians tumbled out of their bunks, and Continental soldiers shot down more, then pursued them into an orchard, continuing to fire until Rall and the three other colonels were killed or mortally wounded. At that point nine hundred Germans put their hands in the air. Some Hessians did escape overland with Colonel Knyphausen, but three regiments were out of the war.[10]

On 1 January Washington won another engagement at Princeton. The American War for Independence had been saved. It was far from won, but it no longer appeared hopeless. Moreover, the battle at Princeton had been a stand-up fight with regulars in full daylight – the British could not dismiss Trenton as a mere Teutonic fiasco.

The Hessians captured at Trenton were marched from Lancaster, Pennsylvania, to the Maryland line by Pennsylvania militia, then told to proceed by themselves. They did so, marching in impressive files – though without their weapons. Since the state governments did not have proper prisons, they rented many prisoners to landowners as indentured servants; the state government also offered inducements to change sides – common soldiers fifty acres of land, officers one hundred. The offer had been drafted by Benjamin Franklin, elegantly translated and placed inside tobacco packages that went into Hessian hands. Few accepted.

The British response to the disaster was to hire more Hessians. They served in Howe's campaign of September 1777, travelling by sea to Chesapeake Bay, then marching up the west bank of the Delaware River towards Philadelphia. When Howe encountered Washington's prepared defences along Brandywine Creek, manned by thousands of militia who had come to assist the regulars, he assigned Knyphausen the task of drawing the attention of the Continental army, while Charles Cornwallis (1738–1805) slipped around the flank. Washington, trying to fight in an improvised position, was soon badly beaten. The Continental army retreated in good order through Philadelphia, leaving the city open to British occupation; Congress fled west, to Lancaster, then to York. With winter coming on, Howe felt sure that both the army and the Continental Congress would soon be ready to parley.

The fierce battle of Germantown in October – Washington's surprise strike against a detached portion of Howe's army – dispelled this optimism: if there had not been a dense fog, the Americans might have won a significant victory. Instead, Washington's troops were bloodied again; afterwards, they withdrew to a strong position just north of Philadelphia where they could interfere with Howe's plans to feed his troops from the prosperous Quaker and Amish farms.

European opinion, especially in France and Prussia, began to follow that of British officers – that the Americans were no longer to be taken lightly. All Washington's army needed was proper training, a task that required proper officers.

The British government was dismayed to learn that not only was Washington's army still intact, but that he had been able detach regulars to assist the northern forces that defeated and captured an entire British–Hessian army in central New York. General Howe pleaded for reinforcements – he had sufficient men to hold Philadelphia (barely) and New York (thanks to the fleet), but too few to undertake any new operations.

Freed from worry about a winter offensive against his well-fortified bases, Washington's main task was to keep enough of his troops together so that the men who went home on furlough (or just left) would have an army to rejoin in the spring. He established this base at Valley Forge; it was easy to fortify, close enough to Philadelphia to strike if opportunity arose, and near rich farming country. If he could not persuade the local farmers to exchange their produce for the increasingly worthless Continental currency,[11] he could at least make it difficult for the British to collect food and fodder. Still, he did not dare just seize what he needed – this was truly a struggle for hearts and minds, and both Washington and Howe understood that many people were still undecided about which party to support.

That winter became a part of American folklore – intense hardship for the enlisted men, with insufficient clothing and worn-out shoes; there was too little of everything except opportunities to complain. There was even an officers' plot to replace Washington as commander-in-chief.[12] It had been a year earlier that Thomas Paine wrote *The American Crisis*, but his words applied better to this moment: 'These are the times that try men's souls. The summer soldier and the sunshine patriot will, in this crisis, shrink from the service of his country; but he that stands it now, deserves the love and thanks of man and woman.'

As disease ran through both armies, Washington took the desperate remedy of inoculating his men for smallpox. The death rate among those inoculated was almost as high as among victims of an epidemic, but Washington was thereby able to guarantee that his men would be ill in winter camp, not in the middle of a campaign.

Yellow fever and malaria had run through camps and cities alike all summer, worse in the south than in the north, and deadly to those already weakened by exhaustion, poor food and wounds; now the diseases were those resulting from close confinement in cold and crowded huts. In each army more men died of disease than in combat, but Americans could at least go home to recuperate – as many who counted as deserters surely did; militia units were rotated in and out, few staying long enough to be turned into reliable troops, but by spring their numbers were so large that new encampments were needed to house them.

Howe, blamed by the government for a failed campaign that was its own concept, was frustrated by the failure of Tory volunteers to appear. Where was the army of loyalists that had been predicted? Alas for him, most of the local Tories objected to the disruptions associated with political agitation and war, or were Quaker pacifists; in short, they did not yearn to fight for the king. Moreover, the British occupation, accompanied by habits of Old World soldiery that no commander could ever curb – looting, robbery, insolence and worse – dampened enthusiasm for the royal cause.

Indians as Mercenaries

There were good reasons for the Indians to support the British. First of all, after the French and Indian War the only alternative employers were Spanish governors, who were far away and still officially neutral. Second, the dominant Indian confederacy in the north was that of the Iroquois, traditional British allies who had swept their native enemies from the hunting grounds of Ohio and the Great Lakes. Third, the British had issued the famous Proclamation of 1763, prohibiting Americans from crossing the Appalachian Mountains, and it was Americans who were violating it. British promises were the last hope the tribes had for survival. Logically, the Indians should have offered their services eagerly. However, it was impossible to persuade rival tribes to join together. Thus, the British promise to pay warriors who made attacks on Americans – either as frontier raiders or auxiliaries – was essential in bringing ancient enemies to support British armies on the frontier.

Indians had long ago become dependent on trade with Europeans – it was a process that had benefited all parties, but the Indians had failed to develop the skills needed to produce trade items themselves (those were female activities, nothing that a hunter and warrior would do). Now they had no alternative to selling furs and hides for knives, axes, cooking pots, clothing and guns. Any tribe that tried to do without guns and gunpowder would fall quickly to traditional enemies. Earning money or taking loot was essential. Protecting lands and exacting revenge had long been important but were still secondary benefits. Now all these motivations came together.

The most famous employment of Indians in the war was in 1777, in the Mohawk valley of New York, when American militiamen attempted to break the siege of Fort Stanwix, thereby reopening the portage that connected the Great Lakes to Albany. Among the besiegers was the

King's Royal Regiment of New York, loyalists led by John Johnson, son of William Johnson, the famed British Indian agent who had children by three different Indian women as well as by an indentured servant. In the French and Indian War William Johnson had kept the Iroquois true to the British alliance; not surprisingly, warriors from the Six Nations of the Iroquois and the Seven Nations of Canada were waiting not far from Fort Stanwix to ambush the American relief column of eight hundred militiamen and their forty Oneida Indian allies.

At this battle of Oriskany, the Americans suffered heavy casualties – 450 killed and wounded. However, the loyalists and Iroquois lost perhaps 150 men, and when the garrison of the fort had sallied out during the fighting to destroy their camp, the Indians had broken off the combat. The British commander, worried about having Fort Stanwix in his rear, chose not to drive down the Mohawk River towards Albany; he retreated back into Canada when Benedict Arnold brought troops from the Continental army to break the siege.

Saratoga, 1777

Three decades earlier the French had barely failed in their efforts to invade the Hudson valley by moving south from Montreal along the string of rivers and lakes that led past Ticonderoga to Albany. Now 'Gentleman Johnny' Burgoyne was certain that he could do better because he expected two other armies to converge on Albany, one coming down the Mohawk and another coming up the Hudson; thus, wherever the Yankees took a stand, a British force would come up from behind. Burgoyne had persuaded the government that this plan would further isolate the rebels in New England from those to the south. Even if everything went wrong, Burgoyne was firmly persuaded that he was competent and a warrior and that Americans were not. He had battle-tested officers leading four thousand proven redcoats, with a fine artillery train; although his three thousand Brunswick mercenaries were of inferior quality and poorly equipped, their commanders, Friedrich Adolf Riedesel, Freiherr zu Eisenbach (1738–1800) and Lieutenant Colonel Friedrich Baum (1727–77), were experienced soldiers who lived up to their formidable reputations. Few Canadians joined the expedition, but several hundred Iroquois did, excited by Burgoyne's promise that they would have a free hand to deal with the Americans. Burgoyne, always the playwright and actor, seducer and social climber, grandly promised Parliament a glorious victory.

His first exploits lived up to his predictions – he took the great fortress at Ticonderoga almost without fighting, then vigorously pursued the retreating Americans, destroying their fleet and their stores of supplies, and dispersing them into the wilderness without weapons, clothing or food. There seemed to be nothing between him and Albany. That 'nothing', however, was a wilderness. Only those who understood what that meant were able to shrug off the panicked reaction of the general public and Congress. Washington, who had a lot of experience on a very similar western frontier, predicted that the deeper Burgoyne penetrated into the forest, the more trouble he would encounter.

And so it was. Burgoyne's army was soon short of everything. The soldiers were able to adjust to short rations, but not the horses. When the cavalry largely dismounted, Burgoyne's plans for battle on the more open ground around Albany were endangered. Moreover, it was disheartening to see the Indians gorge themselves on the remaining supplies, then trot off into the forest, coming back in the evening with scalps and new appetite, but little food. In mid-August he decided to send a raiding party into Vermont to round up horses and cattle, food and fodder.

At this point two professionals and two amateurs made Burgoyne's boasts hollow. The first professional was General Gates, who had experience with the British army in Germany during the Seven Years War before immigrating to America. Washington had replaced the lost arms and equipment, and sent him reinforcements which included Morgan's riflemen – five hundred Scots-Irish and German frontiersmen.[13] This was at a moment when Washington was defending Philadelphia from Howe – Washington knew, as Burgoyne did not, that because Howe had brought his troops to attack Philadelphia, there was not going to be a British offensive up the Hudson River. Washington could use the weapons and men himself, but he understood that Gates needed them to prevent the British from isolating New England. As it happened, his Continentals arrived just in time. But there was also Gates's reputation, which attracted New England militiamen who would not serve under a less-experienced commander, and this was a campaign that could not be lost.

The second professional was a Polish engineer, Andrzej Tadeusz Bonawentura Kościuszko (1746–1817), who designed a defensive system north of Albany at Saratoga that would prevent the British and German troops from advancing into settled country. Volunteer militiamen from New England plied their shovels with a vengeance, confident that proper fortifications would enable them to hold off any number of redcoats. Kościuszko had been unable to find employment in Europe, but in America he would earn fame that later made him the natural leader of Poland's last glorious defence of its independence.

The first amateur was John Stark (1728–1822), a backwoodsman who was a veteran of Roger's Rangers and Washington's army. His New Hampshire militiamen intercepted Baum's foraging party at Bennington in Vermont. Baum, who had expected to overwhelm the guards of an American supply depot, found himself badly outnumbered. Realising that battle was unavoidable, he sent a message asking for immediate help from a following column and formed a defensive line on a hill. Stark, however, chose not to attack head-on, but to envelop the Germans. When the Indians and Canadians saw this, they fled for their lives; the Hessian dragoons, now horseless and clad in awkward cavalry boots, tried to break through the American lines, but, being shot to pieces, raised their hands in surrender. The following column, hurrying to the sound of battle, attacked and almost turned the battle around, but American reinforcements, the Green Mountain Boys – men so fierce and free-willed as to make a mob seem well organised – came onto the scene and made a quick end to the fight. In all two hundred Germans died and seven hundred surrendered. American losses were few.

The second amateur was Benedict Arnold, a Connecticut businessman and merchant whose obvious talents had caught Washington's attention. The most enterprising American officer of the war, he had distinguished himself in the Canadian expedition and was now assigned the task of rescuing Fort Stanwix. Accomplishing this with amazing speed, he then brought his men back to Albany.

Burgoyne was meanwhile learning much about the American wilderness. His men lacked room to form lines; moreover, the bayonet, the weapon upon which he relied for final victory, was awkward to use in the dense trees, shrubs and fallen timber – some of which was cut down by Americans to impede the passage of wagons. Snipers were picking off men, it seemed, at every turn of every path – Britons familiar with London lanes could not figure out where deer trails led. At last arriving at Saratoga, Burgoyne believed that the ordeal was over. It was, in a sense – the American fortifications meant that he was literally at the end of the road unless he could somehow get past them.

Gates gave him that opportunity, crowding all his men into one corner of the works, leaving other parts almost undefended. Burgoyne must have smiled to see his adversary's mistake – he assigned the Germans the task of distracting Gates, while he led his redcoats towards the centre and sent another force around the flank. The plan was thwarted by Arnold, who ordered an attack on the moving columns. The fighting was the hottest that any veteran could remember, and Burgoyne's centre was saved from a massacre only by timely rescue coming from each wing. The next day Burgoyne began building his own entrenchments. Discouragement quickly came in the form of a two-month-old dispatch – informing him that Howe would be moving on Philadelphia, not Albany – and a captured German sent across the lines with a message that Americans had cut his lines back to Canada. Meanwhile, American militia units joined Gates's army in ever-increasing numbers.

The only hope that Burgoyne had was that a relief army would advance north from New York City, but with most of the army in Philadelphia, General Clinton was unwilling to leave his base unguarded; his feeble effort to move up the river was too little and too late.

Had it been up to General Gates, Burgoyne would have been allowed to retreat – he could not imagine Americans standing up to regulars – but the Yankee militias had developed a will of their own, making night-time forays, rounding up half-starved foraging companies, welcoming deserters. Gates was an excellent staff officer, properly praised for having brought order into the Continental army's confused paperwork, but he always advocated standing on the defensive, even retreating into the mountains. Such was the advice he whispered into the ears of congressmen, who came to view him as a potential saviour of the country, a man who would not engage the redcoats with Washington's reckless enthusiasm. His memory of redcoats' murderous efficiency paralysed him when it came to battle; consequently, his subordinates now ignored him.

Burgoyne, torn between the difficulties of retreat and an unlikely victory, chose to make one last attack. The Germans went forward bravely into a murderous fire that concentrated on their officers and horses; the British were likewise shot down in rows – one of Morgan's riflemen, Timothy Murphy, mortally wounded General Simon Fraser at three hundred yards, then shot Burgoyne's aide-de-camp out of his saddle! Only pride and discipline, and Burgoyne's courageous personal leadership, kept the army together sufficiently to make an orderly retreat to a fortified camp. Riedesel advised Burgoyne to abandon the artillery, the stores and the wounded, and push north as rapidly as possible. But Burgoyne insisted on taking everything with them. It was a fatal mistake. The Americans followed, launched attacks on the camp and accomplished the surrender of the entire force. The Germans managed to hide their regimental colours, persuading their captors that they had burned them.

At the banquet following the surrender, Burgoyne raised a toast to his captor's commander, 'General Washington'. At the formal surrender Gates accepted Burgoyne's sword, then returned it to him.

Arnold had been badly wounded in his leg, hence was unavailable for service in the months that followed. Passed over for command by Congress, he fell into the hands of a young royalist (he had a predilection for loyalist women) and became ever more dissatisfied with the patriot cause; the incompetent, Gates-worshipping politicians he met in Philadelphia caused him to wonder whether distant Britons, who now promised a reformed colonial policy, might not provide better government than the rabble in the Second Continental Congress.[14]

The German prisoners went first to Massachusetts, where it is reported that they found the women beautiful, lively and self-confident; they were, however, deeply puzzled by the democratic behaviour of the American soldiers and citizens, who rejected all pretensions to authority except from their women. Riedesel was allowed to retain disciplinary command over his men, which reduced further likelihood of cultural misunderstandings. In early 1778 his troops were marched to Charlottesville, Virginia, for internment; it was a cold and hungry journey, during which a number of his men deserted. Riedesel, who was ill, was exchanged in 1780, but his men remained in their improvised villages until the end of the war. Tarleton made a dash for this location in June 1781, barely failing to capture Thomas

Jefferson, then governor of Virginia, at his home in Monticello. Riedesel and his men were released soon afterwards, but not sent home until 1784; in the meantime, the troops lived happily – good pay being given to their kin at home, no drills, no combat and freedom to earn whatever money their individual skills permitted.

Burgoyne made a very advantageous bargain to free his British troops for service in Europe, but Howe delayed and blustered until the Americans began to suspect that he would immediately incorporate them into his own army. Consequently, they remained prisoners to the end of the war. Some escaped, thanks to a fluency in the language that the Germans did not possess, and to the sympathies of the many loyalists who otherwise kept their heads down. The British government protested the American failure to honour the agreement made by Gates; but the French were very pleased to have so many fine soldiers taken out of the war rather than employed on the Rhine.

Saratoga was the decisive victory that American diplomats had been waiting for to prove that the colonists might win their independence. In February 1778, soon after the news reached France, Louis XVI signed a treaty of alliance with the United States – negotiated by the very Dr Franklin that the Tories had insulted. War with Great Britain followed soon afterwards.

In spite of the American victory over an army of regulars, it was becoming obvious that the Continental army could not rely on militia units – and no one was more aware of this than its commander. Volunteers would flock to the colours at the beginning of a season, then drift away – it was not war that discouraged them, it seems, as much as the discipline required for fighting the war successfully; men with farms and workshops could not neglect them forever. Washington complained that patriotic passion did not last, because self-interest was too strong. He continued to use militias, but the core of his army was now, in the words of Martin and Lender, in *A Respectable Army*, 'folks who didn't have another alternative'. The lures to enlistment were familiar to Europeans, though more generous – a substantial bounty at enlistment, new clothes and a promise of one hundred acres of land. Soon the army had relatively few American-born, middle-class soldiers. Instead, there were immigrants, slaves, ne'er-do-wells, and 'liquor enlistees'.[15]

To their disappointment, these soldiers discovered that they would be paid in Continental dollars that were worth less every month – sometimes much less. Food and clothing came in at intervals – whenever state legislatures could be persuaded to make contributions – rather than regularly. Nevertheless, like their counterparts in Europe, they were the makings of a real army.

French Intervention

The French should have stayed out of the war. Anyone could see that the conflict would be ruinously expensive, and probably would be lost, but the military, the salon patriots and the court desired revenge for being beaten in successive wars. They remembered their ancestors' defeats in the Hundred Years War – fate ordained that they be defeated again and again, but they won in the end. Louis XVI learned that the naval building programme had reached a point where his admirals could challenge their overly committed British counterparts – and if his Bourbon cousin in Spain joined the war, the two fleets would be stronger than the British navy. Perhaps even more important in the royal decision were reports from French volunteers who were serving in the American army. Of these, none was more important than Marie-Joseph-Paul-Yves-Roch-Gilbert du Motier, marquis de Lafayette (1757–1834), a young noble from a military family who had served in the royal household troops; he was an enthusiastic republican, thrilled by the American Revolution. Although the king tried to prevent his departure, Lafayette made his way to America in 1777. Thanks to Franklin's enthusiastic recommendation preceding him, he obtained an interview with Washington, who made him a member of his military family. All the other foreign officers on his ship, except Baron de Kalb, were sent home at American expense. Fortunately for Washington, Lafayette was courageous, loyal and competent; his rank also guaranteed that he could make the court hear of Washington's virtues and hopes.

Johann Henri Jules Alexandre von Robais, Baron de Kalb (1721–80) was a Bavarian serving in a German regiment of the French army. After distinguished service in the War of the Austrian Succession and the Seven Years War, he had left military life to marry the heiress of a manufacturing fortune. In 1768 he was sent to America on a secret mission to determine the public mood; he came home filled with admiration for the country and the people. He had expected to be given an important command, but Frenchmen were rarely allowed to do more than assist American generals.

The most important volunteer may have been Friedrich Wilhelm de Steuben (1730–94). The 'von' so often attached to his name, Paul Lockhart informs us in *The Drillmaster of Valley Forge*, is a time-honoured error, but still incorrect. His father was a Junker – technically not noble, but definitely not ignoble – and an engineer in the Prussian army; he himself had earned the title of *Freiherr* (baron) from the prince of Baden-Durlach. Because de Steuben had spent part of his youth in Russia as an engineer, he had observed how officers made unmilitary recruits into soldiers. As a staff officer he had worked directly under Frederick the Great, but when the Seven Years War ended in 1763, there was a general demobilisation that resulted in his being dismissed from service. He applied to various foreign armies, but the only offer came from Benjamin Franklin and Silas Deane, who warned him that he would have to travel to America at his own expense, and that he could not be promised a command. Washington, fortunately, had an eye for talent: he saw in de Steuben the man who could teach drill to his poorly organised regiments and instruct them in the use of the bayonet. Immediately after de Steuben's arrival at Valley Forge in February 1778, he realised that Americans were neither suitable material for the complicated drills of European armies nor likely to remain in the ranks long enough to master them – the veteran army of 1777 had gone home, its place taken by militias and new enlistees. While the suffering of the army was not as severe as Washington made out in letters intended – successfully – to frighten and/or shame the Continental Congress and the Pennsylvania legislature into providing food and fodder, it was a period of quiet suffering that de Steuben was able to use to introduce modified Prussian and French drills, then teach them to a select company, swearing at them through a translator in a combination of German, French and English. He then assigned those soldiers to teach the drills to the other units, taking on yet another group for personal instruction; his *Blue Book* was published the next year for use by officers throughout the army. His work by itself cannot account for the improved fighting ability of the troops, but, by spring, when great numbers of veterans and new recruits joined the army at Valley Forge, Washington had an army.

At the grand review in May 1778 the troops marched splendidly and fired off salutes that impressed French observers. Subsequently, de Steuben became inspector general, supervising all training, and in 1781 defended Virginia against Cornwallis's invading army. Unlike most foreign officers, de Steuben remained in America after the war – almost penniless, it seems, since Congress had no money to reward veterans – and campaigned for the establishment of a military academy at West Point.

On the whole, however, the process of recruiting foreign officers was badly flawed. Benjamin Franklin was a man of the world, but no soldier; Silas Deane lacked any military experience and was barely able to communicate in French. Many of the men they sent to America were totally useless and a few were quite ready to serve the British crown. Even de Steuben was easier to quarrel with than to like, and his credentials were exaggerated in Franklin's introductory letter.

The problem was not just that American soldiers did not know the drills. As the sturdy farmers and businessmen returned home to care for their personal affairs, those who remained with the army were often landless, day-labourers, immigrants, former slaves – in short, not too different in their social origins from the redcoats and Hessians they were facing. It took drill and pride to make them all into soldiers.

Philadelphia Abandoned

Spring of 1778 saw Washington's army swell in size and confidence, while Howe's position in Philadelphia was becoming increasingly uncomfortable. Loyalists, who had seemed so numerous in the autumn, were noticeably fewer now. Part of this was due to the presence of foreign troops in the streets and homes of the populace. It was no accident that even the British public addressed by Kipling's 1890 poem 'Tommy' disliked having soldiers around ('I went into a public-'ouse to get a pint o' beer/The publican 'e up an' sez/'We serve no red-coats here'). Redcoats were a tough lot, but the Hessians were considered worse – Philadelphians, not knowing German, could not even argue with them. Undoubtedly, some of the Pennsylvania Dutch could make themselves understood, but Hessian dialects are a challenge even for other Germans. The Hessians were the catalyst in the alchemy that turned many loyalists and neutrals into patriots.

Royal government proclamations offering to forgive and forget all offences, if only the rebels would lay down their arms, with promises of titles and rewards to officers and political leaders, might have been effective at the beginning of the revolution. Now they were viewed as an admission of failure. A new policy was needed, and a new commander. Howe had already resigned his commission, and once his successor was named, he sailed home to face hostile questions in the House of Commons.

Henry Clinton took command in May 1778. He had been Howe's second-in-command, but had disagreed that reconciliation with the rebels was possible. Moreover, with the French entering the war, new strategies were needed.

Clinton had been born in Newfoundland, son of the governor, and spent ten of his youthful years in New York City. Though a capable officer with vast experience, he had the reputation of being unlucky; worse, he had the unfortunate knack of alienating almost everyone he worked with. Clinton had long advocated rougher handling of the rebel colonies. News of this only stiffened American resolve, and the patriot faction was strengthened now that loyalists understood that their interests were no longer paramount – earlier there had been few local equivalents of Benjamin Franklin, Thomas Jefferson or John Adams to build a royalist party around; now there was none, the colonial elite understanding that they were all merely Americans. Except in the South – the South is always different.

Clinton had barely taken command before orders came from London to concentrate enough forces in New York City so that he could send men and ships to points threatened by the French fleet and still protect his base. With Washington's cavalry dominating New Jersey, his Hessians had to sally out in large bodies to collect food and fodder – an inefficient process and a dangerous one. Reinforcements were needed. Only Howe's army in Philadelphia was available.

Supplying the army occupying the rebel capital was already difficult, with ships on the Delaware River being fired upon from both the Jersey and Pennsylvania shores, and Washington's army sat just twenty-two miles away, blocking access to rich agricultural districts. If Washington learned of the impending retreat, he would be right on the redcoats' tails; should that happen, could Clinton take with him the thousands of loyalists who now feared for their safety? Clearly, though the British army could capture almost any single place it chose to attack, it was not large enough to hold all of them.

Retreat was awkward because if Clinton went by sea, weather might delay his arrival in New York City for weeks; if that city fell to a lightning strike by Washington, no British government could have survived. Clinton's plan was to evacuate Philadelphia with little warning in late June, sending equipment by sea, troops overland. He had been collecting ships in the Delaware River for weeks; now, almost without warning, he loaded them with supplies and loyalists. When they had sailed, his men made their way across New Jersey as quickly as they could, hoping to stay ahead of the pursuing Continental army. Clinton was unlucky in the weather, his troops first being drenched by heavy rain, then marching through the hottest days that local people could remember. Large numbers of Hessians, after a long winter without much physical exertion and now burdened by heavy packs, fell victim to sunstroke.

Washington was right behind him. Some American officers had spoken against taking any risk, now that the combination of the French alliance and the British flight out of Philadelphia almost surely guaranteed ultimate victory, but Washington wanted a fight. His van – led by recently exchanged Charles Lee – intercepted Clinton at Monmouth Courthouse, but soon retreated before a vigorous attack led by Cornwallis. As soon as Washington arrived on the scene, he had choice words for Lee – and Washington had a military vocabulary to match his physical stature and fiery personality – then sent him off the field. He personally led the army back into action, reinforced by new units hurrying through the heat. Once again Washington lived through the day only because the British lacked sharpshooters. The indispensible man of the American cause, he proved to his men that they could stand up to regulars.

Clinton could claim nothing more about the fight than that it was a draw, and given the assumption that the redcoats were unbeatable, it was an embarrassing draw. After Knyphausen's Hessians had escorted the wagon train safely to New York, Clinton viewed the Continental army's strong defensive lines, then during the night followed the Hessians to safety.

The naval vessels barely reached New York before a French fleet appeared off the harbour under the command of Jean Baptiste Charles Henri Hector, comte d'Estaing (1729–94), a veteran of the wars in India. If d'Estaing had arrived earlier, he could have captured or sunk the many transports. But now, when Richard Howe placed his few ships of the line at the harbour mouth, d'Estaing feared that his own ships could not clear the thirty-foot bar to sail past them. Shortly after d'Estaing sailed towards the Caribbean, Howe resigned his commission.

Public opinion in Europe was stirred – joy in France, followed by the dispatch of a fleet to the West Indies; news such as this made the task of the already popular Dr Franklin much easier. Proclamations by the British government that the successful evacuation of Philadelphia was among the most brilliant military feats of all time were met with general silence. The public was not fooled. Whigs had the sour satisfaction of seeing their direst warnings come true. Meanwhile, American privateers were taking British merchantmen by the hundreds – ultimately over a thousand – and bringing their cargos home as booty. French and Dutch ships began delivering munitions, and commerce resumed without the interference of royal tax collectors; the Royal Navy, which earlier had maintained a blockade of rebel ports, was too occupied with the restored French fleet to chase after small merchant vessels or privateers.

When Spain entered the war in 1780, the energetic governor of New Orleans attacked the British outpost at Baton Rouge, capturing several hundred British troops, among whom were three companies of Germans from Waldeck. The next year he captured Pensacola in Florida, bagging yet more Waldeckers.

Meanwhile, there was domestic unrest in Britain. In the summer of 1780 London was paralysed by an anti-papist riot that was joined by bored bluebloods and criminals; the orgy of drunken looting had dangerous anti-Irish implications. A plan put forward to grant constitutional concessions to both America and Ireland went nowhere. The more obvious it became that the war was not going well, the more determined the government was to win it – reputations were on the line.

These 'Gordon riots' were important for the future – they mentally prepared Britons for the mobs of the French Revolution. That is, the riots made everyone except political radicals aware of how easily popular movements could turn violent; short term, it made the government more determined to crush the rebellion in America. That it could not do so was beyond the government's control – the French had intervened in the war.

In 1780 a small French army landed in Newport, Rhode Island. Led by Marshal Jean-Baptiste Donatien de Vimeur de Rochambeau (1725–1807), its duty was to protect the French naval vessels in the harbour. It was a terrible humiliation for the Royal Navy, part of a series of military reverses – the fleet forced out of the Mediterranean, with Minorca lost and Gibraltar under siege, French privateers everywhere, the French and Spanish fleets too large to contain, the Newfoundland fisheries and Canadian timber reserves threatened, the West Indies sugar islands lost, West Florida lost. Worst of all, the League of Armed Neutrality that included Russia, Prussia and the Scandinavian states appeared likely to join the French, Spanish and Dutch in a war designed for no purpose other than to humble British arrogance. Public feeling was, nevertheless, still strongly in favour of the war – the more enemies, the more honour – but the only hope left for victory in America rested in the army chasing rebels in the southern colonies.

The Southern Campaign

Duke Frederick had specifically insisted that his soldiers not be employed in the Caribbean, where the climate was deadly. He was not pleased to learn that, while the letter of the agreement was kept, in late 1778 some units had been dispatched to Georgia under Henry Clinton and Lord Cornwallis. The Hessian reputation for misbehaviour would have been worse, except that Tarleton's Raiders, a loyalist cavalry unit, set a standard for cruelty so repugnant that by comparison the Germans looked good.

This was an internecine struggle of rebels and loyalists, with Scots on both sides. Their brutality towards one another was exceeded only by their love of the others' cattle. Then there were the Indians, who also fought on both sides, but concentrated their attention on one another.

Clinton and Cornwallis soon found themselves encumbered by escaped slaves, many of whom volunteered to fight for their liberty, but all of whom had to be fed and housed. George III's troops could have recruited even more, but the king, listing to the pleas of loyalist slaveholders, failed to follow up the royalist governor of Virginia's proclamation of freedom for those slaves who would take up arms for the crown. This made little impression on the Germans, who enlisted so many slaves in their forces that some units were called Black Hessians; not all former slaves bore arms, there being a greater need for drummers and teamsters, and many were employed as labourers on fortifications. Some former slaves were well-treated; others, many of whom could not speak English, were sold back into slavery in the Caribbean.

When General Clinton marched north towards Charleston in South Carolina, he left the Hessians to hold Savannah. It was a wise decision, since the rebels soon made efforts to capture his base. In the battle of Stono Ferry, in June 1779, Highlanders and Hessians drove away the American attackers, then in September repulsed a joint assault by American troops and marines from d'Estaing's fleet; black labour had made the fortifications too strong to storm in the brief time the French dared linger. Moreover, d'Estaing was wounded in the attempted storm of the Hessian position, and Pulaski, a volunteer Polish engineer, was slain.[16]

A larger body of Hessians accompanied General Clinton on his voyage from New York to Charleston in early 1780. One of their small boats was so damaged in a storm that it was swept out to sea, ran out of food and, after the men rejected the captain's proposal to resort to cannibalism, barely made it into an English harbour.

Clinton quickly forced the surrender of Charleston, bagging five thousand American prisoners. Thinking the war there was essentially over, he returned to New York City, leaving Cornwallis in command with instructions to invade North Carolina and bring the insurrection in the South to an end. With enthusiastic loyalists hounding the patriots out of almost every county, it seemed that he judged the situation correctly.

The situation was sufficiently critical that all parties in the Continental Congress happily agreed to send Horatio Gates there. Gates had been again intriguing for Congress to replace Washington with himself; hence, his supporters thought this the moment to demonstrate his superior skills, while his detractors were thrilled to have him out of Philadelphia. Gates proved the latter party correct by marching his army to exhaustion in a failed effort to surprise the loyalist base at Camden; since the march took nineteen days, Cornwallis was waiting for him. When the fighting started, Gates led the militia in head-long flight, covering the 130 miles back north in three days; Baron de Kalb was mortally wounded, shot several times and bayoneted. Cornwallis, treating him as a fellow officer, assigned his own doctor to retreat his wounds, but to no avail.

The British press celebrated Cornwallis's victory, undoubtedly one of the greatest in the war, as proof that the tide had turned. On the ocean, meanwhile, Rodney's fleet was capturing Dutch colonies in the Caribbean, making it more difficult for Americans to acquire arms, and taking hundreds of Dutch trading vessels that had been transporting American goods. Stories of American revulsion towards the French alliance were joined with accounts of loyalists taking up arms. There was nervousness upon learning that the French fleet had sailed to the Caribbean, threatening the supply of sugar and tobacco – the staples of the coffeehouse culture, where political discussions were at their liveliest.

Washington, too, understood that this was a crisis moment. He chose as commander of the American forces in the South, such as they were, a young man of unlikely origin. Nathanael Greene (1742–86) had been reared a Quaker, had asthma and a limp, and had no military experience prior to 1775. These obstacles he had overcome by determination and hard work. He had educated himself without formal schooling and made a success as a businessman. When war came, he turned his mind to the study of military books (including de Saxe's *Memoirs*) and raised a militia company. His military career boded to be short when he was informed that his lameness disqualified him from being an officer; undiscouraged, Greene happily shouldered a musket and served as a private. Elected commander of the Rhode Island regiments, he came to Washington's attention at the siege of Boston; soon he was named quartermaster general of the Continental army, an unhappy job for anyone because Congress was unwilling to do more than ask states to provide supplies. When Greene resigned in anger, Washington was so reluctant to lose his services that he assigned him command of West Point, the strategic fortress on the Hudson River that Benedict Arnold had sought to betray. When the southern crisis became acute, he turned to Greene, a general with minimal combat experience, to face two of the most talented British commanders of this era – Cornwallis and Tarleton.

Washington sent with him another officer who had begun the war as an amateur – Daniel Morgan. Fictionalised versions of the decisive battle at Cowpens can be seen in the movies *Sweet Liberty* (1986) and *The Patriot* (2000). Among his men were Scots, some of them exiled after the failed rising of 1745, and Scots-Irish who had settled in the back country, the rough, wooded mountains of the Appalachian chain, and learned to master the famous long rifle. Morgan took advantage of Tarleton's love of the wild charge, luring him into a trap in which most of his troopers were killed or taken prisoner.

When Cornwallis attempted to close with the Americans, Greene united the scattered patriot forces and withdrew across North Carolina. The British commander hoped to recruit more local Scottish loyalists, but a misunderstanding, 'Pyle's Massacre', was followed by a steep decline in support for the royal cause. In a seemingly unimportant contemporaneous incident, a fourteen-year-old Scots-Irish courier named Andrew Jackson was taken prisoner; when he refused to clean a British officer's muddy boots, he was struck with a sabre, leaving lifelong scars on his head and hand. Coming down with smallpox, he was released, together with his brother – perhaps in hope the disease would spread among the rebels. Andrew Jackson survived, but his brother did not; an uncle was killed by Tarleton, and his mother perished in a cholera epidemic while nursing patriots on a British prison ship. In 1815, at New Orleans, he paid the British back.[17]

Cornwallis defeated Greene's army at Guilford Courthouse in March 1781, but he lost a quarter of his small army. Looking at the unpromising situation, he decided to move into Virginia, a patriot stronghold that could be easily ravaged by his skilled troops. Clinton, however, sent him a flurry of contradictory orders, culminating with instructions to find a base on the coast from which his seven thousand men could be evacuated.

Washington and Rochambeau now saw an opportunity to bag the army. Earlier the French commander had been so worried that the British would land in Newport, trapping the fleet, that his army was essentially immobile. Not surprisingly, Americans had interpreted this as a policy of watching Americans and Britons slaughter one another. But recently Washington had persuaded Rochambeau to move closer to New York City, to tie down British troops that could otherwise have been dispatched to the South. When the report came that Cornwallis was at Yorktown, Rochambeau and Washington quietly marched their troops south, not revealing their destination until it was too late for Clinton to stop them. That, and persuading French admiral François-Joseph Paul, comte de Grasse (1722–88) to meet them in Chesapeake Bay, was one of the most brilliant achievements of the war.

While de Grasse's fleet beat off the Royal Navy, thereby preventing Cornwallis's escape, Rochambeau and Washington arrived at Yorktown, bringing the size of the besieging army to seventeen thousand. Only slightly over half were Americans. British dithering and confusion prevented Cornwallis's escape before French artillery was in place; after the big guns quickly demolished his defences, French troops took one key redoubt, Americans another. When cannons fired down on his helpless men, Cornwallis surrendered.[18]

Cornwallis's troops could not believe that they had been beaten, but the fact was that professional soldiers had been bested by the hated French and by rebels they despised as amateurs. They went through the surrender ceremony with unusual bad grace, throwing down their arms, but that was effectively the end of the war.

Impact of the American Revolution on Hesse

Thirty thousand Hessians served in America, along with 60,000 redcoats and 55,000 loyalists. These numbers, nevertheless, were insufficient to defeat a Continental army that never numbered over 30,000 at any one time. About 7,700 Hessians died in the American war, the vast majority from heat and disease, and 4,800 remained in the New World, deserting in order to avoid the long voyage home and perhaps another foreign engagement; 2,400 accepted land grants from the British, who were eager to have loyal soldiers in Quebec and the maritime provinces. Others, liking the places they had been stationed, especially Canada, returned after the war as immigrants.

Knyphausen, who had distinguished himself in later combats and been entrusted with the governance of New York City 1779–80, retired in 1782 after losing an eye. He had earned – in his words – neither fame nor wealth. Unhappy with his new post as military governor of Kassel, where he supervised a rabble of new recruits, he established a winery in the south of Hesse that is still managed by his descendants.

Duke Frederick apparently learned his lesson – in the last seven years of his reign he turned down five offers to rent his troops out. As for the economic benefits that were to have come from investing the subsidy money in economic enterprises, most of those were fleeting: the duke's projects were often poorly conceived and badly administered or put into the hands of swindlers – the typical fate of amateur do-good projects. Government direction of the economy had evolved into bureaucratic despotism; nor had the system of welfare for the poor reduced the number of beggars and impoverished families. These were circumstances beyond any government's control, it being impossible to take into account all the needs and wishes of the population, even for a population that was largely agricultural. The duke and his advisors shrank back from radical measures, and the principal defect of Enlightenment optimism – optimism itself, the belief that everything will work out if one only has the right motives – was not a good basis for an economic policy. Frederick came to realise that Hesse was an agricultural region, not an industrial centre, and that workhouses served the interests of the community better than the dole, because they discouraged the freeloaders that every society seems to produce (and, in Hesse's case, attracted from other states). But it was Frederick's Diet (*Landtag*) that ultimately lost patience – once the subsidies ended, the duke's programmes could be maintained only by greatly increasing taxes; and the Diet was unwilling to pay them. Frederick, having seen that a far more powerful British government could not collect taxes from unwilling subjects, gave in.

As for Americans, the last depredation of the German mercenaries was the importation of the Hessian fly, a small insect that fed on cereal crops. It was believed to have been brought to America in the soldiers' bedding.

The Dissolution of the American Army

Martin and Lender, in *A Respectable Army*, demonstrate that the core of Washington's army was composed of 'down and outers' – lower-class troublemakers and hirelings who constantly complained about pay (because it was in 'Continentals' and usually in arrears); they were mutinous, hard-drinking blasphemers and criminals, and often they were interested only in a pension. There were respectable patriots, but few could leave their farms or trades, and families, for seven long years.

The famous Newburgh conspiracy at the end of the war – which Washington barely quelled by means of subtle theatrical gestures and a quiet speech which left listeners both embarrassed and in tears – almost had the army seizing power, collecting its pay and creating a central national government led by Washington's enemies. The Confederation, the successor to the Continental Congress, eliminated this threat to its authority by reducing the army to six hundred men. Even this tiny force was not put on the frontier, but stationed at West Point and the federal arsenal at Springfield, Massachusetts. The veterans, having only three months' wages in a discredited currency, waited in vain for their reward. Veterans surviving until 1818 received a land grant in one of two 'military districts' in Michigan and Illinois; most, being too old to move west, sold their claims to speculators for pittances, then the speculators had to wait for a decade before they could find anyone willing to settle in Indian country. It was the same all across the frontier. Indian chiefs would 'sell' the land, but their warriors did all not see how this bound them to move away. Removal became the unhappy duty of the army.

In the end, Washington's army came to represent the principle of republicanism upon which the new nation rested. The myth of the citizen-soldier, so often decried by military historians who knew how incompetent untrained troops were when fighting regulars, was so powerful that scholars have overlooked both the importance of the militia for the tradition of self-government and the regulars' willingness to sacrifice their own interests for the greater good. It took generations to find the right balance, and each war required the nation to find that balance anew.

Wider Implications of the Revolution

The impact of the American Revolution on France is obvious. First of all, war expenditures created a financial crisis that Louis XVI was never able to master, requiring him (much like Charles I of England a century and a half earlier) to call the Estates General to pass new taxes; he then mishandled the demands for reforms. Second, America came to represent an ideal that French reformers first sought to copy, then to surpass.

The impact on Great Britain was subtler. Some credit the armed revolt with sharpening the Whig–Tory debate, so that on one hand the king's party slowed its efforts to increase royal power, on the other it provided Edmund Burke and other Whigs occasions for expounding the principle of limited government. Thus, Burke was ready for the more fundamental challenge of the French Revolution, when he could argue for making changes slowly, by consensus – by counting heads, if you will, rather than by lopping them off.

In Ireland the parliament gained new rights and judges became more independent. The 'Constitution of 1782' made the island into a type of dominion. The comparison of Irish unrest with America is misleading – America began its war, then drew the French in; in 1798 Irish rebels took advantage of an existing conflict. There was no Continental Congress, no minutemen, no Continental army. The French force that made its way past the watchful Royal Navy was too tiny to be taken seriously, and French revolutionaries were anything but good Catholics. Most importantly, the British government took the situation seriously, giving Cornwallis almost one hundred thousand men to crush the rebels, then making swift constitutional concessions to Catholics and Dissenters alike. Cornwallis also served in India, earning praise for his forceful administration and military competence.

However, this is the long-term view. As Simms reports in *Three Victories and a Defeat*, the years 1765–85 had been terrible for the king's party. A decade of neglecting continental allies and ignoring the French and Spanish naval building programmes were topped off by making even the Dutch into enemies. The overstretched Royal Navy suffered humiliating defeats, and only by recognising American independence could the War Department withdraw sufficient forces to fight more effectively elsewhere. The first British Empire had fallen.

South Americans watched this debacle intently. Native-born aristocrats and educators, long intimidated by the efficiency of Spain's professional armies, saw in the success of American arms and the Revolutionary army of France a way of taking for themselves the offices held exclusively by foreign appointees. Action was delayed until Napoleon occupied Spain, so that the original revolutionary movement in almost every Latin American country was conservative in nature – to reject Bonaparte's appointees to colonial offices. But their efforts went badly awry and could not be rescinded even when the Bourbons returned to Madrid. A combination of factors – the Spanish army doing rather better than they had calculated, so that many of the revolutionary leaders were shot as traitors; the breakdown of the economy so that no government could pay its army; efforts to impose a federal system on states that knew only central direction, and the resistance thereto; a struggle over the role of religion; and indigenous peoples joining in the civil wars – meant that there were too many problems at one time for the new states to resolve them.

Americans learned lessons, too. Sometimes the wrong ones. The belief that amateur armies could beat professional ones led to many defeats in the war of 1812; and the fear of an all-powerful central authority reinforced the already existing tradition of states' rights. The colonies had co-operated only reluctantly before 1775, a habit that changed little during the War for Independence. In the nineteenth century, proponents of slavery and those who wished it abolished each sought to advance their cause through national legislation, while keeping the federal government too weak to harm them. When the Civil War began in 1861 European officers volunteered their services. However, since the two service academies – West Point for the army, Annapolis for the navy – had turned out numerous professionally trained officers, both the North and the South were able to make their mass armies quickly into capable fighting forces without foreign help.

CHAPTER NINE

Summary

War Evolving Towards What?

Warfare was changing quickly even before the French Revolution burst onto the scene and swept away most of the professional armies of Europe. According to Parker in *The Military Revolution*, three major innovations were already underway – the increased use of skirmishers and light cavalry, the organisation of diverse military units into divisions capable of combined arms operations, and better field artillery; minor innovations such as better roads and maps increased the speed of marches and the ability to supply armies. At the same time the size of armies had increased. The French Revolution speeded up these developments, but it did not create them.

The greatest change in war during this century – according to Brauer and van Tuyll in *Castles, Battles and Bombs* – was not in the military sphere *per se*, but in the ability to organise resources to support it. Strategy, weapons and tactics in 1700 and 1800 would have been equally familiar to Marlborough and Bonaparte, but the former would have been amazed at the systems of taxation, the bureaus for dispensing funds and overseeing expenses, the numbers of fortresses and arsenals, and the size of armies. If this is modernisation, rather than the scope of military innovations, then the protracted debate about when and how it occurred is over.

The 'old regime', McNeill reminds us in *The Rise of the West*, may have been untidy and illogical, but it still worked and was highly effective. There was such comparative stability at home and such obvious superiority to most non-Western states, that European military and economic systems seemed destined to dominate the world. Although the class system was crude and inefficient, religious authorities were often ignorant and superstitious, and the vast majority of people lived in or near poverty while a handful revelled in luxury, on the whole there was much that everyone could be proud of, or at least persuaded that it was not worth trying to make changes. Should dissenters become too noisy, the army would silence them. If young men became too bothersome, there was always the army.

Why would men volunteer to serve such an oppressive system? There was, of course, always the money. That was important, but economic motivations can be overstated. Showalter, in *The Wars of Frederick the Great*, warns us not to forget escaping from the boredom of village life. A young man would run off to the city, then, unable to find work, enlist. Many men went from one army to another. After deserting – usually at night – changing their clothing and name in order to serve in some dull city militia until that became unendurable, they then joined a real army. These men had to be resourceful, since desertion would be punished at least by a severe whipping, and perhaps even a firing squad. There was also the pride of being in a successful army, of fighting national enemies and foreign infidels, or serving the king. Lastly, many young men had no choice – conscription made that decision for them.

If war was the justification for the creation of new state activities, those activities were soon partially redirected to civilian use. Military highways and bridges could be used by merchants, farmers and wealthy tourists; the construction of fortifications stimulated industry and the exploitation of natural resources – the growth of Ulm below one of the greatest fortresses in southern Germany provides a good example of how new industries needed for military construction can stimulate an economy. Armies assisted in policing rural areas as well as cities, creating sufficient peace and order that citizens became confident of keeping more of the wealth they produced; hence, they produced more.

The old-fashioned mercenary, who changed uniforms when it suited him, disappeared. Armies put prisoners-of-war into jails rather than inducted them into their own ranks, regimental pride came to outrank instincts for individual survival, and soldiers took responsibility for seeing that their comrades behaved. It was as if the spirit of the Enlightenment was transforming everything – even armies were becoming more rational and respectable. This was only partially true, of course, and it did not last.

Life was not pleasant in the new army, as Fritz Redlich demonstrates in *The German Military Enterpriser and his Work Force*, volume II. If armies *per se* were no longer feared as greatly as in the past, the public still held individual soldiers in contempt; and feared them. It was not that every recruit came from dregs of society, but after several years of brutal discipline and association with criminal elements, they left the service much like minor felons released from prison – far worse than they had gone in. Changing the conditions of life was not easy – without strict discipline few soldiers would have fought, and fighting was the point of having an army. The armies were so much larger than before that the individual became lost in the mass.

It may have been, as Hall suggests in concluding *Weapons and Warfare*, that states went bankrupt because these larger armies required conscription and heavier taxes; the ensuing revolutions then caused the fall of great powers. That idea, though logical to us, would have struck kings in the 1780s as strange – they knew from history that their ancestors had never been able to rest securely, but however dangerous their external and internal enemies remained, they had thought that the 'modern' world was safer for monarchy. Revolution was far from their minds. Yet it came in 1789, with a suddenness that can stun modern readers as much as it did people at the time.

Still, everyone knew that all familiar dynasties had at some time replaced older ones. Readers of Voltaire's *Candide* did not find it inconceivable that the hero of the novel, eating with six strangers at the carnival in Venice, asked why their servants called each of them 'Majesty'. Removing the masks revealed one to be a former Ottoman sultan, another a Russian pretender, then Charles Edward Stuart, two kings of Poland and an elected king of Corsica. The monarchs who could have saved Louis XVI chose instead to divide up Poland among themselves.

The political earthquake that overthrew the old regime in France liberated the new as well as destroying the old. The advantages of the new have blinded us somewhat to the strengths of the old, because it was under the protection of the traditional practices (modified over time to reduce the dead hand of the past on thought and action) that new ideas were born and nurtured.

The American Revolution, like the French Revolution, was based on concepts that developed over generations. Without the English Civil War, without the Glorious Revolution, there would perhaps have been no protest against royal tyranny. Without the American Revolution, would there have

been demands for reform in France? On the other hand, if reason were
applied to human affairs, would any sensible person have argued for a
continuation of the status quo?

In many ways, these protests were against the military practices of
the royal governments – conscription, forced labour and taxes; soldiers
quartered in homes, Swiss stationed in the Bastille and in Versailles.

Nor was everything changed by the French Revolution. Poles served willingly in the armies of the Habsburgs in Spain, in the armies of Napoleon
in Italy and Haiti. Their hopes were two-fold – first, that their employer
would turn his attention to freeing their homeland; second, that they
would become the nucleus of a new national army. Service as mercenaries
was their means of working towards a noble end. It echoed the hopes and
dreams of Scottish and Irish exiles of earlier times. Equally noble, it was
equally in vain. Militarism would prevail for generations to come.

German Militarism

Hesse-Kassel was the most thoroughly militarised state in Germany,
with more than double the percentage of men under arms in Prussia.[1]
Only because Hesse-Kassel was so small do we think of Prussia as the
embodiment of militarism. Aside from Hessians, today only Americans
are aware of the military skills of the Hessian soldiery – who were not
recruited exclusively from Hesse-Kassel, but from neighbouring lands as
well. In fact, the ranks could not have been filled locally without taking
productive workers out of the fields and workplaces; and the pay was more
than competitive with day-labourers' wages. The government punished
anyone who left the country to serve in a foreign army; foreign recruiters
were subject to harsh treatment, even life imprisonment. Boys were
registered with the government at age seven, then mustered at sixteen
so that recruiting officers could speak with them. While there was no
absolute requirement that young men enlist, considerable pressure could
be applied, especially by the community, which apparently supported the
practice strongly.

It may be tempting to imagine that a militarised regime headed by a self-
centred autocrat would be backward in every sense of that word. That was
not the case. Frederick II of Hesse-Kassel may have been eccentric, but he

was a truly enlightened ruler who worked hard at bettering the life of his subjects, in encouraging industry and the arts and in furthering education. His lands had been harshly treated during the Seven Years War; despite his official neutrality – French soldiers had extracted supplies and money wherever they went, and Marburg/Lahn, the ancient seat of his family, changed hands fifteen times!

Americans considered the Hessian reputation for cruelty well deserved, though the damage they did there would not have been remarkable in Europe. A few rapes, a few chickens stolen, a few places burned down – one Hessian officer viewed these actions as proof that the men had spirit. If their men had some criminal tendencies, what else should one expect of mercenaries?

This judgement was shared by Trevelyan in volume II of *The American Revolution*. Writing of the many men who moved from one army to another, he concluded:

> Without honour, without patriotism, they were thieves and drunkards; seducers in time of peace, and something much worse when during an invasion they had a village or farmhouse at their mercy. Hardly able, some of them, to name a country where they could ever make a home, and settle down to a trade, without the almost certain prospect of being shot as deserters, they lived for the passing moment, intent only on misusing it in some manner agreeable to themselves.

Americans had heard stories of Ireland and Scotland, terrifying tales that reminded American rebels of what everyone had to expect if the War for Independence failed. But they had never imagined an iron tyranny enforced by men who did not even speak their language.

Hessian soldiers were not impressed by Americans, but they did admire America's beauty and wealth. As Ingrao notes in *The Hessian Mercenary State*, they believed that each citizen had the duty to defend his country, and that this was especially true against Catholic enemies, but they could not understand why Americans were fighting. Taxes? They seemed light. Poverty? Hardly applicable. The soldiers had come from impoverished circumstances themselves, with little to look forward to beyond a miserable rural existence or worse conditions in towns. They looked down on Americans because the Hessian military ethos taught that a real man was a soldier, and the colonials had demonstrated repeatedly that they lacked the discipline and staying power of real troops. They would not have been surprised that Americans learned little from them other than an appreciation of band music.

Although the Hessians were earning reasonable wages in the army, there were no jobs waiting for them at the end of the final long ocean voyage. Consequently, desertions increased after 1778, then again in 1783. More might have deserted, but they knew that the Hessian government would seize their property or assess their parents for their share of their inheritance. There were incentives – in some cases deserters received American citizenship, two hundred acres of land, a cow and two pigs; it may be that some replacement troops may have enlisted with the intent of deserting as quickly as possible. However, few had much interest in the ideological reasons for American independence.

The United Kingdom and Empire

Was war equally the defining characteristic of Great Britain in this era? Keegan certainly thinks so in *Fields of Battle*: 'A people numerically weak who challenge the world bind themselves with heavy chains, oppressive taxation, protectionist and costly tariffs, the cruelties of the press gang, fierce treason laws.' The spirit of conquest that subjected Wales, Scotland and Ireland to English law, religion and language was later extended to the wider world. America was the one exception, and when the effort was made to include those colonies to the general pattern, it provoked a revolt.

The hegemony that Britain had enjoyed in 1763 had deteriorated by 1775. Simms notes that France and Spain's shipbuilding programme was outstripping the Royal Navy, Britain was without continental allies and the nation was divided against itself. Unhappiness in America and Ireland could have been cured relatively easily, but imagination was as absent as corruption was pervasive.

The American War for Independence was not the first effort to resist the imposition of English practices and direct taxes, but it was the only one to succeed. The outcome of the war was not accepted easily by crown and Parliament – some historians refers to America's war of 1812 as the Second War for Independence, and some see Britons' enthusiasm for the

Confederacy in 1861 not merely as a matter of weakening a rival, but settling an old score. Even in 1917 Americans – with large minorities of Irish and Germans – had mixed feelings about becoming British allies. The ringing phrase, 'Lafayette, we are here!' was for French ears, not Britons'.

Keegan notes that eastern North America was as heavily fortified a region as any in the world – once one takes into account the difference in scale. Warfare was brutal, too, and ethnic cleansing practised as well, as exiled Cajuns of Louisiana could testify (and those Indian tribes defeated by a combination of one or another colonial power and local enemies). The American Gibraltar was Louisbourg, the great fortress on a barren outcropping of Nova Scotia at the mouth of the Saint Lawrence River, but the great conflict known as the French and Indian War began at the confluence of the Ohio, Allegheny and Monongahela rivers. When Louisbourg was taken and Fort Duquesne became Fort Pitt, France's hope for empire collapsed.

This had not been inevitable. In *The French and Indian War*, Borneman notes many opportunities missed by French administrators and courtiers to save Canada at relatively small cost, but the court was so focused on the war against Prussia that they could not see the larger picture. Under these conditions, it was not easy to recruit officers and men to serve in garrisons where taverns were rare and pretty women had their pick of men with greater promise.

Race or Culture?

It was easy to mistakenly attribute the skills of Western European officers to racial superiority – as was often done. They were superior, arguably, to their native counterparts in India, Africa and Russia, but this was because they had skills that helped transform unsuccessful armies into deadly ones. For the most part the native nobility could have learned these skills, but chose not to. Class feelings and culture stood in the way, much as the high-born nobles of Europe were willing to pose as regimental commanders, but hired professionals to train the troops and give orders when bullets began to fly.

There was another phenomenon in play – the mystique of the superior class. Nobles had long appreciated the advantages of dress, posture and wider vocabulary in keeping the lower classes in their place. Surely, many soldiers believed that their officers, who were almost always reared to believe in their right to command others, must know better than they what had to be done – even when ordered to march towards what seemed like certain death. Officers maintained this fiction by refusing to promote common soldiers, no matter how capable they were.[2]

Pride played a role in this, at all levels. Officers exposed themselves freely to enemy fire, often riding prominently on horseback ahead of their men – as George Washington did at Princeton, miraculously emerging unscathed from the smoke of simultaneous volleys. It helped that marksmanship was almost non-existent and that opposing officers usually discouraged the practice of singling out commanders, but survival through battle after battle impressed common soldiers. And the example was contagious.

In the case of non-white troops, the same principles prevailed. If they came to believe that whiteness was a proof of superiority (a concept that few white men ever sought to discourage) and courage, it stands to reason that they might be sceptical about the abilities of people their own colour.

This is not an idea we would welcome in modern times, but it has given many a modern college graduate a management job that could be performed by a school dropout with experience and training. Moreover, once we accept the idea all Europeans were considered superior to everyone else, it should come as no surprise to learn that some Europeans were considered superior to others.

The Iron Horseman

Peter the Great began the practice of marrying Romanovs to Germans. Anna, who came to power from Courland, favoured Germans from that tiny duchy so extensively during her reign (1730–40) that there was a nationalist reaction under Elizabeth – the anti-German animus that led Russia to war against the new perceived enemy, Frederick the Great. After Catherine became tsarina, there was less Russian blood in imperial veins.

The enthusiasm for all things German was seen in Peter the Great giving German names to new cities, military centres and summer palaces (Saint Petersburg, Kronstadt and Peterhof). He famously required the nobles to wear Western (German) clothing and to cut their beards, but he also imported medical specialists, entrepreneurs who could build up industry and commerce, and officers who could reorganise the army, navy and state bureaucracy on Western models. Though personally very informal in his tastes, after visiting personally many important Western courts, Peter insisted that his court and those of his officials and ambassadors copy their splendour, then exceed it.

In that ironic way that history has, the French orientation of the later Russian nobility had the effect of separating the elite even further from the great mass of peasants and labourers. Soon enough, even their accent in Russian was noticeably different from that spoken in the countryside. While the upper classes of Russia were becoming Westernised, the lower classes mistrusted every effort at reforming their condition or liberating them from poverty or superstition. Eventually, some advanced members of the upper classes came to see the peasantry as the representatives of real Russia; others sensed that if the peasantry awoke, their own services would not be needed. Both groups believed that it would be best to keep the common soldier from seeing how peasants in the West lived, so that they would not try to change their lot.

They did not need to worry. While military service in Europe seems to have had an impact on Russian officers, all of whom were nobles or foreign mercenaries, this was not true of common soldiers. At least there was little noticeable impact, though trying to read the thoughts of illiterate soldiers is guaranteed to be an exercise in frustration. Russian officers remained persuaded that common soldiers would fight only when compelled and when drunk. Therefore, the *knout* (a rope whip) and brandy became part and parcel of their military tradition.

An even more lasting tradition was a belief that all change must come from the top, and a resigned acceptance of the fact that resistance from the bottom would be futile. Rebellions were common in Russia, but they always failed. Extreme methods could force reluctant and even hostile subjects to conform, methods that were continued even when bottom-up progress was showing itself to have superior results in Western Europe. Western individualism and capitalism ran against class prejudices, religious ideals and common sense as Russians understood it. Peter the Great tried to beat change into Russian heads, using methods hardly designed to encourage the kind of change that was motivating people in the West.

The Baltic

The Swedish Empire collapsed. If, as Roberts suggests, the thrust of Swedish policy from Gustavus Adolphus through Charles XII, was to provide security, it was a failure. This is the argument, he says in *The Swedish Imperial Experience*, of the 'old school'. The 'new school', reflecting Marxist influence, attributes economic motives – that is, the effort to control Baltic commerce and the rich Russian trade. Later Swedish efforts aimed to protect the territorial integrity of the nation – if this meant accepting a French general as king when Napoleon was riding high, so be it; if this same French general joined the coalition against Napoleon in 1813, that was also good. Sweden's armed neutrality and its geographic isolation protected it from the winds of war through the next two centuries. That is, there were gales, but no hurricanes.

Peace came to the Baltic states, too, though a very different kind of peace – one imposed by the tsars. There was commercial activity in Reval and Riga, but on the whole the countryside stagnated. Individual incentive was curtailed by rules designed to protect the workers, the employers, the nobles and the interests of the state. Those with an education, mainly German-speaking natives, did well; those with an interest in the military found quick advancement in the tsarist army. But those who spoke neither Russian nor German, nor the French of the internationally minded elite, were condemned to rural poverty and backwardness. And God help the non-Christian communities, especially the Jews, whose contributions elsewhere in Europe were to contribute so much to the arts, culture and science.

The practice of hiring foreigners continued, even foreigners from as far away as Italy. Though Italian architects, artists and musicians were lured north by high wages, a few soldiers came because the north offered safe refuge. Filippo Paolucci, for example, who fought against Napoleon in his native Modena, became commander of Austrian troops in Dalmatia at Cattaro, then was hired by the Russians to command troops in Georgia, and finally made governor of Riga 1812–29. Always discontented, he abandoned his efforts to abolish serfdom when offered the governorship of Genoa. Warm weather, good wine and good conversation won him over. In the end, most sell out. Some just have higher prices than others, and some cannot find a purchaser.

The Balkans

Bad as the situation of the native peoples of the Baltic states was, their experience nowhere equalled the degradation of the peoples in the Balkans. There the incredibly complex mixture of populations and the low levels of education and commerce made it difficult to create those feelings of belonging that are at the heart of nationhood.

The Austrians and Russians watched one another warily, neither eager to eat up regions that might bring on more indigestion than pleasure, but also determined that the other would not get them. This left the Ottoman Turks in possession. Unhappily, there is no worse master than a declining state, for in such a situation those in power have to resort to brutal measures to hold troublemakers down until they can return the state of affairs to their vision of the good old days. One might argue that the Ottoman Turks would have been better off to abandon the Balkans to Christians, who would have fought over it for decades, but one cannot blame them for an inability to see the future clearly enough to sacrifice lands that their ancestors spent blood and treasure to acquire. European states made the same mistakes.

The treasure of generations was exhausted in the wars between 1700 and 1789. Not that the wars were totally useless. Certainly, Protestants facing the bigotry of Louis XIV had little patience with pacifist thoughts. Catholic nuns in the Low Countries considered wounded Dutch soldiers unworthy of their attention because they were Protestants. Germans believed their lands worth defending, as did Swedes and Poles – the only difficulty being to define where their lands came to an end. But they supported national and religious goals and paid for the ambitions and whims of their rulers. They gave up their crops, their homes, their animals, and paid taxes that were often the equivalent of confiscations. As for the soldiers, they were paid in debased coins.

This should have been no surprise. In the end all wars are paid for by inflation. It became a byword in the 1960s that young men die in old men's wars. Even so, John F. Kennedy, the youngest American president ever elected, sent the first ground troops into Vietnam. But it is a good rule of thumb. William III of England, like all those sharing Stuart blood, aged poorly – becoming querulous, disagreeable and unwilling to compromise. Louis XIV became more determined to persist in his wars towards the end

of his extremely long reign. The issue is probably less age than health –
men and women suffering physically tend to tire easily and to make poor
judgements.

An exception, perhaps, was Frederick the Great, who, like Goethe's
Faust, turned to public works in his old age, to correspondence, to learned
conversations about philosophy and to music, only to grow weary of life.
'Der alte Fritz' became increasingly solitary and querulous, but he did not
start new wars.

Universal Peace

The men and women of the Enlightenment were remarkable for their
optimism that rational self-interest would soon bring an end to the outdated dynastic wars of Europe. Between 1784 and 1795 Immanuel Kant
wrote proposals for universal peace. Some of his ideas were revolutionary,
though quite logical for the Age of Enlightenment. A few were errors typical
of the era – first, that men were logical creatures; second, that nature has a
plan which will result in a political constitution that promotes the common
weal and justice; and last, that the human race is moving along the road of
progress towards a better society.

In 1756 Rousseau wrote an essay on 'Paix Perpetuelle', arguing that the
European states were actually in a state of continual war. This was wrong,
he wrote, since Europeans shared so much in the way of culture, religion
and tradition, they should be living in peace. He proposed a confederation
which guaranteed each member protection from every other member, with
regular meetings of a diet to resolve disagreements. An extended peace
would lead not only to prosperity and programme, but also to unlearning
the arts of war.

Jeremy Bentham, the utilitarian philosopher ('the greatest good for
the greatest number') wrote unpublished essays between 1786 and 1789
describing ways to avoid war. His proposals included reduction in the size of
armies and navies, leaving only sufficient numbers to deal with robbers and
pirates, and giving up the colonies. He was astute enough to recognise that
colonies cost more than they brought in, but he also understood that the
public wanted its tobacco and sugar. Hence, being a practical man, he waited
for the right moment to publish his thoughts. That moment never came.

Sugar was the equivalent of oil in the twenty-first century. Once a luxury, it had become a necessity, used in such a wide variety of food products and beverages that even the poorest Europeans had come to rely on its availability. To produce sugar, slavery was tolerated or even considered inevitable, necessary and somehow just. In the end, it seemed that commerce itself was so tied into sugar that giving up the colonies was perceived as inevitably leading to poverty and national decline.

The global economy of that era provoked some of the same concerns, complaints and unrealistic proposals we see today about post-colonial globalisation. We can see in the proposals for universal peace efforts to limit the power of the new national states, with their centralised bureaucracy replacing ancient institutions that limited the authority of dynastic rulers. Why were people dying so that some imbecile or other could rule a province that few people could even locate on a map? Many couldn't even read a map. Now, national interests – that was something else, something that would bring forth new troubles.

It is certainly true, as Bell writes in *The First Total War*, that Napoleon's occupation of Germany awakened a romantic German nationalism, and that this romanticism had baneful results in the future.[3] However, it would be more accurate to say that Germans were awakened from a nap of decades than from centuries of sleep.

Bell noted an even more important point, that the 'culture of war' changed radically, in that war ceased to be seen as something normal, something that was a part of civilian life. Instead, war became a separate profession. He then placed this in its modern context, with modern scholarship treating warfare as something outside, and less significant, than other aspects of our culture.

Black asked a very different question in *Warfare in the Eighteenth Century*: if the eighteenth century led to the rise of the West, which West was this? There had been nothing preordained in British domination of India and North America, or even European industry and commerce. The British were welcomed wherever they could bring law and order, as in India, just as the Ottomans were welcomed in Egypt. Adam Smith, he noted, had credited the modern army with defending civilisation. But there were limits to what Europeans could accomplish, and to what war could achieve – it could not, for example, eliminate all religious practices and ethnic identifications.

Even less could military power suppress the national feelings that accompanied the spread of literacy, wider economic spheres and the greater ease of travel and commerce.

Pacifism

Dreams of peace were most common in America, the land with the fewest outside threats. Leading this movement, but not alone, were the Quakers, a religious society formed during the English Civil War. Their famous statement to Charles II that they would not fight in *any* war was sufficient – along with William Penn's close friendship with that easy-going monarch – for the Stuart monarch to ignore their implicit challenge to his authority. It helped that they never actively opposed any of his military operations. Still, their obstinate insistence on social equality and their refusal to conform in almost any way resulted in many being jailed. Since Charles II preferred getting the Quakers out of England to imprisoning them, he gave William Penn a large colony in America that unfortunately was still occupied by the original inhabitants. Quaker Pennsylvania became famous for its efforts to maintain peace with the Indians, though the infamous 'walking purchase' of a later generation was seen by the Indians as a deceitful trick – the 'walkers' actually being trained runners; the Scots-Irish on the frontier, who were victims of Indian raids, had few good words for a pacifism that blamed them rather than the Indians for their troubles.

Pennsylvania became the refuge of those Protestants driven out of Germany by Louis XIV, especially those pacifist sects that refused even to help drive the French back across the Rhine. Pennsylvania became a leader in democratic movements such as women's rights and opposition to slavery, and Quaker honesty became a byword. Philadelphia was also the home of Benjamin Franklin. His influence on the city was profound – he helped organise the post office, the public library, a public lecture hall, the University of Pennsylvania (all highly innovative at the time) and was a highly respected scientist, sage and political activist. He was also a popular humorist, demonstrating more fully than almost any man except Voltaire that the heart of the Enlightenment was an ability to see the world realistically, then laugh gently at its foibles and contradictions. Franklin was sceptical about religion, but not interested in abolishing it; after a brief flirtation with agnostic notions, he began attending the Presbyterian Church – for him Quakers had too little interest in the world and too much interest in changing it.

When the French and Indian War brought war to Pennsylvania, the Quakers gave up their control of the government and concentrated on their testimonies, one of which emphasised the evils of war. Even the best of conflicts would inevitably bring evil, they said, a position which made them reluctant to support the American Revolution. Still, one Quaker, Nathanael Greene, became Washington's best general. Others took up arms and were expelled from their meetings. This division into patriots and pacifists/loyalists was prominent among the many schisms that transformed the Quakers from one of the largest religious bodies in America to one of the smallest.

This could not be foreseen at the time. The issue was a matter of right and wrong, and it was awkward to be seen as implying that democracy and self-government was wrong; it was even more awkward that the British saw them as potential allies who refused to see their ultimate self-interests. When Dr Franklin went to France, he played on the French belief that he was a Quaker to avoid purchasing expensive court clothing – he wore a simple black outfit such as was widely worn by Quaker men (women wore grey), but he doffed a coon-skin cap, which endeared him to the many followers of Rousseau who believed that the men who lived in America's forest wilderness were closer to nature's intent than they were.

Nevertheless, it was not pacifism that won American independence, but war. And it was war conducted professionally, with Americans relying on European experts and European manuals of war. And thus began, or continued, the American debate over the role of the military in a republican state. How is it possible to defend liberty without a military? And how does one protect liberty from the military?

The answers vary from person to person, from time to time, but the questions remain. What we do know is that political life – and all that flows from it, directly and indirectly – cannot be understood without taking into consideration the events of 1700–89. This is as true in Asia, Africa and Latin America as in Europe and North America.

If the Muslim world was not fundamentally affected by the developments of this time, its isolation led to an intellectual and technological stagnation summarised by Bernard Lewis in the title of his book, *What Went Wrong?* One may or may not agree with his argument, and, according to Faroqhi, in *The Ottoman Empire and the World Around It*, the Islamic world has been misjudged. Still, it is hard to argue that much went right in those states in this period.

Much went wrong in Europe and America too, but it is difficult to imagine (until recently) a best-selling book on the West with that title or thesis.[4] *Bayonets* helped bring one type of society into being in Europe, *scimitars* protected a backward-looking society in the Middle East, and *bayonets* made possible the constitutional republic in North America that inspired thinkers to imagine life without kings, nobles and clergy – it might be added, without a mercenary army.

The Future, or the Past, or Both

Showalter reminds us in *The Wars of Frederick the Great* that although in this era war seemed to be the means of changing the world, the balance of power meant that no state could dominate. As conflicts ground to bloody stalemates, thinking men began to recognise again the significance of diplomacy. Slow changes were possible; sweeping change brought disaster.

Certainly change was not comfortable. As Martin and Lender demonstrate, it was not easy, even under the most favourable circumstances, to create an approximation of the title of their book, *A Respectable Army*. Americans were leery of a regular army, no matter how essential it was or how much it had contributed to defending republican principles. As historians have long noted, Americans could neglect preparations for defence because they had no serious enemies. Still, by 1800, one-sixth of the American national budget went to paying off Barbary pirates, and payments to Indian tribes on the frontier were expensive, too. Eventually, Jefferson – perhaps the most pacific president ever to sit in the White House – authorised war on the first and tried to buy out the second, so that the original possessors of the land (or at least the most recent possessors) would move west.

We live in a complex world, but it is not impossibly more complex than in the past, despite the much larger world population today, the interconnections of economies, politics and thought, and new and occasionally disquieting social and intellectual trends. We live in a world more at peace, with more prosperity and more potential than ever before – but there are parts of the world which could do better. It is not that the developed world does not have good armies, but it lacks the will to use them. Into these vacuums come the irregular forces, mercenaries and criminals.

The immediate future, in the opinion of Brauer and van Tuyll in *Castles, Battles and Bombs*, belongs to alliances and 'security firms'. Policy makers are bedevilled by a combination of new terrorism challenges, public opposition to conscription, casualties and taxes, and a population that increasingly doubts that violence settles anything. Volunteer armies have their internal problems: pay must be higher, commanders must avoid casualties to prevent enlistments from plummeting and equipment must be more sophisticated and expensive. It is a situation made for sharing resources, especially bases, and for a 'rent-a-cop' scenario. Security firms can better provide experienced personnel as bodyguards, to protect buildings and convoys, and move quickly. They provide this at a cost – sometimes a very high cost. Understandably, such security firms are very unpopular with progressives – who call them mercenaries and even attempt to arrest them as war criminals.

We can not yet have a world without armies. Wolves are in the woods, and Little Red Riding Hood still wants to visit her grandmother. When she asks why grandma's teeth are so bright and sharp, must she quietly accept the fact that some will eat and others will be eaten? Or will she call the woodman?

If we cannot do without 'mercenaries', the challenge for us is to find ways to employ them rationally, so that they do the most good and the least harm. For those who prefer to not live in this world, there are still monasteries and nunneries – mostly half-empty, unable to compete with the lure of secular society. Awkwardly, all too often those most likely to denounce the world we live in are loath either to seek to improve it or to withdraw from it. Still, one should not become too pessimistic. In spite of all our collective failures over many years, for many people life is still good and for many others it offers the potential of becoming so. As we look in the mirror of our imperfections, we should remember to smile at ourselves.

Notes

Preface

1   The essays in Frank Tallett and D. J. B. Trim's *European Warfare, 1350–1750* dismiss the traditional view that absolute monarchs were forcing state-building and modernisation, using the army and the new bureaucracy to gather power into their hands. Rather, there was a process of persuasion and flattery, compromise, bribery and mutual benefits that brought the elites to support royal policies. While this thesis might not satisfy readers who think of Peter the Great, it explains much of what was happening across Western and central Europe in the late seventeenth century.

Chapter One

1   Fritz Redlich, *The German Military Enterpriser and his Work Force*, volume I, demonstrated that there was little to choose between soldiers, peasants and townspeople, or soldiers and officers – all were bad. Soldiers drank, fornicated and raped, but when it came to atrocities, civilians gave as good as they got. By 1648 all armies were exhausted – little food, little clothing, few arms and hardly any pay – but if conditions in the countryside had been as bad as described, the armies would have collapsed earlier. There were always enough weapons for killing, food for feasts and alcohol for drunken revelry.

2   An exception is Prussia, where detailed records for recruits were kept – entries for bastards being written upside-down, perhaps to discourage efforts to promote them, but those numerous social outcasts were welcomed into the ranks of cannon-fodder. Redlich uses Prussian records effectively in *The German Military Enterpriser*, volume II. His principal concern, however, was with the men who recruited and commanded the regiments. These entrepreneurs made money in numerous clever ways – the sale of uniforms and equipment, buying and selling horses, sharing in the loot, and using their men as rural labourers and in other employment. Commanders had one major problem – paying the initial bonus to enlistees. This meant drawing on their own resources or finding a patron or borrowing. Only later did the state provide such money in a timely fashion.

3   Maria Aurora of Königsmarck (1662–1728) was foremost among a class of women rising by a variety of talents to positions of influence and occasionally

marrying very well. Augustus had broken off their relationship after coming back from his Balkan wars and learning that she had been flirtatious (or more) during his absence. He had complained to her, saying that Caesar's wife should be above suspicion. Though highly pregnant with his son, the future Maurice de Saxe, she had sufficient spirit, according to White, in *Marshal of France*, to retort that he was not Caesar and she was not his wife.

4 Kazakh and Cossack come from the same word, meaning independent warriors. The Kazakhs, like many steppe invaders before them, were fleeing from more powerful enemies on the Chinese border.

5 Jacques Barzun, in *From Dawn to Decadence*, notes that Macaulay has fallen into disfavour in modern times, accused of being the founder of the Whig school of history, that is, of interpreting history in ways favourable to his political party and suggesting that every change is somehow a step on the way to progress. Barzun noted that Macaulay was a master of anecdote, portraiture and cultural and social history. He also cited Lord Acton (another historian made into a parody because of his skill at minting aphorisms), who once asked the two most prominent German historians, Mommsen and Harnack, who was the greatest historian the world had ever produced; each named Macaulay. As for minor errors, such as are unavoidable even today when more resources are available, Barzun finds it odd that historians consider trivial errors more significant than correctly portraying the big picture.

6 The term Tory began as a derisive taunt, referring to Irish outlaws, but it was soon applied to those who supported royal authority rather than parliamentary supremacy. James II's pro-French, pro-Catholic policies were blamed partly on his wife, Mary of Modena (1658–1718), but the Whigs – generally Protestant and Parliament in orientation – tolerated them as long as their marriage was barren; however, when a son was born in 1688, a party of prominent Whigs invited William of Orange, whose mother was a Stuart, to overthrow the king. After James fled the country, dropping the great seal into the Thames, he took up residence in France.

7 The French language, like French manners and arts, did not go down in defeat with Louis XIV, but came to dominate high society across Europe. Rural England, in contrast, often identified itself more with Squire Western, the hard-riding, hard-drinking, hard-wenching figure in Henry Fielding's comic novel of 1749, *Tom Jones*.

Chapter Two

1 Jeremy Black, *Warfare in the Eighteenth Century*, says that these successes were due to the persistence of two successive emperors who overrode traditional reluctance to fight on the steppe; otherwise, the Dsungars might have become a major empire. Thus, this obscure conflict was one of the most important Asian wars of the century.

2 The exception was a handful of Orientalists who were fascinated by the philosophies, religions and cultures of the East, as well as the history and languages of almost-forgotten empires. Muslim scholars, in contrast, had no interest in pagan lore, either that of the distant past or that practised by their subjects, or in Judaism and Christianity.

Chapter Three

1 It would be a mistake to think of these groupings of interests as modern parties. Tories remained important until the collapse of the Jacobite movement in 1715; after that they would show up at Parliament, cast a meaningless vote against the government, then go back to their estates. Through the era of Walpole and Pitt it was still a matter of 'who got what' rather than principles. With few people eligible to vote, the rich and well-connected fought among themselves for the benefits of office.

2 Louis Joseph de Bourbon (1654–1712) was Prince Eugene's cousin. Given the limited gene pool from which so many competent military commanders came, it is little wonder that people believed talent to be hereditary. Everyone did tend to obey quickly men with impressive titles, but a royal nincompoop was still a nincompoop, and Vendôme never hesitated to say so.

3 Vendôme married a distant Bourbon relative, perhaps to bolster his chances of becoming king of Spain if Philippe V died. His failure to sire children may have been due to her ugliness, or his homosexuality (he had been reputed to have been the lover of his wife's brother, the prince of Conti – an honour he would have widely shared with prominent personages of both sexes), but possibly it was due to her being a spinster of thirty-two (her brother had not allowed her to marry). Even more likely was his departure for Spain, where he died two years later on campaign, apparently of natural causes.

4 Claude Louis Hector de Villars (1653–1734) was the last of Louis XIV's six greatest marshals. He had served under all of the greatest field commanders of his age and had performed brilliantly as a commander, but his father had been only a minor noble and diplomat. Consequently, Villars was so often sent on diplomatic missions that his talents as a field commander were overlooked. After Malplaquet he was entrusted with the most important campaigns and valued for his political advice.

5 It should come as no surprise that Queen Anne chairs have bowed legs.

6 Philippe d'Orléans (1674–1723) began his supervision of the kingdom for the five-year-old heir to the throne only in September, the month the rising in Scotland began.

7 James Francis Edward Keith (1696–1758) fled to France after the failure of the uprising, then to Spain; he joined his elder brother, George, in a failed effort to invade Scotland in 1719. Because he was a Protestant, he was mistrusted by the Old Pretender's inner circle. In 1729 he went to Russia, where he

became colonel of the Guards Regiment and distinguished himself in the War of the Polish Succession and the Turkish war of 1737. George Keith (1693–1778), once among James Stuart's closest associates, ended his life as one of Frederick the Great's most important officers.

8 John Campbell (1678–1743), the tenth earl of Argyll, was the head of the most powerful clan in Scotland, but his reputation can still provoke heated debate. His father, like his grandfather, had been executed by the Stuarts, which goes far to explain his adherence to William of Orange and George I. He had extensive military experience, serving under Marlborough in Flanders, and was later buried in Westminster Abbey.

9 The author admits to having Cahill, Wallace and Stewart ancestry, but grew up without any knowledge of what that meant. An uncle summarised the family history as being 'too Irish to save money and too Scotch to enjoy spending it'.

10 Her influence made court life more enjoyable, while Louis XIV's last mistress had persuaded him to marry her (though in secret), then had encouraged his tendencies towards intolerance and formality.

Chapter Four

1 These imperial officers were called nawabs if they were Muslim, since that was the Urdu version of the Arabic word for 'deputy'; nabob, once considered an acceptable spelling, is no longer so because it has so many wonderfully negative connotations. Hindu rulers were called maharajas. Either title acknowledged that ultimate authority was held by the shah, but the prince's powers were essentially unlimited.

2 Marshman's self-confidence and pride tells us much about his era, the early years of Queen Victoria. He knew India well, having lived there since the age of five, and he was fluent in Bengali.

3 The years 1760–5 certainly make for a powerful exception to Macaulay's generalisation. A parliamentary commission investigated the situation, and Clive became a special target. He defied his interrogators, saying that he had taken steps to halt the worst abuses, even putting down mutinies by British officers. For a strong denunciation of Clive and the East India Company, see Nicholas Dirks, *The Scandal of Empire: India and the Creation of Imperial Britain*; Dirks equates the evils of empire with those of Fascism and slavery. Percival Griffiths, in *The British Impact on India*, praised the ways that the British combined Western principles (such the rule of law and equality before the law) with Indian practices (such as each person being judged by his group's law). He also discussed the practical and moral problems of the moment – the breakdown of law and order, famine and suttee – and the long-term problem of social and political disequilibrium and disintegration. The British managed to stabilise the situation without resolving the underlying problems. Modern scholars often mock Macaulay's words, just as they do Kipling's, suggesting

that East is East and West is West, and East is always Best. Some Britons may roll their eyes, but there is nothing to be gained in politics or academic life by defending colonialism.

4   Hastings spoke Bengali and Urdu, and some Persian (the language of the Mughal court); to prepare civil servants to perform their duties effectively, he encouraged the systematic study of language and literature that native scholars later expanded.

5   William Dalrymple describes the 'complex and politically supercharged debate on empire'. See 'Plain Tales from British India', *New York Review of Books* (26 April 2007). Post-modern analyses change everything, it appears, except people's minds. Modern condemnations of colonial excesses are strikingly similar to those made by contemporaries, as are modern defences of the system's contributions.

Chapter Five

1   Lord Kinross, *The Ottoman Centuries*, reports that the grand vizier had counted on resolving the disputes by diplomacy, but when the Russians demanded free navigation in the Black Sea and to the Mediterranean, the cession of the Kuban, all the coast north of the Dniester, and domination of Wallachia and Moldavia, and the Austrians demanded Serbia and Bosnia, he broke off the talks.

2   Friedrich Heinrich Seckendorff (1673–1763) had served in the armies of Holland (in William III's invasion of England and Ireland) and minor German princes, Venice, Saxony and Prussia before joining the Habsburg army in 1717. After being released from arrest in 1740, he entered Bavarian service, successfully driving back Austrian armies and helping to negotiate the peace settlement.

3   Yegen Muhammed owed his rise to a prominently placed uncle, then to his predecessor's inability to secure a favourable peace by negotiation. After being removed from office in the spring of 1739 by political enemies, he became an exception in Ottoman politics in being sent to govern outlying provinces rather than being strangled. In 1745 he commanded the army in Syria against Nader Shah; after being defeated in the field, he retreated to his camp, where mutineers killed him, then fled for their lives.

4   Lothar Joseph Dominik, Count von Königsegg-Rothenfels (1673–1751). His early career had been brilliant, but he was better at diplomacy than combat. Age must have been a factor in his 1738 failure. After being removed from command, he languished in civilian life until 1743, when Maria Theresa needed him again. He served competently in the Bohemian campaign and was wounded at the battle of Fontenoy, after which he retired for good.

5   One who came to Austria was Ernst Gideon Freiherr von Laudon (1717–90), who was born in Livonia of mixed Scottish and German ancestry to a retired officer in the Swedish army. Enrolled as a cadet in the Russian military academy,

he served at the siege of Danzig, then with the Russian army on the Rhine and in the campaign against Turkey. In 1741 he applied for Prussian service, but was declined, then entered the Austrian army and rose to the rank of field marshal. Frederick the Great had many subsequent opportunities to regret not having employed him. Another, Franz Moritz Graf von Lacy (1725–1801), was the son of Peter von Lacy (1678–1751), an Irishman who rose to the rank of field marshal and commanded Russian armies in some of the most important campaigns of the era; he was sent to Germany as a boy to study the military arts and enlisted in Austrian service in 1743.

Chapter Six

1 Louise-Elisabeth de Bourbon-Condé (1693–1775), a famously quotable and amorous woman, who often quarrelled with her jealous husband, Louis Armand II. It did not help that he believed Maurice's father had stolen the 1697 Polish election from his father by bribing more delegates.

2 A second regiment was raised by his second-in-command, Ulrich Frederik Waldemar von Löwendahl. Louis XV balanced competent foreign commanders like Löwendahl with a bevy of royal bastards, all nincompoops, and more elderly generals who were envious of Maurice having been promoted ahead of them. Löwendahl was named marshal in 1747.

3 Lynn has an extended essay in *Battle* discussing the oft-quoted episode at Fontenoy in which a British officer first saluted the French troops, then invited them to fire first. This is usually cited in support of the principle that whichever side fires last has the most effective volley; that idea, though counter-intuitive, relies on the observation that a volley followed immediately by a bayonet attack was often decisive. Lynn attributes the episode partly to aesthetics (i.e. theatre), partly to the 'military Enlightenment' and partly to a new understanding of the laws of war.

4 Among his disciples was Jean-Armand Dieskau (1701–67), brought from Saxony as his aide-de-camp in 1720. He rose through brilliance and courage to become governor of the naval base at Brest. In 1755 he was sent to Canada with a regiment of regulars. His effort to capture Fort Edward failed. Though he lured the British into an ambush, his Indians betrayed their position too soon; he followed the retreating enemy too hurriedly, running into a larger body that unexpectedly had both cannons and Indians. Though wounded, he continued to fight until his army retreated. Too seriously injured to escape the field, he was captured and returned to France only when peace came in 1763. It had been the best chance the French had to occupy Albany before British reinforcements arrived. The description of his conversation with de Saxe about conducting war in America was widely read. Leach, *Arms for Empire*, has little good to say about those officers who tried to implement European tactics in American forests, but, in fact, when regular troops were not led into ambushes, they proved their worth again and again. They were facing either regular French

troops, who were familiar, or irregular forces of Canadians and Indians who were reluctant either to assault a fortification or to withstand a bayonet charge.

5 Wayne Lee, *Barbarians and Brothers*, notes the increased emphasis on discipline and restraint, part of which was intended to protect taxpayers. No one wanted subjects prevented from contributing the maximum to royal coffers.

6 The Drummonds were a powerful clan located near Sterling and had long feuded with the MacGregors. James (1615–75), the earl of Perth, had been a Covenanter, but later became a Jacobite; his son James (1648–1716) became a Catholic and joined James II in France. The grandson James (1713–46) commanded the left wing at Culloden and his brother, John (1714–47), commanded the centre. Other sources cite Louis Drummond as commanding the Scots regiment.

7 Americans called them Scotch-Irish, though that is now politically incorrect. They were, like the tape, strong, cheap and useful.

8 Historians who venture an opinion on this subject are certain to offend someone. This is occasionally true for comments summarising attitudes in central Europe, where zealots do not customarily read histories in English, but regarding the Celtic peoples of the British Isles, it's 'Katy bar the door!'

9 Native Americans had practised slavery since time immemorial, but had not bought and sold slaves until they saw that colonial settlers would give weapons, cloth and other products for people they had captured from other tribes.

10 Christopher Clark, *Iron Kingdom*, writes that fifty-three males of the Kleist family perished in battle, twenty-three Bellings, and seventy-two Wedels. This presented the Berlin Cadet School a difficult task, since it could train only 350 noble sons at a time. Frederick did what he could to rescue the Junker class from the debts acquired from changing economic conditions, destruction of estates by invading armies and the division of property among numerous children.

11 Lawrence Henry Gipson, in *The British Empire Before the American Revolution*, credited Pitt's lavish expenditure for his loss of office, but Fred Anderson, *Crucible of War*, sees the death of George II, Pitt's insistence on a pre-emptive war with Spain (a war that came anyway) and the foolish defection of his closest partner, the First Lord of the Treasury as the cause. But most of all, it was the hostility of the new king, George III – a 'thick-headed adolescent' Anderson called him – who considered Pitt a corrupt liar who was leading his country into bankruptcy and destruction.

12 John Stuart (1713–93), the earl of Bute, was in the House of Lords, so leadership in Parliament fell to George Grenville (1712–70), Pitt's brother-in-law; Bute was a Scot, Grenville dutiful but untalented. Neither was popular; neither was respected.

13 Gipson, *The Great War for the Empire*, volume VIII, says that Tyrawley – too young, too inexperienced and with too few troops – accomplished little. However, he was named field marshal in 1763, which suggests that the government thought otherwise. James O'Hara (1682–1774), the second baron of Tyrawley, was an Irish professional soldier, as was his father, but he knew Portugal well and had a

child by a Portuguese woman. His illegitimate son, Charles O'Hara, was given the unpleasant duty of surrendering Cornwallis's sword to George Washington at Yorktown in 1781. Chesterfield was quoted in 1773 as saying, 'Lord Tyrawley and I have been dead these two years, but we don't choose to have it known.' Obviously, Tyrawley was not an important figure in his later years.

14 Though Havana was taken relatively quickly, half the British troops there died of disease. The word quickly spread among English and continental publics that deployment in the Caribbean was little better than a death sentence.

15 Educated men and women now routinely thought of the ancient gods. For literature and off-hand conversation, that was much safer than making any reference to the Christian god. Besides, some leaders of Enlightenment thought already considered a personal god something suitable for the lower classes, but unworthy of their own time and dignity.

16 William McNeill, *The Pursuit of Power*, recounts the British advantages in industry and commerce that made it possible to equip and supply both a large army and the world's dominant navy. There was much more to war than raising soldiers and pointing them at the enemy. In the American War for Independence Britain could supply ninety thousand soldiers overseas, as well as perhaps as many as sixty thousand sailors.

Chapter Seven

1 On the other hand, John Keegan in *The Second World War* reports that: 'In the eighteenth century the French army had typically found its source of such fit men among the town-dwelling artisan class rather than in the peasantry. The peasant, physically undernourished and socially doltish, rarely made a suitable soldier; he was undisciplined, prone to disease and liable to pine to death when plucked from his native hearth.'

2 Dennis Showalter, *The Wars of Frederick the Great*, has good observations on the practical details of providing food to the army. Wheat does not grind itself into flour, nor does bread bake itself. Transporting mills and ovens was as essential (and difficult) as hauling the great twelve-pound siege guns.

3 Christopher Duffy, *The Army of Maria Theresa*, calls these free companies the equivalent of naval privateers. The prospect of unsupervised plunder attracted adventurers from many nations, though everyone understood that employment ceased whenever a peace treaty was signed. There were also volunteer groups of partisans, who were sometimes difficult to tell from free companies. Duffy notes that the Croats supplied a much larger percentage of troops for their numbers than other people in the empire (more than a quarter of the army), that they were considered by far the best troops, and that their loyalty never wavered. Their officers were either foreigners or rejects from line units, but the Croats often preferred such men, who were less partial to favourites than their own countrymen.

4 Awkward for the consistency of Frederick's enlightened beliefs, he wanted only nobles as officers. Redlich, in *The German Military Enterpriser*, volume II, called the idea that noble blood ensured virtue a superstition; perhaps the belief that commoners lacked patriotism was a reflection of observations that they fought better in defence of their homeland, but it left the army less well prepared for the military operations of the future than the revolutionary armies of France. Frederick's encouragement of celibacy caused many officers to be much like himself – childless, but dedicated to their careers. The king's admirable Enlightenment principles, Niall Ferguson notes in *Civilization*, allowed freedom of thought, but not of action – everything was intended to enhance the power of the state.

5 Czech is not that hard to pronounce, except for a couple letters, but it takes some courage to make the first try. Beer helps.

6 Johann Baptist Serbelloni (1697–1778) was a Lombard aristocrat best known for his pride and arrogance, attributes that stood him well in the imperial court. A dashing cavalry general, he performed well as a subordinate (when he was not being insubordinate), but was lethargic in command. Simon Millar, in *Kolin 1757*, remarks that he never fully mastered German, but became angry when aides repeated messages that they were not sure he had understood.

7 Franz Leopold Nádasty (1708–83) was a Hungarian, the best light cavalry commander of the era, Franz Moritz Lacy (1725–1801) came from Irish ancestry via Russia as a protégé of Maximilian Browne, Gideon Ernst Loudon (1717–90) was a German Balt of Swedish ancestry who had served in the Russian army before being rejected by Frederick the Great and applying with the imperial army; many of the Italians were fiery warriors too, only not the one the empress trusted most – Serbelloni. Alas, Lacy and Loudon hated one another. Duffy, *The Army of Maria Theresa*, noted a few exceptional officers from Maria Theresa's hereditary lands, then commented that it seemed as though Austrian soil seemed incapable of producing good generals.

8 Long descriptions of Maximilian von Browne's career were published, the first in the very year of his death: *Zuverläßige Lebenbeschreibung U. M. Reichsgrafen, v. B. K-K General-Feldmarschall*, and in 1785 by Baron O'Cahill, in *Geschichte der großen Herrführer*. Later generations often confused him with two distantly related half-brothers, both named Johan Georg Braun, who left Russian service for the Austrian army.

9 Because Anna had warned every court not to seek a marriage with Elizabeth, she had no children of her own. And while she had very good relations with the army, including affairs with prominent officers, this assisted her only in seizing power – she had not become pregnant. After becoming tsarina, she could not marry – there was no one her equal and there were plots and intrigues everywhere. This situation required Elizabeth to find an heir among her nephews. The choices were not good – Ivan VI was too dangerous and Peter was feeble-minded; so she disposed of the first and tried to make the second into another Peter the Great. She was a typical Enlightenment ruler –

strong-willed, eager to improve the lives of her subjects and dependent on her favourites for information about the actual state of the country.

10   Germans were still acceptable as spouses – it being too dangerous for the tsarina, Elizabeth, to marry her heir, the childlike Peter III (1728–62) to a Russian, she sought out a wife from a minor principality, Anhalt-Zerbst. Peter was technically duke of Holstein-Gottorp, the result of marriage alliances that made Catherine (1729–96) his second cousin. Frederick the Great assisted in the arrangements, thinking that a Lutheran princess would be less likely to favour Catholic Austria, but like everyone else he underestimated Catherine's willingness to conform to the practices of her subjects.

11   Stanisłas August Poniatowski (1732–98) went to the Russian court at a time when Catherine was still a grand duchess. He quickly won her heart. The 1764 election was a complicated affair, with Poniatowski's family finally seizing power in a *coup d'état*. Clark, *Iron Kingdom*, attributes the growing anarchy in Poland to Frederick the Great's suggestion to Maria-Theresa and Catherine to take the nation apart like an artichoke, leaf by leaf.

12   François de Tott's (1733–93) Hungarian ancestor had served in the Ottoman army before emigrating to France. In 1755 he had gone to Constantinople in the company of the ambassador to learn Turkish and to look into the strengths and weaknesses of the empire. His skills attracted the attention of Ottoman officials, who put him in charge of producing cannons and training artillerymen. He later wrote a four-volume work on his experiences in the Islamic world.

13   Grigory Potemkin (1739–91), a handsome and talented member of the imperial guard, became the tsarina's lover, then her most important advisor. He became famous as governor of the Ukraine, when he repaired and painted the façades of buildings to impress her, knowing that she would not see the collapsing sides or backs. Such 'Potemkin villages' became proverbial both for efforts to deceive visiting bureaucrats about real conditions and as a metaphor for Russia itself.

14   A confederacy was a traditional method for nobles to resist a 'tyrannical' king. Surprisingly, the insurgents maintained an army in the field until 1772, hoping against better judgement that Austria or Prussia would come to their aid, expel Russia from the Commonwealth, then in a disinterested manner restore the national sovereignty, together with necessary military reforms.

15   John Paul (1747–92) left Scotland for the life of a sailor at age twelve. In 1773, accused of murder in Tobago, he fled to his brother's home in Virginia. There, knowing he would be hunted by the British authorities, he adopted the name John Jones; when he joined the Continental navy, he took the name John Paul Jones. His exploits in the American Revolution were honoured, but the American navy almost ceased to exist after the war ended. Therefore, he went to France in an effort to collect compensation for American ships which had been confiscated. Without money and with no prospect of employment, he accepted a commission in the Russian navy.

Chapter Eight

1 Fred Anderson, in *A People's Army*, describes the special characteristics of Massachusetts troops – the importance of religious fervour, legal obligations and dislike of the regular officers' quick employment of the lash. Veterans went home proud of their victories, proud of being part of the empire, and thanking God for their delivery from French and Indian attacks, but they quickly recognised in British policy the same attitudes they had experienced from British officers – and were determined not to give up their liberties to men who regarded all Americans as an inferior sort of human being.

2 Anderson, *Crucible of War*, blames Montcalm's having treated the Indians as subjects rather than allies. Unable to understand their needs and desires, unable to make gifts or even offer goods for sale, he found himself without any Indian allies when the British army and navy arrived. Later, the commander of Montreal discovered that the Indians had joined with the advancing British forces to overwhelm all the western posts. Amherst then copied Montcalm's mistakes. Timothy Shannon, in *Indians and Colonists at the Crossroads of Empire*, dates the crisis earlier, in the 1720s, when new trading posts bypassed the Mohawk monopoly. The Iroquois, unable to buy trading goods except by selling land, began complaining that the colonists had broken the Covenant Chain by failing to observe the proper condolence rituals – that is, gifts of clothing, food, alcohol and war supplies, and speeches honouring fallen warriors (accompanied by compensation to the tribe for the losses). Rum was central to every discussion, in that some Indians, seeing alcoholism as a serious problem, wanted the trade banned; others demanded access to it.

3 Thomas Gage (1719–81) had served at Fontenoy and Culloden. Only Amherst noted his lack of talent at war or public relations, but Amherst was too eager to get home himself to call this to his superiors' attention. Soon Gage found himself enforcing the 'Intolerable Acts', which included new taxes and requiring colonies to provide quarters for his men; the growing hostility of the people led to the 'Boston Massacre', a incident that provoked public protests across the colonies.

4 Technically, the government ministers were all Whigs, but in practice they were picked by the king, who encouraged them to expand royal authority at home and in the colonies; since prominent Whigs like Pitt were now in opposition, Americans began calling the king's supporters Tories.

5 Members of Parliament were elected by a relatively small number of wealthy people living in boroughs that no longer reflected the distribution of populations. In theory, they represented national and imperial interests, not the concerns of their voters; in practice, so many members accepted money or posts in exchange for voting as directed by leaders of factions, that corruption was almost the essence of the system.

6   Richard Montgomery (1736–75) was an Irish-born veteran of the British army who had participated in the 1759 capture of Montreal; after the war he had settled in America and married into the prominent Livingston family of New York. Benedict Arnold (1741–1801) had been sent with a second army to Quebec; wounded in the attempted storming of the fortress, he commanded the besieging army until the arrival of British reinforcements. His skilful delaying tactics in his westward retreat prevented the British from retaking Canada quickly. The commander of the British army in Canada, Guy Carleton (1724–1808), became commander-in-chief of all British forces in North America 1782–3.

7   Although American mythology emphasises the Americans' skills at irregular war, in *Barbarians and Brothers* Wayne Lee describes Washington's determination to fight a disciplined war, and some of the contradictory and nuanced aspects of this policy.

8   Howe had not expected Washington to have cannons, but once volunteers had dragged cannon though the snow from Fort Ticonderoga (the 'Gibraltar of America') and Crown Point, he faced the destruction of the town and the fleet. Washington had sent Benedict Arnold to upper New York with militiamen, but the Green Mountain Boys led by Ethan Allen insisted on accompanying them. Arnold's plan of overwhelming the small garrisons by surprise got no farther than the gate of Ticonderoga, where Allen ran up to the guard and demanded the post's surrender; if the guard's pistol had not misfired, that would have been the end of one of America's most colourful figures, but within moments Allen was pounding at the commander's door, demanding his surrender. The commander opened the door, his trousers in his hands, and asked in whose name he was acting. Allen roared, 'In the name of the Great Jehovah and the Continental Congress'. The cannon were then transported to Boston by a young bookseller, Henry Knox, whom Washington had appointed chief of artillery – this demonstrated Washington's ability to measure character and talent, and the enthusiasm and loyalty of those he gathered around him.

9   Banastre Tarleton (1754–1833) was a stereotype of the dashing cavalryman. Son of a merchant and slave trader, he wasted his education and his inheritance except for enough money to buy a commission. Later he arrived in South Carolina at a moment when local rivalries had escalated into atrocities and Howe's efforts at reconciliation had been abandoned. Tarleton decided that intimidation and terror were the only policies left. 'Tarleton's quarter' was a synonym for massacre. Losing three fingers to a backwoods sharpshooter did not improve his temper.

10 Charles Ingrao reports in *The Hessen Mercenary State* that enlistments fell sharply when news of the disaster at Trenton reached Hesse. By 1782 the five-thaler enlistment bonus had to be increased to twenty, and the height requirements were lowered from five foot four inches to four foot eleven inches. Neighbouring princes complained that his recruiters used abduction

and kidnapping to meet their quotas. David Hackett Fischer, *Washington's Crossing*, remarks on the difficulties of transporting the prisoners back across the Delaware. He also notes that the Hessian court martial put all the blame on the four deceased officers, thereby allowing the survivors to evade the fury of their embarrassed prince.

11   This necessary but inept use of paper currency inevitably led to inflation, then to British counterfeiting.

12   Conway's Cabal was based on anonymous letters to congressmen. Thomas Conway (1734–1800), born in Ireland, left his homeland to serve in the French army; because of his experience he was made inspector general of the Continental army. He was persuaded that only Gates could save the situation; and Gates agreed with him. Washington bore the insults stoically, refusing to give in to the temptation to strike back at his enemies; by doing this, he became more popular than ever. When Lafayette was assigned to invade Canada, in hopes he could rally the French population there, he refused to have Conway as his second-in-command; shortly afterward Conway resigned from the army. In the summer of 1778 Conway fought a duel with General John Cadwallader and was shot through the face. He then returned to France, was governor of the French possessions in India, and during the French Revolution commanded royalist forces.

13   Daniel Morgan (1736–1802) was a Virginian who had recruited the first company of riflemen from his fellow backwoodsmen; according to legend, he put a picture of King George on a target, then accepted only those marksmen who could hit the picture in the head at a hundred yards on their first shot. The British regarded him as little better than a criminal because he had his men concentrate their fire on officers.

14   Arnold was angry over Congress's unwillingness to promote him or even repay the debts he had incurred to supply his troops in Canada, but the Continental Congress had no money, many political intrigues and little patience with proud and querulous officers, while Arnold, who had witnessed the massacre of the surrendered British garrison of Fort William Henry in 1757, had an abiding hatred of the French which caused him to oppose the alliance with Louis XVI that his leadership at Saratoga had made possible.

15   No history describes the differences between regulars and militia, between the wrangling of democratic politics and a kingdom, better than Bernard Cornwell's novel, *The Fort* (2010), which describes the 1779 battle at Penobscot Bay in Maine. An overwhelming American force was totally destroyed by a combination of courage, an effective chain of command, luck, and the Royal Navy's timely rescue.

16   Kazimierz Pulaski (1746–79) had been an officer in the 1768 uprising against Russian occupiers, fleeing to Turkey when the insurrection collapsed in 1771; he took refuge in France, where Lafayette recruited him for service in America. In 1778 he organised Pulaski's Legion, composed largely of foreign adventurers

and deserters, which quickly became Washington's finest cavalry unit; after Pulaski's death at Savannah, the legion was absorbed into Armand's Legion, a crack cavalry unit of foreign volunteers that fought effectively to the end of the war in 1783. Charles Armand Tuffin (1757–93), the marquis de la Rouerie, was less a democrat than Pulaski, dying during the French Revolution while fighting for the royalist cause.

17 Jackson always said that he was born somewhere between his parents' village in Ulster and America, but his parents had immigrated from Antrim two years before his birth. His father had been entranced by a brother's stories of service in the 49th regiment of foot during Braddock's expedition and the capture of Quebec; his mother by letters from her four sisters in America. Because his father died shortly after his birth, Andrew Jackson grew up among his strongly patriotic Crawford uncles.

18 The 2,500-man-strong Royal Deux Ponts Regiment in the French army was composed largely of German mercenaries (Deux Ponts was the French rendering of Zweibrücken). Thus, German mercenaries faced German mercenaries in Virginia.

Chapter Nine

1 Azar Gat argues in Roger Chickering and Stig Förster, *War in an Age of Revolution*, that 2 per cent of a population under arms was unsustainable. Prussia's 150,000 peacetime soldiers represented 3 per cent.

2 Redlich, *The German Military Enterpriser*, volume II, notes a small number of exceptions: NCOs with many years of experience and regimental adjutants of middle-class origin who presumably did the paper work, again after many years of service. Promotion was easiest in the artillery and irregular troops, but very few commoners reached positions of high command.

3 The review by Adam Gropnik in *The New Yorker* (12 February 2007) is recommended reading, especially for his reminder that although the future would belong to the conscript armies, the general most responsible for defeating Napoleon was a thoroughly old-fashioned professional, and his British army was equally traditional. As Gropnik summarises both the past and present, 'Perhaps war makes culture as much as culture makes war, and the farther off the war is the less we notice its effects'.

4 Jacques Barzun, in *From Dawn to Decadence*, believes that Western civilisation has been on a downward path since the end of the long double decade 1890–1910. There have been technological advances only. In today's debate over the environment and world population growth even the wisdom of technological advance has been questioned.

Bibliography

Anderson, Fred. *A People's Army: Massachusetts Soldiers and Society in the Seven Years War*. Chapel Hill and London: University of North Carolina Press, 1984.

—— *Crucible of War: The Seven Years' War and the Fate of Empire in British North America, 1754–1766*. New York: Vintage, 2000.

—— and Cayton, Andrew. *The Dominion of War: Empire and Liberty in North America, 1500–2000*. New York: Viking, 2005.

Aronson, Theo. *Kings Over the Water: The Saga of the Stuart Pretenders*. London: Cassell, 1979.

Axworthy, Michael. *The Sword of Persia: Nader Shah from Tribal Warrior to Conquering Tyrant*. London: I.B.Tauris, 2006.

Ballard, George Alexander. *Rulers of the Indian Ocean*. Reprint, Lahore: Al-Biruni, 1979.

Barker, Thomas. *Double Eagle and Crescent: Vienna's Second Turkish Siege and its Historical Setting*. Albany: State University of New York Press, 1967.

Barzun, Jacques. *From Dawn to Decadence: 500 Years of Western Cultural Life, 1500 to the Present*. New York: HarperCollins, 2000.

Baxter, Stephen. *William III and the Defense of European Liberty, 1650–1702*. New York: Harcourt, Brace & World, 1966.

Bell, Daniel. *The First Total War: Napoleon's Europe and the Birth of Europe*. New York: Houghton Mifflin, 2006.

Bickham, Troy. *Making Headlines: The American Revolution as Seen through the British Press*. DeKalb: Northern Illinois University Press, 2009.

Black, Jeremy. *European Warfare, 1660–1815*. London : UCL Press, 1994.

—— *Warfare in the Eighteenth Century*. London: Cassell, 1999.

Bodle, Wayne. *The Valley Forge Winter: Civilians and Soldiers in War*. University Park: Pennsylvania University Press, 2002.

Boot, Max. *War Made New: Technology, Warfare, and the Course of History, 1500 to Today*. New York: Gotham, 2006.

Borneman, Walter. *The French and Indian War: Deciding the Fate of North America*. New York: HarperCollins, 2006.

Bose, Sugata. *A Hundred Horizons: The Indian Ocean in the Age of Global Empire*. Cambridge, MA: Harvard University Press, 2006.

Bovill, Edward William. *The Golden Trade of the Moors*. London: Oxford, 1968.

Braudel, Fernand. *Civilization and Capitalism, 15th–18th Century, Vol. I: The Structures of Everyday Life*. New York: Harper and Row, 1979.

Brauer, Jurgen, and van Tuyll, Hubert. *Castles, Battles and Bombs: How Economics Explains Military History*. London and Chicago: University of Chicago Press, 2008.

Buchanan, Brenda (ed.). *Gunpowder, Explosives and the State*. London: Ashgate, 2006.

Calloway, Colin. *The Scratch of a Pen: 1763, and the Transformation of North America*. Oxford: Oxford University Press, 2006.

Carlyle, Thomas. *History of Friedrich the Second Called Frederick the Great*. Vol. IV. New York: Harper, 1859–64.

Cashin, Edward. *The King's Ranger: Thomas Brown and the American Revolution on the Southern Frontier*. New York: Fordham, 1999.

Chase, Kenneth. *Firearms: A Global History to 1700*. Cambridge: Cambridge University Press, 2003.

Chickering, Roger, and Förster, Stig (eds). *War in an Age of Revolution, 1775–1815*. Washington, DC: German Historical Institute, and Cambridge: Cambridge University Press, 2011.

Churchill, Winston. *Marlborough, His Life and Times*. New York: Charles Scribner's Sons, 1968.

Citino, Robert. *The German Way of War from the Thirty Years War to the Third Reich*. Lawrence: University of Kansas, 2005.

Clark, Christopher. *Iron Kingdom: The Rise and Downfall of Prussia, 1600–1947*. Cambridge, MA: Belknap, 2005.

Collins, James. *The State in Early Modern France*. New York: Cambridge University Press, 1995.

Cracraft, James (ed.). *Peter the Great Transforms Russia*. Lexington, MA: D. C. Heath, 1991.

Creveld, Martin van. *Supplying War: Logistics from Wallenstein to Patton*. Cambridge: Cambridge University Press, 1977.

Curtis, Edward E. *The British Army in the American Revolution*. New Haven, CT, Yale University Press, 1926.

Darwin, John. *Unfinished Empire: The Global Expansion of Britain*. New York: Bloomsbury Press, 2013.

Davidson, Basil. *Black Mother: The Years of the African Slave Trade*. Boston: Little, Brown and company, 1961.

Davies, Brian. *Warfare, State and Society on the Black Sea Steppe, 1500–1700*. London: Routledge, 2007.

Davies, Norman. *God's Playground: A History of Poland*. New York: Columbia University Press, 1982.

Dippel, Horst. *Germany and the American Revolution, 1770–1800*. Chapel Hill: North Carolina University Press, 1977.

Dirks, Nicholas. *The Scandal of Empire: India and the Creation of Imperial Britain*. Cambridge, MA: Harvard University Press, 2006.

Douglas, Hugh. *Jacobite Spy Wars: Moles, Rogues and Treachery*. Bodmin: Sutton, 1999.

Duffy, Christopher. *The Army of Frederick the Great*. New York: Hippocrene Books, 1974.

—— *The Army of Maria Theresa: The Armed Forces of Imperial Austria, 1740–1780*. New York: Hippocrene Books, 1977.

—— *The Fortress in the Age of Vauban and Frederick the Great, 1660–1789*. London: Routledge and Kegan Paul, 1985.

—— *The Military Experience in the Age of Reason*. London: Routledge and Kegan Paul, 1987.

—— *The Wild Goose and the Eagle: A Life of Marshal von Browne, 1705–1757*. London: Chatto & Windus, 1964.

Faroqhi, Suraiya. *The Ottoman Empire and the World Around It*. London: I.B.Tauris, 2004.

Ferguson, Niall. *The Ascent of Money: A Financial History of the World*. New York: Penguin, 2008.

—— *Civilization: The West and the Rest*. New York: Penguin, 2011.

—— *Empire: The Rise and Demise of the British World Order and the Lessons for Global Power*. New York: Basic Books, 2002.

Finkel, Caroline. *Osman's Dream: The Story of the Ottoman Empire, 1300–1923*. NewYork: Basic Books, 2005.

Fischer, David Hackett. *Washington's Crossing*. Oxford and New York: Oxford University Press, 2004.

Fisher, Godfrey. *Barbary Legend: War, Trade and Piracy in North Africa, 1415–1830*. Oxford: Clarendon Press, 1957.

Fleming, Thomas. *Beat the Last Drum: The Siege of Yorktown, 1781*. New York: St Martin's, 1966.

Flores, Jorge, and Vassallo e Silva, Nuno (eds). *Goa and the Great Mughal*. London: Scala, 2007.

Flowers, Desmond (ed.). *The Memoirs of Louis de Rouvroy, duc de Saint-Simon, Covering the Years 1691–1723*. New York: Heritage, 1959.

Forrest, George. *The Life of Lord Clive*. London: Cassell and Company, 1918.

Fortescue, John William. *A History of the British Army, Vol. I: To the Close of the Seven Years War*. London: Macmillan, 1910.

Foster, Robert Fitzroy. *Modern Ireland, 1600–1972*. London: Penguin, 1988.

Gagliardo, John. *Reich and Nation: The Holy Roman Empire as Idea and Reality, 1763–1806*. Bloomington and London: Indiana University Press, 1980.

Gilmour, David. *The Ruling Caste: Imperial Lives in the Victorian Raj*. New York: Farrar, Straus and Giroux, 2006.

Gipson, Lawrence Henry. *The British Empire Before the American Revolution*. 15 vols, Caldwell, IN: Caxton, 1936–70.

—— *The Great War for the Empire, Vols VI–VIII of The British Empire Before the American Revolution*. 15 vols, Caldwell, IN: Caxton, 1936–70.

Glubb, John. *Soldiers of Fortune: The Story of the Mamlukes*. New York: Dorset, 1973.

Goffman, Daniel. *The Ottoman Empire and Early Modern Europe*. New York: Cambridge University Press, 2002.

Gray, Richard (ed.). *The Cambridge History of Africa, Vol. IV: From c.1600 to c.1790*. Cambridge: Cambridge University Press, 1977.

Green, Nile. *Islam and the Army in Colonial India: Sepoy Religion in the Service of Empire*. Cambridge: Cambridge University Press, 2009.

Griffin, Patrick. *The People with No Name: Ireland's Ulster Scots, America's Scots Irish, and the Creation of a British Atlantic World, 1689–1764*. Princeton: Princeton University Press, 2001.

Griffiths, Percival. *The British Impact on India*. London: Cass, 1952.

Hall, Bert. *Weapons and Warfare in Renaissance Europe: Gunpowder, Technology and Tactics*. Baltimore, MD: Johns Hopkins University Press, 1997.

Hellie, Richard. *Enserfment and Military Change in Muscovy*. Chicago: University of Chicago Press, 1971.

Herrmann, Gerd-Ulrich. *Freiherr von Derfflinger*, Berlin: Stapp-Verlag, 1997

Hodgson, Marshall. *The Venture of Islam: Conscience and History in a World Civilization, Vol. III: In the Gunpowder Empires and Modern Times*. Chicago: University of Chicago, 1974.

Hughes, Lindsey. *Peter the Great: A Biography*. New Haven, CT: Yale, 2002.

Ingrao, Charles. *The Habsburg Monarchy, 1618–1815*. Second edition, New York: Cambridge University Press, 2000.

—— *The Hessian Mercenary State, Ideas, Institutions, and Reform Under Frederick II, 1760–1785*. London: Cambridge University Press, 1987.

Jasienica, Pawel. *The Commonwealth of Both Nations, Vol. III: A Tale of Agony*. Miami: American Institute of Polish Culture, 1992.

Jardine, Lisa. *Going Dutch: How England Plundered Holland's Glory*. New York: Harper, 2008.

Kagan, Frederick, and Higham, Robin (eds). *The Military History of Tsarist Russia*. Basingstoke: Macmillan Palgrave, 2002.

Karger, Johann. *Die Entwicklung der Adjustierung, Rüstung und Bewaffnung der österreichisch-ungarischen Armee 1700–1809*. Reprint, Buchholz: LTR, 1998.

Keegan, John. *The Face of Battle: A Study of Agincourt, Waterloo and the Somme*. New York: Viking, 1978.

—— *Fields of Battle: The Wars for North America*. New York: Knopf, 1996.

—— *The Second World War*. New York: Penguin, 1990.

Kenny, Kevin (ed.). *Ireland and the British Empire*. Oxford: Oxford University Press, 2004.

Khodarkovsky, Michael. *Russia's Steppe Frontier: The Making of a Colonial Empire, 1500–1800*. Bloomington: University of Indiana Press, 2002.

Kinross, John. *The Ottoman Centuries: The Rise and Fall of the Turkish Empire*. New York: Morrow Quill, 1977.

Kirby, David. *Northern Europe in the Early Modern Period: The Baltic World, 1492–1772.* London: Longman, 1990.

Lamphear, John. *African Military History.* London: Ashgate, 2007.

Laroui, Abdallah. *The History of the Maghrib: An Interpretive Essay.* Princeton: Princeton University Press, 1977.

Leach, Douglas. *Arms for Empire: A Military History of the British Colonies in North America, 1607–1763.* New York: Macmillan, 1973.

LeDonne, John. *The Grand Strategy of the Russian Empire, 1650–1831.* Oxford: Oxford University Press, 2004.

Lee, Wayne. *Barbarians and Brothers: Anglo–American Warfare, 1500–1865.* Oxford: Oxford University Press, 2011.

Lewis, Bernard. *What Went Wrong? The Clash Between Islam and Modernity in the Middle East.* New York: Oxford University Press, 2002.

Liddell Hart, B. H. *The Great Captains Unveiled.* Freeport, New York: Books for Libraries, 1967.

Lockhart, Paul. *The Drillmaster of Valley Forge: The Baron de Steuben and the Making of the American Army.* New York: HarperCollins, 2008.

Lord, Robert Howard. *The Second Partition of Poland: A Study in Diplomatic History.* Cambridge, MA: Harvard University Press, 1915.

Lowell, Edward. *The Hessians and German Auxiliaries of Great Britain in the Revolutionary War.* New York: Harper and Brothers, 1884.

Ludwig, Karl, Freiherr von Pöllinitz. *La Saxe Galante, or the Amorous Adventures and Intrigues of Frederick–Augustus II.* New York: Garland, 1972.

Lynn II, John. *Battle: A History of Combat and Culture from Ancient Greece to Modern America.* Cambridge: Westview, 2003.

—— *The French Wars, 1667–1714: The Sun King at War.* Oxford: Osprey, 2002.

—— *The Wars of Louis XIV.* New York: Longman, 1999.

—— *Women, Armies and Warfare in Early Modern Europe.* Cambridge: Cambridge University Press, 2008.

Macauley, Thomas Babbington. *Lord Clive.* New York: Harper, 1878.

McCullough, David. *1776.* New York: Simon & Schuster, 2005.

McKay, Derek. *Prince Eugene of Savoy.* London: Thames and Hudson, 1978.

McNeill, William. *Europe's Steppe Frontier.* Chicago: University of Chicago Press, 1964.

—— *The Pursuit of Power: Technology, Armed Force, and the Society Since A.D. 1000.* Chicago: University of Chicago Press, 1984.

—— *The Rise of the West: A History of the Human Community.* Chicago: University of Chicago Press, 1963.

Mahan, Alfred Thayer. *The Influence of Sea Power Upon History, 1660–1763.* Boston: Little, Brown and Company, 1898.

Majumdar, Ramesh Chandra, et al. *An Advanced History of India.* London: Macmillan, 1960.

Malleson, George Bruce. *Lord Clive and the Establishment of the English in India.* Oxford: Clarendon, 1907.

Marshman, John Clark. *The History of India.* London: Harrison and Sons, 1867.

Martin, James Kirby, and Lender, Mark Edward. *A Respectable Army: The Military Origins of the Republic, 1763–1789*, second edition. Wheeling, Illinois: Harlan Davidson, 2006.

Massie, Robert. *Peter the Great: His Life and His World*. New York: Knopf, 1980.

Mill, James. *The History of British India*. New York: Chelsea, 1968.

Millar, Simon. *Kolin 1757: Frederick the Great's First Defeat*. Oxford: Osprey, 2001.

Miller, James. *Swords for Hire: The Scottish Mercenary*. Edinburgh: Birlinn, 2007.

Mitford, Nancy. *The Sun King*. New York: Harper and Row, 1966.

Murphey, Rhoads. *Ottoman Warfare, 1500–1700*. New Brunswick, NJ: Rutgers, 1999.

Namier, Lewis Bernstein. *England in the Age of the American Revolution*. London: Macmillan, 1930.

Pancake, John. *1777: The Year of the Hangman*. Montgomery: University of Alabama Press, 1977.

Parker, Geoffrey. *The Military Revolution: Military Innovation and the Rise of the West, 1500–1800*. Cambridge: Cambridge University Press, 1996.

Parvev, Ivan. *Habsburgs and Ottomans Between Vienna and Belgrade (1683–1739)*. New York: Columbia, 1995.

Redlich, Fritz. *De Praeda Military: Looting and Booty, 1500–1815*. Wiesbaden: Franz Steiner, 1956.

—— *The German Military Enterpriser and his Work Force: A Study in European Economic and Social History*, 2 vols. Wiesbaden: Franz Steiner, 1964–5.

Roberts, Michael. *The Swedish Imperial Experience, 1560–1718*. Cambridge: Cambridge University Press, 1979.

Roider, Karl. *The Reluctant Ally: Austria's Policy in the Austro–Turkish War, 1737–1739*. Baton Rouge: Louisiana State University Press, 1972.

Ross, John. *War on the Run: The Epic Story of Robert Rogers and the Conquest of America's First Frontier*. New York: Random House, 2009.

Saxe, Maurice de. *Reveries, or Memoirs on the Art of War*. Westport, CT: Greenwood, 1971.

Schama, Simon. *Citizens: A Chronicle of the French Revolution*. New York: Alfred A. Knopf, 1989.

Schuster, O., and Francke, F. A. *Geschichte der Sächischen Armee von deren Errichtung bis auf die neueste Zeit*, 3 vols. Leipzig: Duncker & Humblot, 1885.

Setton, Kenneth Meyer. *Venice, Austria, and the Turks in the Seventeenth Century*. Philadelphia: American Philosophical Society, 1991.

Shannon, Timothy. *Indians and Colonists at the Crossroads of Empire: The Albany Congress of 1754*. Ithaca, NY, and London: Cornell University Press, 2000.

Sharp, Tony. *Pleasure and Ambition: The Life, Loves and Wars of Augustus the Strong*. London: I.B.Tauris, 2001.

Shay, Mary Lucille. *The Ottoman Empire from 1720 to 1734 as Revealed in Despatches of the Venetian Baili*. Urbana: University of Illinois, 1944.

Showalter, Dennis. *The Wars of Frederick the Great*. London: Longman, 1996.

Simms, Brendan. *Three Victories and a Defeat: The Rise and Fall of the First British Empire*. New York: Basic Books, 2007.

Staël-Holstein, Anne-Louise-Germaine de. *Germany, by Madame the Baroness; with notes and appendices by O. W. Wight*. Boston, New York: Houghton, Mifflin and company, 1859. Reprint Ann Arbor, MI: University of Michigan Library, 2005.

Stember, Sol. *The Bicentennial Guide to the American Revolution*, 3 vols. New York: Dutton, 1974.

Stone, Daniel. *A History of East Central Europe, Vol. IV: The Polish–Lithuanian State, 1386–1795*. Seattle and London: University of London, 2001.

Sutton, John. *The King's Honor and the King's Cardinal: The War of the Polish Succession*. Lexington: University of Kentucky Press, 1980.

Szechi, Daniel. *1715: The Great Jacobite Rebellion*. New Haven, CT, and London: Yale University Press, 2006.

Tallett, Frank, and Trim, D. J. B. (eds). *European Warfare, 1350–1750*. Cambridge: Cambridge University Press, 2010.

Tanner, Marcus. *Ireland's Holy Wars: The Struggle for a Nation's Soul, 1500–2000*. New Haven, CT: Yale University Press, 2001.

Thomson, Janice. *Mercenaries, Pirates and Sovereigns: State-building and Extraterritorial Violence in Early Modern Europe*. Princeton: Princeton University Press, 1994.

Tilly, Charles. *Coercion, Capital, and European States, A.D. 990–1990*. Oxford: B. Blackwell, 1990.

Tombs, Robert, and Tombs, Isabella. *That Sweet Enemy: The French and the British from the Sun King to the Present*. New York: Knopf, 2007.

Toohey, Robert. *Liberty and Empire: British Radical Solutions to the American Problem, 1774–1776*. Lexington: University of Kentucky Press, 1978.

Trevelyan, George Otto. *The American Revolution*, 4 vols. London: Longmans, Green and Co., 1917–20.

Turberville, A. S. (ed.). *Johnson's England: An Account of the Life and Manners of his Age*. Oxford: Clarendon, 1933.

Voltaire. *The Age of Louis XIV*. New York: Dutton, 1926.

—— *The History of Charles the Twelfth, King of Sweden*. Philadelphia: Lippincott, 1865.

—— *History of Frederick II*. New York: Putnam, 1915.

Warraq, Ibn. *Defending the West: A Critique of Edward Said's Orientalism*. New York: Prometheus, 2007.

Waterson, James. *The Knights of Islam: The Wars of the Mamluks*. London: Greenhill, 2007.

Webb, Stephen S. *Lord Churchill's Coup: The Anglo-American Empire and the Glorious Revolution Reconsidered*. New York: Knopf, 1995.

Webb, Stephen S. *Marlborough's America*. New Haven, CT: Yale, 2011.

White, Jon. *Marshal of France: The Life and Times of Maurice, Comte de Saxe*. London: Hamish Hamilton, 1962.

White, Reginald James. *The Age of George III*. New York: Walker and Company, 1968.

Wolf, John. *Louis XIV*. New York: Norton, 1968.

Index